WHO'S AFRAID OF
MARIE CURIE?

THE

CHALLENGES

FACING

WOMEN

IN

SCIENCE

AND

TECHNOLOGY

LINLEY ERIN HALL

SEAL PRESS

D0188323

WHO'S AFRAID OF MARIE CURIE?

The Challenges Facing Women in Science and Technology

Copyright © 2007 by Linley Erin Hall

Published by
Seal Press
A Member of the Perseus Books Group
1400 65th Street, Suite 250
Emeryville, CA 94608

Library of Congress Cataloging-in-Publication Data

Hall, Linley Erin.
Who's afraid of Marie Curie? : the challenges facing women in sci-
ence and technology / by Linley Erin Hall.
p. cm.
Includes bibliographical references.
ISBN-13: 978-1-58005-211-5
ISBN-10: 1-58005-211-8
1. Science—Vocational guidance. 2. Technology—Vocational guid-
ance. 3. Women in science. 4. Women in technology. 5. Women—
Employment. I. Title.

Q147.H35 2007
305.43'5--dc22

2007039521

Cover design by Gia Giasullo, studio eg
Interior design by Domini Dragoone
Printed in the United States of America by Malloy
Distributed by Publishers Group West

FOR MY GRANDMOTHER,

NADINE PULLIAM

CONTENTS

INTRODUCTION

Women have poured into many occupations over the past several decades, making significant contributions to the advancement of their fields. But in science and engineering, highly innovative professions of great importance to our economy and society, women remain underrepresented, particularly in the highest ranks. Too many women who are interested in these fields receive a "women not welcome" message and take their talents elsewhere.

The debate about the reasons behind these low numbers of women in science intensified in 2005 when Larry Summers spoke at a conference on women in academic science. Although he acknowledged that he was making hypotheses, guesses, and conjectures, conference participants heard the president of

Harvard, one of the most influential figures in the American academic community, say that women don't have the same intrinsic scientific and mathematical abilities as men and that discrimination isn't a big issue.[1] The firestorm that erupted brought much-needed attention from beyond the academy to the inequalities that women in academic science and engineering face. But this is only part of the issue, for bias begins when girls are young, continues throughout an education, and affects women who work in a wide variety of settings. It's also important to note that many of the conditions in science and engineering that are difficult for women also hinder men; the problem is much larger than simply getting more female bodies into laboratories.

From elementary school to doctoral programs, academia to industry, this book explores the wide range of challenges and successes that women experience in science, technology, engineering, mathematics, and medicine. Although in some fields women are nearing parity in numbers with men, at least at the bachelor's degree level, these disciplines are still largely set up on a male model that presents obstacles for women. While progress has been made over the past several decades, *Who's Afraid of Marie Curie?* examines the influences (both subtle and overt) that continue to hamper women's advancement, discusses what is working, and suggests how we can transform our schools and workplaces into more supportive environments for both men and women.

What exactly is the problem? Although women have flooded into America's universities and workplaces, they are still scarce in many science and engineering disciplines, particularly in positions of leadership. Fewer women than men start down the path toward a career in science or engineering, and women leave these fields at a higher rate.

The reasons for this are wide-ranging. Discrimination, both overt and subtle, plays a large role. Bias, some of it unconscious and unintentional, begins in childhood, as teachers interact with girls and boys differently, and continues throughout a woman's career, affecting hiring, promotion, mentoring, networking, and the availability of resources and opportunities. Increased awareness of discrimination has decreased blatant injustices; now more bias is subtle and hard to fight. It's also difficult for many women to battle society's perceptions about women's abilities (or lack thereof) in mathematics and science. And since the demands of a scientific career are so intense, particularly given the lengthening time needed to earn a PhD and the postdoctoral training requirements in many fields, a workable balance between career and personal life is not easy to achieve.

However, many of the problems that women in science face are not unique to science, or to women. Women in all fields are looking for careers that allow them to achieve success both at work and in their personal lives. Many K–12 classrooms are failing to adequately educate both boys and girls, and the American university system needs an overhaul on the undergraduate and graduate levels. The fact that many American men are turning away from science and engineering, as evidenced by the influx of foreign students into American universities, certainly suggests that the problems facing these disciplines are larger than many realize. But these issues often hit women in the sciences harder, and solutions have been slower to come than in some other fields.

This book examines the experiences of women in science, technology, engineering, mathematics, and medicine—particularly their challenges, but also the ways some women have navigated the system to become happy and successful in their careers. (I define "science" here as life and physical sciences only; the social sciences are beyond the scope of this book.) In addition to exploring the experiences of female students and faculty members, I also talk to women who work in industry and government, and look at the reasons why women choose to leave science and engineering, as well as what they do afterward.

In addition to gathering data from published research studies, I interviewed ninety-four women, ages fourteen to eighty-one, currently and formerly in a wide variety of scientific and technical fields. They worked at universities, corporations, government laboratories, hospitals, and other institutions. They studied at liberal arts colleges, universities of various sizes, schools focused on science and engineering, women's colleges, and schools abroad. While my sample of interviewees is not statistically representative, I have attempted to represent a diversity in age, race, socioeconomic background, field, undergraduate and graduate institution, and occupation. Since so few women work in many scientific fields, names and identifying details have often been changed or obscured to protect privacy.

Some of the women I spoke with loved their careers in the lab. Others decided to leave science behind completely, as I did;

I earned a bachelor's degree in chemistry before deciding to pursue a writing career. Some of the stories I heard were full of anger, frustration, and sadness. Other women's stories were inspirational, full of hope and triumph. Most were a mix of positive and negative experiences.

Each woman I talked with faced a different set of hurdles to overcome—some huge, some tiny. I looked for patterns in the stories they told me, and I found some, although no one characteristic was true of all the women to whom I spoke, apart from their being female. Some schools, companies, and laboratories are incredibly supportive of women; some are not. Change is happening: A wide variety of programs recruit and support women in science and engineering, but these operate in the shadow of the status quo and do not change the underlying institutional climates. Some of the most vital changes that need to happen would alter the structure of institutions that have been designed to meet men's needs, and changing an institution is a slow process.

This book offers a window into what it's like to be a woman in a science or engineering career. While very real difficulties continue, we've had some success in creating environments that nurture women and provide a springboard for them to succeed. We also still have a lot of work to do.

A DIFFERENT
EDUCATION

GIRLS

IN THE

SCIENCE

CLASSROOM

Four-foot DNA molecules made out of pipe cleaners and strips of brightly colored construction paper line the walls of a suburban California classroom. Clay models stuck to the windows show the different phases of cell division. It's spring 2007, and the seventh graders are learning about genes and heredity. Today they're extracting DNA from wheat germ.

The students line up to receive graduated cylinders containing wheat germ and hot water. After stirring for several minutes, they add a bit of dish detergent. A few minutes later they pour cold rubbing alcohol into the cylinder so that it forms a layer on top. This is the hard part: waiting fifteen minutes without touching the mixture, allowing the white, gooey DNA to slowly rise from the lower layer into the alcohol. As a distraction, the students take a short quiz while they wait.

I watch four classes do the same experiment. Once they have their materials, the girls seem as interested as the boys. Ms. B tells the students they can work in pairs of their choosing, but the majority of the girls decide to do their own experiment, although they chat and compare with a small group of others. Research suggests that boys are likely to hog laboratory equipment, relegating girls to observers. But in these classes, very few girls work with boys, and those who do are more hands-on than their partners. This is despite the fact that the mixture looks disgusting; students use the words "snot" and "barf" to describe it, but most girls don't mind the grossness. Some of the girls are quite assertive: When a boy walks over and starts to poke at the experiment of a girl–girl pair, one of them not only tells him to quit it but hits his arm. He backs off.

After the students finish the quiz, they write observations about the experiment in their notebooks and then use a bamboo skewer to remove some of the DNA from the alcohol. "Aw, it fell," whines one girl as her DNA slides off the stick and back into the alcohol. A girl sitting nearby tells her, "Try again. That was really working." Then she turns back to her own experiment and says, "I don't think mine is going to work." No one responds to her statement.

A redheaded girl with glasses is also having trouble getting her DNA out. Although most students are simply disposing of the experiment afterward, she wants to take some DNA home. She turns to the boy working next to her. "Will you try to get some out for me, Greg?" she asks. He barely responds, intent on his own experiment. She tries again: "Can I have some of yours?" He shares.

A tall girl with a brown ponytail and heavy mascara is startled by the sudden appearance of the DNA in her graduated cylinder. She tells several other students, as well as Ms. B, that it "jumped" at her. She asks if the white goo is DNA, and Ms. B assures her that it is. Her eyes light up, and she nearly bounces in her seat before leaning down to peer at the cylinder once again. Later, after she has removed a large glob of DNA from the mixture, she walks up to the front of the class to show it to Ms. B. "That's good and gross. You did it well," the teacher assures her.

Ms. B's classroom contains both typical and atypical elements as compared to other classes across the country. The students are a racially diverse group divided about evenly between girls and boys, with a range of ability levels. Ms. B is probably more aware than the average teacher of the bias and barriers that girls experience in science; she has a master's degree in exercise science (the study of human movement and fitness) and worked in the field for several years before going into teaching. She works hard to make sure that girls receive attention and encouragement in her class. But for many students, the experiences of their previous twelve years have already shaped their behavior in ways that are difficult to change.

From the time a girl starts school, she is likely to receive a different education from that of the boy sitting next to her. Observations of classrooms over the last twenty years have repeatedly shown that girls receive less feedback on their work and ideas than do boys, and when they do receive feedback, it's usually less specific and useful.[1] In general, boys receive more attention than girls because they're louder and rowdier. Lessons may be geared toward learning strategies that fit boys better than girls. In textbooks and other materials, noteworthy women may be discussed only as a special case or not at all. Throughout their education, girls experience bias in subtle and overt ways, though many of them may not notice it. I asked each of my interview subjects if she remembered experiencing gender bias in the classroom while growing up. Most said no. But it's almost certain that most or all of them did experience it, even though their age and maturity level kept them from consciously noticing those subtle messages.

When women do recall gender bias, it is usually of an overt and often sexual nature. Ayyana, for example, remembers her biology teacher in high school in the 1990s. "By the end of the first week, we had gone from being seated alphabetically to all five of the cheerleaders being in the front row. He was always remarking on the clothing that the girls wore that he liked." That's hard to miss. Other women weren't sure if bias was truly the motivation behind behavior they experienced. Amy recalls a middle school math teacher during the 1990s: "He tended to call on the girls a lot to come up to the board and solve problems. We used to joke that he was staring at our butts when we walked up there because he hardly ever called on guys, and it just seemed sort of strange." While this may seem an obvious case of inappropriate behavior from the outside, it can be very confusing to a thirteen-year-old who hasn't encountered such situations before.

Overt gender bias need not be sexual, of course. Tess took an introductory computer science class at her high school in the

2000s. Although the course was supposed to presume no knowledge of computer science, Tess was one of only a few students without programming experience. "I remember having difficulty with one of the programs. And the teacher told me that he thought I would never understand computer science, so I should just stop working on the program altogether and use the remainder of the course as an extra study hall. Of course I didn't give up on the program, but I had to pretty much teach myself for the rest of the class, because he wouldn't really give me help."

It's possible that this teacher would have said the same thing to a boy who was having trouble. But research suggests that teachers, even those who are supposedly unbiased, are more likely to help boys and give them useful feedback, whereas they will tend either to do the assignment for girls or tell them that it doesn't matter how they do.[2]

Teachers provide four different categories of feedback to students. One type is praise for a correct answer or a job well done. Another is remediation, when a teacher suggests that a student fix an incorrect answer or elaborate on a response. Teachers may also criticize, explicitly stating that something is wrong. The final type of feedback is acceptance, when teachers merely offer a brief acknowledgement of a correct answer.[3]

The amount of each type of feedback varies from classroom to classroom. In their book *Failing at Fairness: How Our Schools Cheat Girls*, David and Myra Sadker discuss several years' worth of classroom observations in which they found that praise and outright criticism are generally rare and may be absent altogether.[4] Acceptance and remediation make up the bulk of classroom interactions. Researchers have found that boys are more likely to receive remediation, which promotes learning by prompting students to think about their mistakes, whereas girls are more likely to have their answers accepted by the teacher without more explicit feedback.[5]

Ariane, who graduated from high school in the 2000s, found that her female calculus teacher offered the boys more praise as well as more help. "When students struggle, that's when you start to see where the teacher's attention really is. More attention was always exerted towards the boys' questions in class. A boy would say, 'Oh, I don't understand this,' and the teacher would reply, 'Why is that? Let's work this out.' If I or one of the other female students asked a question, the response would be something along the lines of, 'In this chapter you can find . . .' It was a seek-out-your-own-answer kind of deal."

Boys are more likely to receive attention in K–12 classrooms because they demand it. When answering questions, boys tend to raise their arms high in the air, sometimes waving them, while girls tend to keep their elbows on their desks. Boys are more likely than girls to call out answers without raising their hands. They're also less likely to be told to stop this behavior. For example, a boy who calls out an answer may have the answer accepted, while the girl who calls out is told to raise her hand, and a quiet girl is often ignored simply because the teacher has his or her hands full with other students.[6]

When students aren't calling out answers, teachers are often more likely to call on boys than girls. Girls often don't notice this, but Sarah sensed that something was wrong in her seventh-grade science class in the 1990s. "If a male and a female student had their hands up, [the teacher] would always call on the male," she explains. "He would belittle a girl's answer if it was wrong—not encouraging. I don't think that I recognized it then. I knew that I didn't like him in particular, but I didn't see it for what it was."

"I think that boys do speak out more in class," says Suzi, a current high school student. "I don't know if that's because they're smarter or if they're just more outgoing. A lot of the girls at our school are very self-conscious about their reputation."

In fact, some girls are afraid for their reputations. Although it has become more socially acceptable to be an intelligent woman, the degree of acceptability varies depending on location and social group. Being a "nerd" or "geek" of any gender still has a stigma attached to it in many schools. Some girls are not willing to risk being socially ostracized for being smart, so they stay very quiet in class, even if they have the answers. Even if girls have developed a social group in which intelligence is accepted or even celebrated, they may fear jeopardizing relationships by being too smart. "I thought that people might be a little bit jealous of my skills because they made it easier for me to get good grades in math classes, and I wasn't quite sure how to handle that dynamic," says Justine, who graduated from high school in the 1990s.

On the other hand, girls may also avoid answering questions in class because they fear being made fun of if they are wrong. In another of Ms. B's classes, she reviewed for a test later that week by asking the students questions about skin. All students offered answers, the boys more enthusiastically than the girls. After a brown-haired girl successfully answered an easy question, Ms. B asked a follow-up question that was more complicated. The girl's expression changed from one of pride to one of fear; she wasn't sure of the answer. Rather than risk being wrong in front of the class, she asked the teacher to come over, look at what she had in her notes, and verify that it was right before she answered aloud.

Although differences in how often boys and girls contribute can and do arise in all subjects, it can be even harder for a girl to participate actively in a male-dominated class. The National Assessment of Educational Progress found that the number of twelfth-grade girls who had taken both biology and chemistry increased from 38 percent in 2000 to 42 percent in 2005; the number of girls who had taken biology, chemistry, and physics increased from 28 to 29 percent.[7] Yet while more girls are choosing to take advanced math and science classes in high school, a gender imbalance still exists at the highest levels in some schools. For example, at Catherine's math- and science-focused high school in the 1990s, she was the only girl in her advanced physics course of ten students and was one of only two girls in her advanced calculus class of twelve students. While this sort of experience can be good preparation for college, where women are more likely to be outnumbered by men in science and engineering classes, it can also suggest that math and science are male endeavors, and it can prompt a girl to look at other fields for a potential career.

The lack of women may also prompt extra encouragement—of a sort. At Bitsy's private high school in the 2000s, where none of her advanced placement calculus and physics courses were more than 25 percent female, she got the distinct impression that she was different. "I got a tremendous amount of—I don't know if I'd call it praise or encouragement. I don't think it was so much that as positive surprise: 'You're a female and you can do this!?' My teachers seemed overly amazed at me and overly impressed with my abilities because I was female."

Classroom experiences like this can reinforce the perception of science and math as male fields. Science classes usually include laboratory activities in which students perform experiments, and while such hands-on projects can be quite good at getting girls excited about science, boys are more likely to take over and do these experiments when working in mixed-gender groups. (This result doesn't reflect the mixed-gender pairs dynamic I observed in Ms. B's class during the lab, when the girls did most of the work, but in that case, the boys seemed to be of the "too cool for school" mentality and not interested in doing any work at all.) In one study, researchers observed the fifth- through eighth-grade science classrooms of six different teachers, three male and three female, twice a month throughout the school year. These teachers had taken training in performance-based learning and were known as exceptional educators committed to eliminating gender bias from their classrooms. The researchers found that during group activities, boys and girls were equally likely to exhibit leadership behavior such as instructing other group members or explaining a scientific concept. Boys, however, were more likely to handle the equipment and sometimes prevented girls from participating in the activity. By the end of the year, girls had less confidence in their scientific ability, even though there were no gender differences in grades.[8]

Although most discussions of girls in school focus on classroom interactions, the materials that students use are also important. Textbooks are often a student's first introduction to the material being learned, and what is in the text often determines what a teacher includes in the lesson. Texts can come with workbooks, worksheets, laboratory exercises, quizzes, exams, study guides, websites, or other materials. If these materials are biased, students may not consciously notice, but they'll still receive a subtle message. Bias can take many forms; for example, photos of laboratory experiments may consistently show a boy doing the experiment while a girl records data or simply looks on.[9] Drawings and photos used as illustrations may consistently depict more men than women, or show them only in traditional gender roles, and texts may use only male pronouns, or discuss the achievements of men more than those of women.

For much of the relatively short history of modern science, men did not allow women to read books about science, to enter science classrooms, or to use scientific equipment. Some women surmounted these barriers and made significant contributions, and in the last fifty years, women's discoveries have been growing, but it remains true that men have made the vast majority of scientific discoveries, especially the ones likely to be covered in a precollege science class. A science textbook that discusses the experiments and ideas that led to the formulas and principles that are the foundation of science today will inevitably end up talking about a lot of male scientists, presenting students with a vision of science as a male-dominated or even exclusively male world.[10] Consider, for example, common scientific units: watts, joules, kelvins, hertz, newtons, pascals, coulombs, ohms, teslas . . . all named after men. The only unit I could find named (partially) after a woman is the curie, named for Marie and Pierre

Curie, and since the becquerel (named after a male physicist, of course) is the more commonly used unit of radioactivity, a girl is unlikely to encounter the curie.

Although giving students a skewed view of scientific history by overemphasizing the contributions of women is not appropriate, a girl who sees science as a male endeavor is unlikely to aspire to a career in a science field. Many textbooks have tried to counter this imbalance by including profiles of modern female scientists, but these are often limited to sidebars or enrichment sections that teachers do not necessarily include in their lessons. Still, the women I spoke with were generally happy to find any reference to women in science. "Every once in a while my science book would have, in the middle of the chapter, a little box: 'Special Issue: Women in Science.' It would give a blurb on Marie Curie or Rosalind Franklin. Those were always kind of exciting for me," says Alicia, who graduated from high school in the 2000s.

Educational publishers have made a lot of progress toward creating materials that are free of bias, but they're not there yet. I compared three chapters of two recently published middle school life science textbooks. The books covered essentially the same material, although it was organized somewhat differently. In each text I examined chapters on genetics and heredity, animals, and systems in the human body. Although the photos and drawings that featured men and women were about the same in number, their context differed in noticeable ways. For example, one book illustrated different ways to build strong bones with a boy rollerblading and a girl eating yogurt. In another section, a photo showing sweating as a way to regulate body temperature depicted a girl lifting a small free weight; later in the chapter, the section on muscles included a photo of a man lifting a heavy barbell. Even in the series of photos that showed two boys and two girls playing baseball, the girls were waiting passively, as catcher and batter, while the boys were active—one winding up to pitch, the other sliding into base. While these differences may seem insignificant and are not specific to science or math ability, taken together they do suggest that women are weak and passive while men are strong and active, reinforcing traditional gender roles.

Bias appears in the texts as well. One textbook included a timeline of knowledge about the human body that started with ancient Egyptians. Only one of the fifteen or so entries discussed a woman, Rita Levi-Montalcini. Instead of focusing on her Nobel Prize for the discovery of growth factors, it told how she set up a laboratory in her bedroom during World War II after being forced to leave her position at a medical school because she was Jewish. The men discussed in the timeline "implant," "discover," "repair," "publish," "prove," "determine," and "receive a Nobel." Levi-Montalcini "studies."

Since the 1980s, researchers have been using the Draw-A-Scientist-Test (DAST) to evaluate the perceptions that people, particularly children, have about scientists. It's very simple: Participants are asked to draw a scientist. The researcher then evaluates the drawing, looking for stereotypic and more realistic elements. When the DAST was first conducted with elementary school students in 1981, only 28 of the more than 4,800 drawings were of women.[11] The typical scientist drawn by students was male, Caucasian, had facial hair, and wore glasses and a lab coat.

Although more recent studies have shown that the percentage of female scientists drawn is increasing, it's still far less than 50 percent. A 1999 study found that students' scientists were male 58 percent (grades K–2), 73 percent (grades 3–5), and 75 percent (grades 6–8) of the time.[12] Studies suggest that if simply asked to draw a person, one is highly likely to draw someone of the same gender,[13] so the fact that so many girls draw pictures of male scientists indicates how firmly entrenched the idea of science as a male domain can be.

Perhaps more disturbing is a 1999 study in which college students majoring in education—future K–12 teachers—completed the DAST. Although nearly half of the students drew a female scientist, almost all were Caucasian, and many stereotypical elements were included, particularly eyeglasses, lab coats, and other symbols of research, such as test tubes.[14] When the classes discussed the results of the DAST, many of the students did not see any problem with the stereotypic drawings they had produced. Textbooks may be improving by showing scientists as a diverse group, but if teachers in their lessons portray science as something that white men do, this will be a huge influence on students.

Bias extends outside the classroom to extracurricular activities as well. Participation in a science club, math team, or other science- and engineering-related activity can give a girl additional opportunities to explore subjects she's interested in and to gain experience. (It looks good on college applications too.) But sometimes it can feel as if there's a glass wall separating the girls and the boys, or even a NO GIRLS ALLOWED sign on the door. For example, Tess, who graduated from high school in the 2000s, joined her high school's robotics team. "The advisor's first comment was, 'Oh, excellent, we have somebody to write our press releases now,'" she says. "He just couldn't let go of the idea that I was going to be doing all sorts of nontechnical activities. Later in the season, some kids were showing me how to wire together something on the chassis. Our advisor came up to me and said, 'Are you planning on actually doing anything, or are you just going to stand here and look pretty for all these boys?' I was pretty taken aback by that."

Girls also encounter bias from other students. "The guys on the math and science team were just the dorkiest nerds. But they were, in spite of it, almost chauvinists sometimes in how they would say that, since there aren't very many girls on the team, girls obviously aren't that smart," says Alicia, who graduated from high school in the 2000s. "Over time, hearing that a lot—it was hard to deal with."

Although the subtle and not-so-subtle messages that girls receive about math and science not being for them can certainly turn them off of those subjects, bias is not the only problem for girls in today's science classrooms. Poor teaching is also a concern. According to the National Science Foundation, in 1999–2000 only 71 percent of public school grades 7–12 mathematics teachers had an undergraduate or graduate major or minor in mathematics or math education. The corresponding statistic for science teachers was 77 percent.[15] Although the No Child Left Behind Act has instituted new standards for teacher credentialing, some K–12 science and math teachers are still not comfortable with the subjects they teach and therefore are much less likely to communicate an enthusiasm for science and math to their students.

Many women also reported being bored by or frustrated with the slow pace of their science and mathematics classes. Of her elementary school classes in the 1980s, Kelli says, "I remember [math class] being very repetitive; we would learn the same things year after year. I got bored fairly easily, and in fact I once got a D in science because I was so bored, I was doing other things during science time instead of science. It wasn't challenging or inspiring in any way." Some school districts allow students to accelerate, taking particular classes with students one or two grades ahead, but other districts resist allowing students to work ahead, turning some of the brightest students, male and female, off of math and science at an early age.

Although laboratory activities and collaborative learning strategies have been shown to increase learning and are more akin to what scientists actually do in their careers, they are scarce in or even absent from some classes. In my high school's advanced placement physics class in the 1990s, for example, we did not do a single hands-on activity until after taking the exam in May. Our teacher explained that we had too much material to cover to take time for any labs. In recent years, the No Child Left Behind Act has increased schools' focus on standardized testing, particularly in the areas of reading, writing, and mathematics. In some schools, this has resulted in students doing fewer laboratory and hands-on activities and even reduced the amount of time they spend on science learning.

In general, classes at the K–12 level tend to present science and math as a collection of facts and formulas. Rather than experiencing science as a way to explore the world around them, students memorize facts and spit them back out. When lab activities are included in the curriculum, they are often cookbook-style, with an expected result, so students may never experience the thrill of discovery that is at the heart of scientific endeavors. Furthermore, K–12 curricula generally do not expose students to the open questions and controversies in a field, many of which are well within students' understanding. Many students also don't have contact with practicing scientists or engineers while they're growing up, and if they do, it's not in the classroom.

Although this dry teaching style and lack of exposure to real-world science affects all students, it's particularly detrimental to girls, who are already at a disadvantage because of the gender biases discussed thus far. Not only can girls sometimes not envision themselves as scientists, but they also may not know what scientists actually do, or that it's possible to make a career out of certain areas of science. Tara, for example, got hooked on astronomy in elementary school but didn't seriously consider it as a future career until finding it on the SAT registration form as a possible college major. Similarly, Brianna loved her eighth-grade earth science class but thought that scientists had already figured out everything. "Studying the earth and rocks—it seems like something that's been done. We understand how the earth works, so is there more to discover? . . . I just had this assumption—I don't know where I got it—that people didn't do anything in geology as a field."

Given bias, poor teaching, and the inadequate introduction to what math and science are about in the real world that many girls experience in school, how do they actually perform in these subjects? It depends on how you measure performance. On average, girls receive higher grades than do boys in mathematics and science classes. But they tend to receive lower scores on standardized tests such as the mathematics SAT and the statewide achievement exams required by the No Child Left Behind Act.

Despite the bias that many girls face in the classroom, many of them are achieving, but too often they don't think they are. The idea that girls aren't good at math and science gets into kids' heads early. "I was shocked at the number of my girls who would say, 'Math is too hard for me,' on the first day of school," says Ayyana, who recently taught middle school mathematics in the South through the Teach for America program.

Some girls experience what is known as math anxiety, the discomfort that students may feel when performing a mathematics-related task. Math anxiety can arise from a number of factors, including difficult experiences in classrooms and with teachers, or issues with self-esteem and negative attitudes toward mathematics. Although both boys and girls can experience math anxiety, some research suggests that it is more persistent among girls.[18] In a study of fourth through sixth graders, University of Illinois psychologist Eva Pomerantz and colleagues found that although the girls performed better in school than the boys, they evaluated themselves more negatively than the boys in every subject except language arts. Even the girls who excelled were more vulnerable to internal distress.[19]

While Allison was a fifth grader in the 1980s, her math confidence took a nosedive for a while. "I felt like I wasn't good at math because I wasn't getting 100s on things; I was getting 90s," she says. "I got really scared, because I wondered if I would ever be able to do the math that you do in high school. If I was only getting 90s and not 100s in fifth-grade math, how would I ever be able to do calculus?"

What does a gender-fair classroom that encourages girls to be successful look like? To begin, teachers should offer girls and boys similar amounts of praise and criticism, making sure that girls receive feedback and encouragement that they can use to improve, rather than simply saying "okay" to them all the time. They also need to push girls to keep working at problems that challenge them. "Rescuing" girls does them no favors and can imply that they aren't smart enough to figure it out.

Furthermore, teachers should also call on girls and boys with equal frequency, and after giving students enough time to think about a question. Studies suggest that teachers wait only about 0.9 seconds for a student to provide an answer.[20] Waiting four or five seconds gives students more time to think and put their hands up. Since boys are more likely to shoot up their hands immediately (whether they know the answer or not), waiting will give girls a better chance of getting in on the action.[21]

Girls also need opportunities to take on leadership roles in the classroom and to work with both genders on collaborative projects. Teachers should avoid separating boys and girls or pitting the genders against each other in competition. No teacher would put all the white kids on one team and all the minority students on another, and yet girls and boys often compete against each other in classroom spelling bees and other informal contests.

Perhaps most importantly, teachers need to be aware of their own biases and work to overcome them. Even if they are careful to be gender-fair in classroom interactions, bias may be communicated to students in their assignments and grading. For example, a teacher may expect that girls will perform better when writing essays, whereas boys will perform better during hands-on science experiments, an assumption that can affect the amount of assistance offered, as well as the grades given.

Educators have tremendous power to influence their students, not only through the material but also through their attitudes. Some of the women I interviewed could not remember a single woman they saw in their community while they were growing up who was a scientist or engineer—including a few interviewees who graduated from high school in the past decade. The only women they saw interacting with math and science were their teachers. Teachers who are uncomfortable with the material or who see math and science as male domains are unlikely to inspire girls, whereas good teachers can be powerful role models who encourage girls to pursue careers in these fields. "Both my biology and chemistry teachers in high school were very personable, very easy to interact with and even be friendly with. They just had this infectious enthusiasm for the subject. You could tell they loved it. But there wasn't anything extraordinary about the teaching style," says Jennifer, who went on to earn a PhD in biology.

Furthermore, teachers need to incorporate teaching methods that work particularly well with girls into their classrooms, such as collaborative learning. Many strategies that work well with girls are useful for boys as well. For example, all students can benefit from hands-on laboratory experiments in which they use the scientific method. But these are infrequent in many classrooms, because many school districts do not have the resources to fund regular lab projects.

"I do a lot of labs, which is different, apparently, than a lot of other schools," says Cate, a middle school science teacher. "I get kids from other schools, and they do maybe three or four labs a year. I do one a week. I get the kids a lot of hands-on exposure. And sometimes, yeah, we light things on fire or we totally trash the room. Sometimes there's cornstarch everywhere. I'm not very popular with the custodians on those days. But I don't think you're doing a good job as a science teacher if you're not getting into trouble on a regular basis."

Another obstacle to hands-on activities is teacher inexperience in the techniques needed. Some programs have attempted to address both this and the funding issue by offering teachers training in specific laboratory experiments and then providing them with the materials to do them. These programs generally do not pay for chemicals and other materials that may be used up, but they do provide reusable equipment.

Of course, in a classroom that's not gender-fair, more laboratory activities may simply be an opportunity for boys to hog the equipment. Some educators and psychologists, among them Leonard Sax, author of *Why Gender Matters: What Parents and Teachers Need to Know About the Emerging Science of Sex Differences*, have suggested that the real solution to the problem of gender fairness is not to try to fix coeducational classrooms but instead to separate students into single-sex classes. Until recently, single-sex education was solely the province of private schools, but in recent years public and charter schools have begun experimenting with single-sex classrooms.

The results are mixed, with some schools experiencing significant improvements in academic achievement while other schools declare single-sex classrooms a failure. Results from established single-sex schools, however, show important gains for girls in science and math. Girls in single-sex schools are more likely to take courses and engage in extracurricular activities in areas that have been traditionally male. At an all-girls school, the top scorer on the physics exam is always female. Girls get all the spots on the math team. Girls can't just look on during group experiments, or nothing will get done. As a result, girls have more opportunities to engage with math and science and become more confident in their abilities.

And it does make a difference in girls' career choices. The National Coalition of Girls' Schools surveyed more than 1,000 women who had graduated from all-girls high schools in 2004. They found that 15 percent intended to major in science or math, and an additional 4 percent intended to major in engineering.[22] According to the National Science Foundation, in 2004 overall, 11.9 percent of female college freshmen intended to major in science, and 2.9 percent in engineering.[23]

One argument against single-sex schools, however, is that girls and boys need to be able to interact with each other. This may be especially true for women who go into fields that are male-dominated. But even girls who go to coed schools can be overwhelmed by a college science or engineering department that operates on a masculine style of teaching and testing. Although girls may learn better using certain teaching strategies, they should still be exposed to others and should learn how to learn within them so that they are not blindsided when they attend college. Programs for precollege girls usually highlight the more exciting and fun aspects of science and engineering, but girls also need to be prepared for the frustrations and barriers they may face when they leave the K–12 environment, or they will be less likely to overcome them. This is a difficult thing to balance against trying to build girls' enthusiasm and confidence, however.

K–12 education has come a long way in the past few decades. Educators have learned a lot about child development, learning methods, pedagogy, and gender issues. More teachers are not only aware of the problems that girls face in the classroom but are also making progress in removing those hurdles. Change is slow, however. Especially with the renewed focus on standardized tests, some of the strategies that improve science and mathematics learning for both boys and girls are being shoved aside. The precollege years provide an important foundation for success in college and a career. Girls who have poor experiences with science and math during childhood are unlikely to go into these fields later. And those who do discover a love of science and mathematics will find that they still must overcome many hurdles to achieve and succeed in a technical career, including the idea that women aren't good at science and math simply by virtue of being female. The next chapter looks at the facts and biases behind the debate over how (and whether) biological and environmental factors contribute to scientific and mathematical ability.

NATURE, NURTURE

WHAT'S
BEHIND
SCIENTIFIC
ABILITY?

The evidence regarding the degree and causes of gender differences in mathematical and scientific ability is pretty murky. When reporting on the latest study, the media often makes it sound so simple: Males outscored females on this test, or men have more of that ability than women do. But such reports rarely indicate how large these differences are, whether there are any limitations to the data, or how the findings compare to other research in the field. In fact, there is a lot of research, a lot of bias, a lot of confounding factors, a lot of people trying to be the loudest in the room, and a lot of tantalizing questions. The common stereotype is that men are better at math and science than women are. Women in these fields fight this stereotype every day. But does it have any basis in reality?

While the bulk of this book is devoted to women's experiences in their education and careers, this chapter focuses on research into the nature and causes of gender differences that may influence women's choices and success in technical fields. The thicket of competing studies and theories may feel alternately irrelevant, frustrating, or overwhelming, but it's important to realize how much this backdrop frames how women perceive themselves and are perceived by others. Perhaps the scientific method itself will ultimately help expurgate the bias toward women in the sciences that still permeates our schools and workplaces.

Proponents of the equal rights movement assert that women are no less capable than men but that they are not given opportunities to develop and use their skills and talents because of prejudice. Others believe that innate biological differences in the abilities of men and women do exist; indeed, this was what Larry Summers suggested in his infamous speech. If such differences do exist, they argue, and they are deficiencies for one gender or the other, then choosing the best person for the job by gender wouldn't be discrimination. But differences do not have to be negative, nor do they have to be biological in origin. There are two separate and distinct issues here: Do men and women have different amounts of scientific and mathematical ability, and, if so, what is the source of these differences? Unfortunately, the answer to both of these questions is unclear.

Various measures of scientific and mathematical ability, most notably standardized tests such as the SAT, but also course grades and other assessments, do show some differences in the performance of males and females. But these differences are not necessarily consistent: Men perform better on some measures and women on others. The size of the disparity between male and female abilities on an exam can vary depending on the age of the test-takers, as well as when and in which country a test was administered. For most of the skills relevant to success in science and engineering, the differences are quite small, but when people start arguing about their causes, these tiny disparities often become a big deal.

Some people use these variations in men's and women's performance to claim that biological differences between the genders occur in a wide range of characteristics and abilities, proving that men are inherently better equipped to achieve success in technical fields. On the other end of the spectrum, others claim that gender differences end with the obvious physical ones and that any differences beyond that are due to how men and women are taught to behave, explicitly and implicitly, by the people around them, a process known as socialization.

Each of these positions is extreme. Based on decades of research in many different fields, it appears that biological and environmental factors combine in each individual to produce a unique set of abilities and characteristics. What is still in question is how precisely these factors interact and how important each is. Although scientific advances such as improved brain imaging techniques are providing us with new ways to explore these questions, brains are incredibly complex structures, and drawing causal relationships can be quite difficult.

Part of the problem, as psychologists Jeremy and Paula Caplan put it, is that "the only way to estimate ability is to examine samples of performance, but performance is often treated as though it perfectly reflected or corresponded with ability."[1] Performance on a math exam, for example, can depend not only on mathematical ability but also on test-taking skills, confidence, and even amount of sleep. While it's possible to control for some of these variables, a pure measure of ability is unlikely to be found. Although we should utilize the measures we do have available, caution is in order when we draw conclusions about ability from tests.

Mathematical and spatial reasoning abilities are widely considered the two most important skills for success as a scientist or engineer. Math is an important component of most science and engineering disciplines. Although some scientific fields such as biology may not appear to be mathematical, researchers must perform data analysis, calculate statistics, and draw on logic and problem-solving skills that are also crucial to mathematics. However, mathematical ability is not a single skill. Similarities exist, for example, between solving a long division problem, determining if two triangles are similar, or integrating a function, but these problems draw on diverse skill sets.

Spatial reasoning is the ability to visualize mathematical relationships and models of physical things. A person uses spatial reasoning when drawing a diagram or a graph, solving an algebraic word problem, or looking for patterns in numbers or shapes. It's also useful for determining what happens when one ball hits another, when two molecules come together to react, when two tectonic plates rub against each other, when a surgeon's scalpel cuts in a certain way, and so on. Some mathematics problems require the use of spatial abilities, but they can also be tested separately from mathematics.

When presented with the results of a mathematics or spatial reasoning test, or any other measure of ability, researchers usually use two methods to look at any gender differences in scores. The most common is to take the average of the scores for men and for women and compare them. The other method is to look at any differences in variability—how likely men and women are to score at the high end or at the low end rather than in the middle. This is useful because people with high ability in an area are more likely to go into and be successful in fields that use that ability. In mathematics, gender differences between averages are quite small and may favor males or females, whereas males exhibit higher variability more consistently.

Average gender differences are small in many areas outside mathematics as well. University of Wisconsin-Madison psychologist Janet Shibley Hyde examined major studies on gender differences not only in cognitive measures such as mathematical and verbal ability but also traits such as communication, self-esteem, and competitiveness. She found that 78 percent of the gender differences in these studies were small or close to zero.[2] In only three areas were gender differences large: motor performance (such as the distance one can throw a ball), some measures of sexuality, and physical aggression. Gender differences in math were all small, some so near zero as to be trivial, whereas some differences in spatial abilities reached the moderate range. This work has led Hyde to advance the gender similarities hypothesis: "that males and females are similar on most, but not all, psychological variables. That is, men and women, as well as boys and girls, are more alike than they are different,"[3] a finding consistent with that of other researchers over several decades.[4]

Many factors influence both the size of a difference in performance between genders, as well as whether it favors males or females. One of these is age. The media most frequently reports on gender differences found in high school students and often implies that these disparities are fixed. But standardized tests of elementary school students often show no difference in math abilities, and when they do, it's an advantage for girls. An advantage for boys doesn't begin to appear until middle or high school.[5] The SAT, generally taken near the end of high school, is one of the standardized tests with the largest gender differences in scores and also one of the best-known exams because of its role in college admissions.

On the math SAT, the gender gap in average scores has hovered around 35 points since the mid-1990s.[6] The SAT illustrates several of the problems inherent in using standardized tests as a measure of ability, particularly if one wants to show a biological source for gender differences.

The first problem is that although more than two million students take the test each year,[7] it's not a representative sample, because only college-bound students take it—a fraction of the student population. Thus, we should hesitate in using these results to make generalizations about all men and women. On the 2005 National Assessment of Educational Progress, a set of tests given every other year to a representative sample of high school seniors, male twelfth graders' average score on the mathematics section was 151, while females scored 149 (out of a possible 300).[8]

This is a clear case of different testing measures' yielding different results, and yet the SAT scores continue to dominate our understanding of high school test performance.

Second, to measure differences in mathematical ability using a test, that math exam needs to be designed so that it is fair and truly measures what it claims to measure. Since mathematical ability is not a single skill, an exam should contain a wide variety of problems that draw equally on different parts of mathematics. This is particularly important when discussing gender differences, as some researchers have found that men and women typically perform differently on certain types of math problems, in particular that women do better on arithmetical computation and men on mathematical word problems.[9] These differences are generally small, and they have not been found reliably in all studies, but even a small difference can add up to a larger disparity if a test focuses on questions on which one gender tends to perform better.

For example, the math SAT used to have a section that required students not to solve a problem but to determine if they had enough information to solve it. Women did very well on this type of problem, better than men. But the Educational Testing Service, which develops and administers the SAT, eliminated the section, claiming that it was too easily coached. As Susan F. Chipman, a cognitive psychologist at the U.S. Office of Naval Research, writes, however, "In any case, the historical fact that the Educational Testing Service chose to drop a class of items that consistently favored females from a test that consistently favors males should cast doubt on the tendency to treat the SAT as if it were some gold standard of mathematical ability."[10]

Third, many educators argue that a timed, standardized test such as the SAT, with problems that fit easily into a multiple-choice answer format and a structure that rewards test strategies such as guessing based on partial information, does not truly represent a person's ability to do mathematics. Being familiar with the format of an exam and test-taking strategies can improve performance without changing the amount of math a person knows; the brisk business that test-preparation classes do is certainly a testament to this. In addition, mathematicians do not speed through problems but think long and hard about complex questions, carefully developing their results until they are sure of them and explaining their thought process so that others can follow it. Students act more like mathematicians in class than when taking standardized exams, because achievement in mathematics courses is rarely about guessing, especially since many teachers require students to show their work to earn full credit on homework and tests. Many studies have found that on average, girls and women get better grades than boys and men do in mathematics classes, including those in college.[11] In fact, women's math SAT scores underpredict their performance in college math courses—their grades are higher than those of men with the same SAT scores.[12] The fact that grades and test scores suggest different gender differences in mathematics performance raises serious questions about the reliability of the tests we most frequently use to measure ability.

It's also important to note that gender differences in mathematics and spatial abilities are not the same now as they were several decades ago. Some exams that have been given to students in particular grades for years show a pattern of decreasing average differences between the genders over time.[13] While differences in the composition of exams may be one factor in this change, another explanation is social—women are now encouraged to take more math and science courses, so they are more likely to have the knowledge necessary to do well on certain exams. A woman may have a great deal of mathematical ability, but if she's never been exposed to a certain kind of problem, she will likely need longer to figure it out than would someone whose math classes had covered such problems. And that hurts on a timed test.

Gender differences also vary between nations, as a number of studies show. In 2000, the Program for International Student Assessment tested fifteen-year-olds in thirty-one countries on verbal, mathematics, and science literacy.[14] Boys outscored girls in mathematics in twenty-eight of the countries, but the gender differences were statistically significant in just fifteen countries (and not in the United States)—hardly suggestive of a huge, innate male advantage. Scores on science literacy were about even, with three countries showing a significant male advantage and two countries showing a significant female advantage. These differences between nations (and thus between cultures) suggest that many different factors, including environmental ones, are influencing performance on these exams.

So far, the focus has been on average gender differences. These are small in most cases, and various environmental factors—as well as limitations of the tests used to measure ability—may be as much as or more of an influence than any innate differences that exist. But because a person with high science and math ability is more likely to pursue a career in these fields than one with average ability, it's also important to look at how many men and women are among the top scorers on exams, and why differences between the genders might exist. If men outnumber women at the high end of scientific and mathematical ability due to biological factors rather than environmental ones, then the low numbers of women in science and engineering disciplines would be expected, but if environmental factors are the cause, then changing those factors should improve women's performance and bring more women into technical fields.

Many studies suggest that men's test scores are more variable than women's. Variability is low when most test-takers score around the average—when 80 percent of a class receives Cs, for example. Variability is high when test-takers have a wide range of scores, including a significant number that are both very high and very low. Men's more variable test results mean that on some exams men outnumber women in the top five or top one percent of test-takers, although they do not always outnumber women by the same amount.

Much of the research on gender differences in mathematics or spatial abilities has focused on students with known high abilities, who are often identified in talent searches. In the early 1980s, the ratio of boys to girls among thirteen-year-olds who scored 700 or above on the math section of the SAT was 13:1. In recent years, the disparity has decreased to 2.8:1.[15] As with average differences, changes to the test content and format may be responsible for some of this decrease. But another explanation is that more girls are taking advanced math courses, and they're taking them earlier, so they are better prepared. That is, the huge disparity seen in the 1980s was in large part a result of environmental rather than biological factors.

But in a study that contradicts this conclusion, Yu Xie and Kimberlee Shauman examined data from six large-scale tests of middle and high school students conducted over three decades. (This is the study that Larry Summers referred to in his controversial speech.) They found that among high school students, more men than women were in the top five percent for both math and science achievement. Among students who were tested in multiple grades, the disparity is generally greater for older students than younger ones. No clear patterns, such as a decrease over the decades in the ratio of high-achieving boys to girls, emerge from comparing the tests to one another. Furthermore, Xie and Shauman found that girls took math classes similar to those taken by boys and were actually more likely to take biology and chemistry courses, so a lack of access to classes cannot explain the gender differences seen on these tests.[16]

In the realm of gender-differences research, studies are often contradictory. Researchers can obtain very different results depending on the data they use and the methods they use to analyze it. For this reason, it's important not to leap to conclusions. While it seems that variability in scientific and mathematical ability could be, at least in part, a biological phenomenon, researchers have not yet investigated all the variables that may be influencing the results they get (and variables that might explain why different data sets yield such different results).

Many factors beyond pure ability also go into a test score or grade in a class. For example, practicing a skill usually leads to improvement in it, even if we do not realize that we're practicing. Very few twelve-year-olds play video games to improve their spatial skills, for example, but various studies have suggested that these games can do just that. Since many more boys than girls play these games, this may be one reason for the large gender difference seen in this area.[17]

Other research has shown that children from a low socioeconomic background do not exhibit any gender differences in spatial ability, whereas children from high socioeconomic backgrounds exhibit a difference favoring males on certain tests.[18] The researchers suggest that children from low socioeconomic backgrounds may not have as many opportunities to play video games, build with LEGOs, or put together puzzles, which can all improve spatial skills (and are more likely to be engaged in by boys). Playing sports can also improve spatial abilities; given that more girls are participating in sports than in the past, it will be interesting to see if and how women's scores on tests of spatial ability change.

While practice is likely to improve performance, negative stereotypes are likely to decrease it. Stereotypes about women's lower math and science performance are still prevalent and can affect women's performance without their realizing it. A phenomenon known as "stereotype threat" occurs when someone is in a situation where others can judge her behavior based on a negative stereotype about a group to which she belongs, usually gender or race. The additional pressure caused by the fear of being judged can cause a drop in performance, even if the person is not consciously thinking about the stereotype. Researchers have measured the effects of stereotype threat in a variety of different groups and situations, including women taking mathematics exams.

In one study, several groups of college women and men who had scored well on the math SAT took a math test. The administrator told some groups that men generally scored better on the exam than women. Other groups heard that men and women generally did similarly. The researchers found that, on average, women who heard that men performed better did worse on the exam than women who were told they would do as well as the men around them.[19] But such explicitness is not necessary. Other researchers have found that women taking a math test simply with men in the room experienced stereotype threat, performing worse than women tested in a same-sex group.[20]

Psychologist Nalini Ambady and her colleagues at Tufts University have conducted a couple of very interesting experiments on stereotype threat. Asian American women encounter two conflicting stereotypes: Females are bad at math, and Asians are good at math. In one study, Asian American girls in early elementary and middle school first did an activity to subtly activate one distinct identity: female, Asian, or neither. For example, the elementary school girls colored a picture of a girl holding a doll, children eating with chopsticks, or a landscape scene. Then they took a math test. The girls reminded of their race got the highest scores, followed by the girls with no identity activated, and then the girls reminded of their gender.[21] A similar experiment with female Asian American college students yielded the same results.[22]

Stereotype threat affects only those people who identify with the discipline: It's important to them, it forms part of their identity, and they want to do well in it. A woman who long ago decided that math isn't important will not experience stereotype threat during a math exam. But stereotype threat can cause a woman to decide that doing well in a discipline is not an important part of her identity and thus lead her to underperform for reasons unrelated to stereotype threat, such as low motivation or insufficient preparation. Stereotype threat does not appear to occur when a test is easy or ridiculously difficult, but when an exam is difficult to the point of being at the edge of someone's abilities—when doing well requires some work, and failure is a possibility. Some researchers have also found that gender differences in mathematics occur only on difficult math problems, not easy ones. They suggest that this is because hard math problems require more spatial skills, so the difference between men's and women's performance in math is actually a spatial difference rather than a mathematical one.[23] But since stereotype threat also acts on difficult problems, it could also be affecting the results— a possibility that the authors do not mention.

Researchers generally begin a study with an expectation about what they will find; forming hypotheses is a crucial part of the scientific method. But this also means that if research does not show the results researchers expect, they may be tempted to disregard them or to present their results in a manner that lends credence to their theory, even if the data could be interpreted in other ways. There is also what has sometimes been called the "file drawer issue": A study showing no difference is generally considered less interesting than one showing a difference, so studies that don't produce differences often sit in a file drawer rather than being published.

Some gender-differences researchers have accused others in the field of flat-out bias or poor science—of setting up experiments to get the result they want, of not publishing results that do or do not demonstrate differences between men and women, of using sample sizes that are too small, of not replicating their work, of writing papers to imply that the differences they found are larger than they really are, and of simply ignoring any other studies that contradict the ideas they want to promote.[24] Research on potential gender differences is already contradictory; these accusations of bias make it even more difficult to separate the truth from the hype.

Although most people focus on mathematical and spatial abilities when discussing gender differences related to success in science and engineering, other abilities and even preferences may also play a role. For example, the ability to communicate is also essential to learning and practicing science. Newton, Darwin, and other great scientists may have spent time in solitude to think about ideas and develop important new theories, but their ideas were influential only when they were able to communicate them to the rest of the world.

The ways in which aspiring and practicing scientists and engineers communicate are numerous; they may write lab reports, journal articles, review papers, conference reports, grant proposals, manuals, project reports, emails, book reviews, and textbooks, as well as use posters and PowerPoint slides. They may give presentations during classes, during lab meetings, at conferences, during job interviews, at other universities, to funding agencies, and to clients. They may communicate information to students by teaching, holding office hours, and mentoring. They may talk to the media, to K–12 students, and to the general public. They may mentor colleagues, sit on committees, attend department meetings, and work in teams to complete projects. They may review the journal articles and grant proposals of other researchers, as well as write recommendation letters and other evaluations of their and others' work. They may discuss work with their lab group, collaborators, and clients. Those who rise to administrative or managerial positions often find that communication is most of the job. And although writing in C++ is very different from writing in English, well-written, readable computer code is crucial in creating a functional program that others can use.

If a scientist cannot communicate her work to others, she doesn't get any grant money, she doesn't get a job, and she doesn't get others to work with her. Of course, there are exceptions to this rule, just as with any other. Some incredibly intelligent scientists' utter lack of communication skills is tolerated because they are so brilliant. Often one or more people do their communicating for them. But most scientists have to write their own grant proposals. While measurements of gender differences in verbal ability pose the same challenges of interpretation as those for mathematical ability, many tests show a small advantage for women in this area. If women truly are better communicators on average, this could be a tremendous asset in their scientific careers.

It's also important to consider whether attributes beyond the ability to get the job done may be influencing whether women enter science and engineering. Larry Summers suggested that women and men may have different innate "taste differences" that account for their preferring some fields to others. Some researchers have seconded this claim.[25] One often cited "taste difference" is that men are more interested in objects while women are more interested in people, both interacting with them and doing things to help them. Science and engineering careers outside of biology focus on things—atoms, rocks, computers, bridges—and generally involve some amount of independent, solitary work. Research in many areas of mathematics and science is highly theoretical, with no obvious direct application to society. While understanding how the universe began is quite interesting, it doesn't feed starving children or cure disease. If women are, on average, more interested in working with and helping people than men are, then this could be a reason why women choose careers outside science and engineering, as well as why those in these fields tend to cluster in biology and related areas. But even if this preference does exist, it could certainly be the result of environmental influences rather than biological ones, or a combination of the two.

One environmental influence may be inaccurate perceptions of science and engineering. Contrary to common assumptions, many jobs in science and engineering do require a lot of communication and interaction with other people. Truly independent scientific work is becoming less and less common. An individual scientist might spend a few hours or even a day not talking to anyone else, completely focused on an experiment. But many problems are too big for any one person working alone in a lab to solve. Researchers can have a lot of interaction with others if they want it—and some end up with more than they would prefer. In addition, engineering is both a very applied science and a discipline with few women. Engineers develop new products and solve problems, often helping people and society by doing so. For example, they design safer cars, determine how to remove pollutants from water, develop better prosthetic limbs, create new recyclable materials, and invent technologies to keep people in touch. The fact that so few women are in engineering suggests that a "taste preference" for helping people is not the only thing keeping women out of technical careers.

These preferences are part of a larger set of traits that are now known as "instrumental" and "communal," previously referred to as "masculine" and "feminine." Other instrumental traits include self-confidence, independence, competitiveness, leadership skills, ambition, self-reliance, self-assertiveness, and analytical ability, whereas communal traits include helpfulness to others, emotionality, understanding, cheerfulness, tenderness, and sympathy.[26] Are these traits truly different in men and women because of biological factors? The instrumental traits sound a lot like the characteristics one needs to be successful in a high-powered career. Indeed, when researchers first began to measure these traits, few women were in the workforce. But times are changing, and women's instrumentality is changing as well, challenging suggestions that it is purely biological.

Jean Twenge, a psychologist at San Diego State University, looked at more than one hundred studies conducted between 1973 and 1994 in which college students rated themselves on instrumental and communal characteristics. She found that over time, women increasingly reported that they possessed instrumental traits; in surveys conducted during the 1990s, men and women received almost identical average scores on instrumentality.[27] Twenge conducted a similar analysis of studies on the assertiveness of girls and college women over time. She found that women's assertiveness was high before World War II, was lower between 1945 and 1965, and then began to rise again.[28] Women's assertiveness levels correlated with their status, especially when college women's assertiveness was matched to women's status ten years prior, when they were children and their personalities were still forming. Twenge offers two possible explanations for her results. First, girls may absorb ideas about women's roles and status, then develop a personality to fit. Second, ideas about women's roles and status may cause parents to treat girls differently and encourage different activities.

While it appears that environmental factors can and do have a large impact, biological factors almost certainly have some influence, however small. What is the source of the biological influences that may be at work? While we know that the X and Y chromosomes determine sex, no one has discovered a gene that makes someone good at math or spatial reasoning or independent work. Nor is there any evidence that such genes exist on the Y chromosome.

A large body of scientific work does document a variety of differences between men's and women's brains, however. For example, while most people know about the impact of hormones like testosterone and estrogen on the male and female reproductive systems, certain structures in the brain also contain receptors for these hormones, and their different levels in men and women do appear to have an impact. A lot of research has been done on girls and women with congenital adrenal hyperplasia, or CAH, a genetic disorder in which the body produces excess testosterone. Women with CAH perform better than the general female population on certain tests of spatial abilities; on other tests, no difference is seen.[29] Interestingly, girls with CAH show deficits in mathematical ability.[30] These results point to a role for testosterone in spatial and mathematical reasoning, but they also suggest that it is not the only factor. Some research also suggests that different areas of the brain develop at different rates in males and females. In general, female brains mature more quickly than male brains do.[31] This finding may help to explain why different patterns and magnitudes of gender differences are found at different points in childhood.

Furthermore, some brain structures exhibit different activity levels or are different sizes, on average, in men and women. A promising line of research uses functional magnetic resonance imaging (fMRI), during which people complete tasks, such as solving math problems or mazes, while researchers monitor their brain activity. Research suggests that in some cases, women and men use different parts of their brains to solve the same problems. While this could suggest a source of observed gender differences in ability, often no difference in performance is observed.[32] Some of these results are controversial—questions arise about instrument settings, numbers of subjects, and so on—but brain imaging has the potential to teach us much more about the impact of biology on cognition.

We simply don't know enough to make definitive claims about gender differences, and even if we knew more, the answer is unlikely to be simple. Ability in math and science, just as in any field, results from a complex mixture of environmental and biological factors. Whether (and if so, how and how much) the biological factors differ between men and women is still an open question. Considering that some of the differences found so far are tiny, we may find that although innate gender differences exist, they are so overwhelmed by environmental factors as to be insignificant. And even if they do make a difference, this does not necessarily imply a deficiency. So what if some women scientists and engineers don't think about their work the same way their male colleagues do because of biological differences? We need to stop seeing this as a bad thing and start celebrating it. Women can offer science a great deal precisely because they often do look at problems in different ways. It's obvious that some women are not only interested in these fields but are also quite good at what they do. We need to make sure that women are encouraged and supported in academia, in industry, and in whatever other setting they choose. Scientists should continue to investigate the brain and learn more about how biology influences abilities for all people. But to truly improve the experiences of women in science and engineering, we need to focus not on what may or may not be different about a woman's brain, but on the barriers she faces outside her head.

COMPETING
CLOCKS

STRUGGLING

FOR BALANCE

IN SCIENCE

CAREERS

In the 1960s and 1970s, the women's movement told women that they could have it all, a career and a family and a rich, full life that involved their talents and skills in a wide variety of areas. But now it has become abundantly clear that, given the current structure of the American workplace, women can have it all only for certain definitions of "all." This is especially true in science and engineering because of these fields' intense demands on a woman's time and energy. Most of the women I interviewed had struggled with or expressed fears about balancing a career and a personal life.

"We think as superwomen that we're not going to be subject to those kinds of basic fears," says Cathy, who left engineering after working in the field for only a few years in the 1990s. "[But] it doesn't matter how smart you are. You still have to juggle having a career and having a family."

The problem is that a female scientist's or engineer's life is full of competing clocks that are not synchronized and are often in direct competition with each other. There's the education and career clock, which dictates how long she spends in college and graduate school, when her profession expects her to focus on building a career, when she goes up for tenure or promotion, when to retire, and so on. There's the partner and family clock, which drives her to find a partner and to have children if she wants them before biology makes it impossible, and then to spend time with the children before they're suddenly adults. And there's the personal clock, which includes a wide variety of goals and timelines that a woman sets for herself and may relate to neither career nor family.

Consider a woman who begins college at age eighteen with dreams of becoming a professor. She spends four years as an undergraduate and then goes immediately to graduate school. PhD programs generally last between four and eight years, depending on the discipline and circumstances. Let's say she finishes her degree in six years. Then she does a two-year postdoctoral fellowship before obtaining a position as an assistant professor. Tenure is granted (or not) after six years. Do the math: She's thirty-six years old.

When Ingrid was a graduate student in math in the late 1980s, a male professor gave her "what he said was the only workable advice for having a life while being in academia, which was: You can't afford to fall in love until both of you have tenure." But most scientists and engineers, whether they plan to go into academia or not, would prefer not to wait until their late thirties to find a long-term partner and have children. On the other hand, employers typically see a man's family as evidence of his stability and dedication to work—he has to feed those kids, after all—while a woman with a family is often viewed as less serious about her career.

Career and family are not the only two things competing for a woman's time. Having kids often rests on finding a partner and creating a stable relationship, which can be a time-consuming process. Of course, a woman doesn't need children or even a partner to desire a balance between work and personal time. Most women want to pursue interests outside of science, to perform volunteer work, to develop friendships, to travel, and so on, a balance that is important to overall well-being.

Marie Curie enjoyed bicycling and going to the theater. Albert Einstein played the violin and liked to sail. Other iconic scientists also had interests outside of test tubes and equations. And yet many people, scientists included, have an image of a scientist as someone who spends all of his or her time in the laboratory, someone who lives and breathes science and can think of nothing else.

Unfortunately, in some areas of science this is not just a stereotype but a reality. This is because science and engineering are greedy fields, ones that demand as much time and energy as their workers can give. From the time an undergraduate starts college, the educational path of a scientist requires huge amounts of dedication. Preparing for a high-powered science career requires many more years, with PhD plus postdoc, than the three years of law school or two years to earn an MBA. Then, during their careers, scientists and engineers are expected to perform as ideal workers who are willing to work long hours and have the flexibility to do whatever their employers need, including travel on short notice.[1]

This means that the ideal worker has traditionally been a man with a wife who stays home and does all the childcare and housework. To function as ideal workers, most of the pioneering generation of women in science and engineering did not have children, and some did not even marry. But many female scientists now in their twenties and thirties refuse to remain single and childless for the sake of their careers.

A woman with a partner who does all the childcare and housework could also function as an ideal worker, but this is rare, as most women would not want to be so disengaged from their children. Unfortunately, an even split of childcare and housework between partners is still elusive. Even in dual-career households, men often function as near-ideal workers, leaving women with more household responsibilities. A study of University of California faculty found that female professors spent an average of fifty-one hours per week on childcare and housework, while male faculty averaged thirty-two hours a week on these tasks. For women, this household work is on top of an average work week of fifty-one hours.[2] Due to these intense demands, for many women, life becomes super-scheduled, with very little time spent on activities beyond career and family. Many of the professor-moms (not all scientists) in one study reported wanting time just to think.[3] Cecilia, a tenured engineering professor with two young children, loves flying alone, because it gives her a few hours to read or do whatever else she wants.

Even when employers don't expect long hours from all employees, they may expect them from some. In particular, managers may assume that the person without kids will be the one to stay till midnight and get the project done after those with children have gone home for the day. "I had this experience of working through my thirties as the only person in my group who did not have children, and having to frequently make the statement when we did our scheduling that while I did not have children, I still had a family and still had a life," says Jenni, a physician in her forties. "I had to fight against this idea that having children is the only legitimate reason to adjust your work schedule."

These long hours have consequences for balancing career and family long before the birth of a child. While some women choose to have children on their own, most would prefer to be in a stable relationship before becoming pregnant. A woman who is putting all her energy into her education or career will have fewer opportunities to meet potential partners and build a relationship. "I put my career before dating," says Carolyn, a computer scientist who is still single in her late forties. "I always thought that I could get married later. But once you get out of college it just gets harder and harder to meet a compatible man."

Female scientists and engineers are more likely than their male counterparts to marry other scientists and engineers, or at least other professionals. A 1990 survey showed that 68 percent of married female physicists were married to other scientists, compared to only 17 percent of male physicists.[4] A 2001 survey of chemists under forty showed that 52 percent of married women were married to scientists, whereas only 37 percent of men were.[5]

Female scientists marry other scientists and engineers for many reasons. One is opportunity: Male scientists are nearby—in classes, in the lab, in the cubicle down the hall. Another is understanding: Many women enjoy being able to "talk shop" with their significant other, and if your partner also has four hours of homework every night, or works twelve-hour days in the lab, he's less likely to feel neglected when you're not available. "I think the best thing is having somebody who understands where I'm coming from. Not only is my husband a techie, but he was in grad school," says Miranda, a computer scientist in her thirties. "He understands the whole academia thing. He understands the need to work long hours, to go where the jobs are."

Not only may this sort of understanding be lacking in men in fields outside science, but they may also be intimidated by female scientists. One woman told me that she and her friends, all MIT alumnae, discovered that they all use the same tactic on dates. "When we're meeting someone for the first time and the subject of where we went to school comes up, we say, 'Oh, I went to school in Boston. Have you ever been to Boston?' We avoid admitting for as long as possible that we went to MIT," she says. "We were raised to be proud of being smart women. But in the dating world that doesn't work. It does intimidate men, or alienate us from them."

Women in science and engineering also marry other professionals because, in general, women tend to marry partners who are a few years older and as well or better educated than they are. A 1998 survey of dual-career physicists found that women were on average 2.1 years younger than their partners; only 15 percent were older.[6] This is one reason why women may have trouble finding partners as they become older; the pool of older, unattached men becomes smaller, and the women must compete against younger women as well. Many high-achieving men also prefer to marry women who are less ambitious and more willing to let their careers take a backseat to their partners'.

Once a female scientist enters a long-term relationship, she must navigate other obstacles. For one, science and engineering assume that their practitioners are able to move freely around the country and even to other nations. In general, a woman aiming for a high-powered science career attends one university as an undergraduate and another as a graduate student. Most science fields then require at least one postdoctoral fellowship, and in some fields it's now common to do two or even three. Each of these is generally at a different university, national lab, or corporation, resulting in more moves. Finally, a woman obtains the coveted faculty or staff scientist job—but depending on tenure decisions, promotions, layoffs, corporate reorganizations, and other factors, a woman may be uprooted again. A similar runaround can occur for physicians as they complete their undergrad, medical school, residency, and fellowship in different places before settling down in a medical practice. Staying in one geographic area is sometimes possible, but this can severely limit options and increase the potential for rejection.

Tara's husband, a city planner, followed her across the country when she started graduate school in astronomy several years ago. "He's perfectly willing [to move] and very encouraging about astronomy being my passion. I think he's even proud of my ambitions," she says. "But I don't want to take advantage of his generosity. I want him to be in control of our lives as well."

Couples who meet while they're still students often try to apply to graduate programs and/or postdocs at the same universities. A school with a great program in microbiology may not necessarily be strong in mechanical engineering, however. Applying to schools in the same metropolitan areas can sometimes solve this problem, but many couples find that one of them has been accepted to schools in Seattle, Chicago, and Boston, while the other has been accepted to schools in Los Angeles, Austin, and Atlanta, and thus they end up with a commuter relationship. No one has conducted a large-scale survey on the frequency of long-distance relationships during science careers. However, more than half of my interviewees who entered long-term relationships prior to or during graduate school had spent time apart from their partner—or made sacrifices in their careers to keep the couple in one place.

In the 1990s, after being in a long-distance relationship for two years, Linda took a year off from graduate school in computer science to be with her husband, who was in medical school in another state. When she went back to school, her husband was able to do some of his fourth-year medical school rotations near her university.

"And then we had the match," Linda says, referring to the process by which med students are matched to residency programs. "That was really stressful because we basically knew that wherever he matched I was going to go. We weren't even sure if I was going to get to stay [in my graduate program] or if I was going to have to transfer." Fortunately, Linda's husband was matched to a residency at the same university as her graduate program, so she was able to complete her PhD there.

Attempting to get accepted to graduate programs and post-docs in the same area is an example of the "two-body problem": the issue of finding satisfying jobs or educational opportunities in the same city for two people with specialized abilities, such as scientists and engineers. Since graduate school and postdoctoral positions are finite, couples are more willing to spend time apart. The two-body problem becomes a bigger issue when couples pursue permanent positions, such as tenure-track professorships. Although the two-body problem is often discussed solely in the context of faculty positions, it applies to industrial and government jobs as well. Women are disproportionately affected, both because they are more likely to be married to other scientists than their male colleagues and because women have traditionally been expected to sacrifice their careers for the sake of their husbands' aspirations.

Unless at a very large university, a science or engineering department is likely to have only one faculty position open at a time. If both halves of a couple are in the same field and looking for professorships, things become difficult quite quickly. On the other hand, if multiple positions are open, the university must judge that both halves of the couple are the most qualified candidates. A large city with multiple colleges may offer opportunities for faculty positions at different universities, but competition for positions in urban areas is usually higher than for those in rural areas, so this is no guarantee. Ultimately, one half of the couple often makes a sacrifice and takes a non-tenure-track position, or gives up on academia and finds a job in industry or government.

Laurie and her husband applied to faculty jobs only at small colleges, since they agreed that a large, research-intensive university wasn't the right place for them. Her husband got a tenure-track position at a small state university, which offered Laurie a part-time position. "The part-time pay is just ridiculous, almost nonexistent. There's absolutely no reason to teach part time unless you're really enjoying what you're doing," she says. Laurie teaches two classes that she likes and has been applying for grants (so far unsuccessfully) that would fund undergraduates to do research with her. She's also had a baby. "All this stuff is so much work, and no one is paying me to do it," Laurie says. "I feel the added stress of not wanting to let down my colleagues, but I'm not really enjoying the work so much right now."

In some relationships, both spouses make career sacrifices at different times. When Maria married her husband, she left a tenure-track position to join him in industry. Both are computer scientists, and at the time, her husband was much better known in the field. "What I hadn't figured out was that the only reason they made me an offer was because they wanted [my husband]. It was sort of a shock when I started working there," she says. But their three most recent moves (within academia) occurred to advance Maria's career. "[My husband] has been amazingly willing to make changes and to do very different things for my career," she says.

In the midst of dealing with the issues surrounding having a relationship and a career in science, a woman must decide if and when she will have children. "I've never gotten to a point when I've felt that this would have been a good time to have a baby. I don't know that that exists," says Paula, a tenured physics professor who had her only child while in graduate school. "You just sort of live with the situation you have and figure it out."

In a study of Canadian women professors, sociologist Carmen Armenti found that before maternity leave was common, many women tried to give birth at the end of the spring term so that they could spend the summer with their infant before resuming teaching duties in the fall.[7] (Of course, not everyone was able to conceive at precisely the right time for this to work.) In recent years women have been more willing to give birth in the middle of the semester, but many women in academia still feel that they would be jeopardizing their careers by giving birth before getting tenure. Some women in nonacademic positions similarly feel that they must get to a certain point on the career ladder before a baby comes along, although a woman who waits until her late thirties has a higher chance of not being able to have children at all. About one-third of couples in which the woman is older than thirty-five have difficulty conceiving.[8] While we frequently hear about the increase in women having children later in life, the truth remains that older women are also more likely to miscarry or bear children with birth defects.[9] Although assisted reproductive technologies (ART) such as in vitro fertilization can allow older women to become pregnant, they are expensive and invasive and have low success rates. In 2004, 37 percent of ART cycles with mothers younger than thirty-five resulted in live births, but only 11 percent of cycles with forty-one- to forty-two-year-old mothers did.[10]

Given these statistics, fewer women are willing to risk not being able to have children because they waited to try. As a result, more women are giving birth as junior faculty. "We actually have a plan that fits around the tenure and promotion cycle," says Carmen, an assistant professor of engineering in her early thirties. She hopes to have her first child after the third-year review process and then a second one after she receives tenure. "Now, I realize that these things can't be quite strictly as planned, but you kind of have to move forward with a plan and see what happens."

Some women are choosing to have children even earlier, in graduate school or during postdocs. This is in part because the increasing number of postdocs required in some fields is raising the age at which a woman can expect to get a tenure-track position. In addition, a graduate student's children may be preschool- or even school-age by the time she starts as an assistant professor or industry scientist, which can make childcare easier.

In some disciplines, having kids in grad school makes a lot of sense. Women in mathematics and computer science, whose work often doesn't require specialized equipment, can frequently work from home or at odd hours. "You have an amazing amount of flexibility because you can do it at night after the kids are asleep; you can write that code or that paper," says Linda, a computer scientist who had her first child in grad school.

But some kinds of research are more difficult to do while pregnant or with a child. Many chemicals are more toxic to fetuses than to adults, so performing certain kinds of chemistry and biology experiments safely can be difficult for pregnant women. It's also harder to do geology research in a remote mountain range with a baby on your hip. But women with these restrictions may still be able to have children toward the end of graduate school, when they are focused on analyzing data and writing up their dissertations. Having a child often does increase a student's time to graduation, regardless of field, however.

One downside of having a child while in graduate school is that most universities do not have formal maternity leave policies for graduate students. The Family and Medical Leave Act of 1993 (FMLA) requires employers to provide twelve weeks of unpaid leave per twelve-month period for medical reasons, birth of a child, adoption, or care of an immediate family member.[11] Many companies, universities, and other institutions offer a partial or full salary for part or all of the twelve weeks required by FMLA. But depending on how graduate students are paid—often out of their research advisor's grants, or by the department for teaching—they may not qualify for FMLA leave. They thus must negotiate with their advisor or department for leave time. Since graduate student stipends are generally no more than $25,000 per year, many students can't afford to take unpaid leave. Some university health insurance programs don't cover dependents, creating an additional financial burden.

Of course, what all maternity leave policies fail to take into account is that it takes many years to raise a child, not six weeks or twelve weeks, or even a year. The United States requires employers to offer far less maternity and paternity leave than many other countries do. Lena, for example, gave birth to her children while doing graduate work in Sweden in the 1990s. At the time, parents of newborns received twelve months of leave at 80 percent of their salary to split between them as they wished. (Sweden now offers more leave time and requires that each parent take some of it.) During her leave, Lena chose to continue to work at a slower pace and usually from home; other times she brought her baby to work with her.

Women have used a variety of methods to extend their

maternity leave. Claire, an associate professor at a private university, worked right up until she gave birth in the 1990s and then went on sabbatical for a year. Miranda, an assistant professor at a liberal arts college, cobbled together seven months of leave when she had her first child in the 2000s. This included a one-term sabbatical, a summer, and her paid maternity leave. While some women find inventive ways to make the balance work, others don't feel as if they can truly go on maternity leave without causing harm to their careers.

SAMANTHA, 30

As a PhD student, Samantha, an engineer, met her now-husband while at a summer job doing consulting work in another state. They began to date long distance when she returned to school. Soon, however, commuting across the country became frustrating. "He was doing this start-up company," she says. "The idea was that he just needed one more year, because this was the year that they were going to make it big."

Samantha thus applied for an exchange scholars program that allowed her to do a year of graduate work at a university near her partner while remaining enrolled at her science and engineering school. She found that she loved the new lab she was in—and being near her partner—so she transferred schools. "I lost probably one or two years in the process, so I took a lot longer to finish overall."

As Samantha drew near to completing her degree, she considered her options. She enjoyed her consulting work and could see herself in industry. But she also thought that academia was something she might really enjoy. "There are certain things about it that you can't get in industry, like complete freedom to work on whatever you are able to get funded. And I thought that it might give me a lot more flexibility in my family life," she says. Samantha decided to try the professor route first, figuring that she could return to industry if academia was a poor fit.

The university she ultimately chose was attractive because it had many women faculty with children as well as excellent leave policies. Unfortunately, it was in a different state from her husband's company, so they were back to a long-distance relationship until he was in a position to telecommute.

Samantha and her husband had planned to have their first child before she finished graduate school. It didn't work out that way, but not for lack of trying: She suffered two miscarriages. Samantha gave birth to a healthy baby girl a few months after she began her faculty position. "If I had only been thinking about my career, I would have waited until after I had tenure," she says. "I know that other women have had kids pretenure and gotten tenure, but are they happy people? I'm not sure."

Samantha never had a proper maternity leave. She was writing grants and a conference paper the week before giving birth, and attended a conference the week after. "I was on email, writing work email, three days after she was born. I bought myself a BlackBerry so that I could send and receive email while I was nursing," Samantha says.

Attending conferences has also been difficult. One, held a couple months after Samantha's daughter was born, was in a nearby city on a Saturday. Seems like ideal conditions—except Samantha was breastfeeding. Her husband was willing to bring the baby to her, so Samantha called the conference hotel and asked if they had a room where she could breastfeed. "They wanted me to pay for two nights of a $200-a-night hotel room so that I could feed the baby three times during the day." The hotel also said she was welcome to breastfeed the baby in the lobby. "I thought that it would be such a terribly embarrassing situation if any male colleague from the conference came upon me while I was breastfeeding my baby," Samantha says. "I was thinking to myself, five years from now, this guy is going to be writing a tenure letter for me and he's going to remember me as the woman who was breastfeeding her baby at the conference." Samantha ended up feeding her daughter at a friend's house nearby, missing significant chunks of the conference.

Although Samantha thought that being in academia would give her more flexibility, she has found that it's harder to have a child there than in industry, because no one can do your job for you. "There's someone who might step in and teach your class, but there's nobody who's advising your grad students, there's nobody who's applying for grants for you, and there's nobody who's writing papers for you," she says.

"I want to make my family decisions independent of my career decisions. If the best time to have my kids is now, then I'm going to have them now. If I don't get tenure because I didn't have the time to put in it, so what?"

Samantha is not alone in her problems balancing childcare with travel. Academics are expected to present their work at conferences, which also provide many opportunities for networking.

These conferences are held all over the world and may last from a day to a week or more. Women who want or need to bring their children to a conference must often also bring a spouse, other relative, or nanny to provide childcare. Some conferences provide information about local childcare centers, but on-site childcare is rare.

Some kinds of research are also more likely to require travel. During graduate school, Paula needed to spend time observing at various telescopes. "That's what you do when you're an observational astronomer. You go off to the mountain for a week or two weeks or whatever to get your data, and then you come home and you spend all your time in front of a computer," she says. During her first observing run, she left her daughter with her parents, who lived in a different state from either Paula's graduate school or the telescope. Her husband's mother came to visit during another observing run—different accommodations every time.

Because of the challenges inherent in balancing a scientific career with children, some women make the decision to stay home with their children for a few years—or permanently. But trying to reenter the scientific workforce is extremely difficult. New discoveries and developments occur constantly. Especially in rapidly changing fields such as molecular biology, if you're six months behind, you're way out of date. Thus, some women instead attempt to balance their careers and personal lives by working part time. While this may seem like the ideal compromise, in practice, working part time is often far from perfect.

Jane, a biomedical researcher, considers the period in the 1990s when she worked part time to be the unhappiest of her life. "When you work part time, you often get tracked into a real mommy-track job," she says. "When I was at work, I had really mundane stuff to do that kept me busy all the time I was there. And then when I was at home, I was with my kids a lot, but I didn't fit in with the mothers who weren't working. I liked being home more hours, but it was both not enough and too much."

Part of the problem is that since full time is much more than forty hours per week in many science and engineering careers, part time is more like full time. Jenni, a physician, has worked part time since adopting her daughter several years ago. "Part of my own personal maturation process was figuring out a way that I could take care of myself emotionally so that I could be available to a child in the way that I wanted to be, and that meant that I couldn't work full time. That's my own personal calculus," she explains. But as a primary-care doctor, she has a part-time schedule that is suspiciously close to what would be considered full-time work in other jobs. "If I see patients 36 hours a week, which is full time, I'm working 50 hours a week, minimum, because of the paperwork and the phone calls," Jenni says. "So I see patients 22 hours a week. I sometimes teach outpatient 4 hours a week, so at most I am scheduled to work 26 hours a week. That means I work between 30 and 35 hours a week. I have full-time daycare."

At many universities, all tenure-track faculty positions are full time. Although policies that permit part-time work are on the books at some universities, many faculty don't know about them. Those who do are often afraid to inquire about, much less take advantage of, such policies, for fear of being seen as not serious about science. Universities offer some part-time faculty positions off the tenure track. However, they are generally poorly paid and often focus on teaching.

Regardless of how many hours a woman works, she will need childcare for the hours she is unavailable to her kids. In the 1970s, Chris, then an industrial materials scientist, and her husband split the cost of a nanny with another couple who had children the same age and lived two blocks away. "One week we would have kids at our house and the next week at the other house. [The nanny] would come from something like 7:30 to 4:30, and then we hired a college student to cook dinner and watch the kids from 4:30 to 6:30, and then we'd all come together, at whichever house had the dinner, and then take our kids home." The joint childcare arrangement lasted thirteen years, all with the same nanny.

Not all families are able to afford a nanny, so many children end up in childcare centers. Some universities and companies offer on-site childcare or recommend daycare centers in the area. But these generally have far fewer slots than employees have children who need them. Furthermore, many daycare centers serve children only in a limited age range, and they may not be open the hours that scientists need.

"Many of the faculty with young children aren't able to enjoy the wine and cheese following our colloquia," says Tara, a graduate student in astronomy. "They have to leave right away to pick up their kids from daycare. We've talked about setting up a better daycare system at [this university] for the 5–7 PM time."

Many women feel extremely uncomfortable with the idea of bringing their child to their job. Certainly some universities and companies are more child-friendly than others, but sometimes bringing a child to the lab regularly can work.

"My daughter was in the lab with me for the first sixteen months. I didn't have any daycare by choice," says Paula, a physicist who gave birth during her second year in graduate school in the 1980s. "Everybody else in the lab was at least polite enough not to complain about it. Some of them seemed to like it." Other grad students would watch the baby when Paula went to class. Later, the little girl zoomed around the lab wing in her walker, and they cleaned out a closet for her to use as a playroom. Paula's desk was right outside. "I was doing mostly image processing, so I was available and interruptable. It was like working at home, except that home was in the lab."

Paula's daughter accompanied her to the lab until she wanted to be with other kids, at which point the toddler started going to a babysitter three times a week. Paula's husband worked at a restaurant, so he was on the evening shift on the days they didn't have childcare. Paula explains, "I would go into work early, come home at 2:30 or 3 or whatever it was, he'd go off to work, I'd stay home until dinner, and then after dinner my daughter and I would go back to the lab when if she wanted to be noisy she wasn't going to bother anyone else. That went on until she was about four." In all, Paula's husband did about half the childcare. They called it tag-team parenting.

Men are increasingly putting more time and effort into parenting. Overall, this only occasionally means being the primary caregiver: The U.S. Census Bureau estimates that there are 143,000 stay-at-home dads in the United States out of the more than twenty-five million fathers with kids under age eighteen.[12] However, in my interviews I talked with five mothers whose partners are the primary caregiver, plus two women who don't have children yet but whose partners plan to stay home with the kids when they do. My sample isn't representative, but I was still surprised at how many times this situation came up.

Of course, these arrangements vary wildly. Brianna's husband, for example, is taking care of their daughter just during Brianna's postdoc; when she obtains a permanent position and they settle down, he plans to work full time again. In Miranda's case, her husband continues to consult part time from home while taking care of their child. She explains her husband's decision: "He understands that at this point my career has to take precedence until I get tenure."

Traditionally, mothers have stayed home in part because their husbands earned higher salaries. Although some of the women I spoke with had the potential to outearn their partners, this wasn't always true. Vera and her husband both have PhD degrees in physics. They married while in graduate school, and she had a child as a postdoc. When she and her husband applied to positions in industry, they made a pact that they would stay together in the same place. Unfortunately, they didn't find jobs in the same city. Vera really liked one offer she had received, while her husband was generally discouraged about his career. "He said, 'You know, why don't I take a year to take care of the baby, because I think that would help you get established in your job, and then I'll look for a job,'" Vera explains. "I was willing to let him do that because I had been [a full-time parent] for a few months, so I was going to be ready to go back to work."

Her husband found that he liked being a stay-at-home dad, so he continued after the year was up. When I talked to Vera, she was pregnant with their second child, and her husband was going to continue to be the primary caregiver for both kids after she gave birth. "My husband truly—truly, truly, truly—was willing to let my [career] be as important as his, or more," Vera says. "And I see my husband paying a price. Somebody has to give in."

Sometimes the stresses on a marriage are too much, and a separation occurs. According to the U.S. Census Bureau, about 20 percent of adults have been divorced.[13] Researchers at the University of California, Berkeley, found that female tenure-track faculty were significantly more likely to divorce than were male tenure-track faculty or female faculty not on the tenure track.[14] For women in science and in high-powered jobs in general, the woman's career can certainly be a factor in a breakup in a variety of different ways. The intense demands of a science career may mean that a woman has less time for her spouse. Some men still expect that their careers will take precedence over those of their wives, which can create conflict if the woman is unwilling to play a supporting role and the husband is unable to change his expectations or otherwise adapt. Furthermore, some men expect to be more successful than their partners and can become frustrated if their wives outperform them, especially if the two are in the same field.

Jane is a biomedical researcher; her former husband is a physician. "Just as I'm publishing in *Science*, he's getting fired," she says. "The mythology of our relationship had always been that I was smart but he was smarter. And I was way outperforming him." The two went through a very messy divorce. "That derailed my career in large measure for several years," Jane says. "The people with whom I worked were so supportive and so helpful. The community of my women colleagues there really was what got me through. . . . And it was my self-esteem that I got from my work that allowed me to leave a really failed marriage. Aside from the financial aspect of it, that I made a reasonable living, I had a sense of self that was completely separate from my family."

After couples divorce, women often have to adjust their career–personal life balance because of the additional responsibilities of being a single mom. When Kelsey, an assistant professor of biology, was married, she relied on her husband a lot for childcare. Now that they are divorced, she has her kids every other week. "I try to cram as much work as possible into the weeks I don't have them and then scale back when they're here and with me."

After a divorce, a woman may also be less willing or able to pick up and move for her career. "After I split from my son's dad, it was important to me that I be in the same city as my ex, because I felt strongly that even though I don't need his dad, he does," Bridget explains. She was lucky to already be at a university that is a major player in the type of physics she does, but some women end up extremely confined by their lack of mobility.

Young women in science and engineering today seem to be more aware of the challenges of balancing a career and a personal life. They have seen the tough choices that their predecessors have made and know that having it all is an elusive goal. But the best strategies to handle these challenges are not always clear, and discussing them is sometimes taboo. "Being able to talk to someone about my concerns without them judging me—I think that's really difficult to find," says Rose, a graduate student in biology who wants to have children eventually. "There are times when I don't feel like I can talk to some female professors about my reservations or worries, because their attitude is, well, you should be able to do it all. If I even think about taking a little time off, that makes me less of a scientist."

Some women have found ways to make their lives full and balanced, even if some trial and error was required. Others are opting out rather than fighting the prevailing norms in science and engineering. To retain women in technical fields, flexibility and support for interests and responsibilities outside of science are crucial. But achieving a balance between work and a personal life is not the only challenge that female scientists encounter. Bias and discrimination, some hidden, some related to marriage and motherhood, also play a large role in the underrepresentation of women in science and engineering.

SWIMMING
UPSTREAM

BIAS

AGAINST

WOMEN IN

SCIENCE

P rior to the civil rights and women's movements, people and institutions did not generally hide their prejudices. When Irene went job-hunting after earning a bachelor's degree in engineering in the 1940s, she was literally shut out. "When I'd go to apply, they'd send a secretary down to say, 'We don't hire women for those jobs.' Close the door, that was it," she says. Women were prohibited from using many scientific facilities; in the 1950s, astronomer Margaret Burbidge gained access to the Mount Wilson Observatory in California only by posing as her husband's assistant. Until the passage of Title IX in 1972, few university engineering programs admitted female students, and those that did generally imposed quotas.

Citing antinepotism rules, many universities forced women who married other academics to give up their faculty positions.

Policies have changed. Universities, companies, and other institutions do not officially restrict women's access or opportunities. Many women now learn and work in environments that appear to be free of discrimination. They are treated similarly to the men around them and receive the same types of projects and support. Many women told me that they have experienced no gender bias or didn't experience bias until they reached a certain point in their careers. "While I was an undergrad I was pretty well convinced that gender bias was a thing of the past," says Kathryn, now in her thirties.

Unfortunately, not all those attitudes have changed, and some people continue to discriminate against women. This discrimination is more likely to occur in male-dominated environments, which many science and engineering fields still are. Some of this discrimination is overt and directed, such as sexual harassment. But discrimination is more likely to be subtle and hidden. For example, the head of the faculty search committee may rank male candidates higher in his evaluations just for being male. The graduate advisor may meet with his male graduate students more often and help them network with others in the field. The boss may offer less interesting and less challenging projects to his female employees, so when promotion time comes the male employees are stronger candidates. Since these actions often occur behind closed doors, a female scientist may not realize that she is being treated differently.

People can also discriminate without realizing it. In her book *Why So Slow? The Advancement of Women*, Virginia Valian discusses the concept of gender schemas, unconscious hypotheses that people hold about the characteristics of men and women.[1] These schemas, which start to take root in childhood, are based on both overt and inadvertent messages from society about how men and women behave. Because gender schemas are unconscious, someone who consciously believes in gender equity can still take actions that are biased.[2]

One consequence of standard gender schemas is that men are overrated and women are underrated in professional life. A manager holding a standard gender schema may assume that men are more competent and have better ideas, for example, even though the manager has no evidence to support this. While these assumptions may at first appear to be minor annoyances, over time, small instances of subconscious favoritism can accumulate into large disparities between women and men. Women are poorly represented at the highest ranks in most science and engineering fields. For example, in 2003 women represented only about 19 percent of full-time tenured faculty members in science and engineering.[3] A 2000 study of top research universities found that women composed only 2.7 percent of engineering department chairs and 5.7 percent of mathematics and physical sciences department chairs.[4] While these low numbers can be attributed partly to other factors, the accumulation of disadvantage is at work as well.

"Very few people will say it out loud, but discrimination happens every day. You have to work two times, three times harder to gain the same level of respect for your work and to get people to understand what you are there to do," says Rachel, an engineer in her twenties.

Applied psychologist Richard Martell and colleagues created a computer simulation of an organization containing eight levels with a varying number of positions. The simulation began with equal numbers of men and women awaiting promotion. In each round, 15 percent of the employees left the company, creating promotion opportunities. Each employee received a performance score based on a normal distribution, and employees with the highest scores were promoted to the next level. The researchers found that when men received just a 1 percent gender bonus to their performance scores, women clustered at the bottom of the organization and men at the top. Women could not achieve more than 35 percent of the top positions in the organization.[5] Thus, if unconscious bias on the part of supervisors gives men in an organization even a small advantage, that advantage can build over time and have a large effect on who ends up at the top. And indeed, women are most severely underrepresented at the highest levels of most companies and other organizations.

"For a long time I had this theory that a lot of [the different treatment] at least partly was due to your own attitude," Laurie says. "If you acted like you weren't any different from men and that you had no reason to think you were, then people were more likely to treat you that way. Now I'm not so sure."

Conscious discrimination, both overt and subtle, can combine with the subconscious workings of gender schemas to create a hostile or "chilly" climate for women in science and engineering. Such an environment can make it much harder for a woman to perform well and be successful. This is particularly true for women of color, who often must overcome not only gender discrimination but racial discrimination as well. When overt discrimination occurs, many women do not report it. When more subtle discrimination occurs, women may not notice it, or may not be sure whether they're experiencing bias or something else. For example, a few years ago, after Helen, an Asian-American woman, received her master's degree in mathematics, the director of graduate studies asked to meet with her. "He told me that it was best for me to transfer to another school [for my PhD]," she says. "He said that some faculty were doubting my research abilities. I asked him which faculty, and he wouldn't tell me. And then he said that given the fact that my boyfriend was in [another state], it was best for me to transfer back to [that state]."

Helen admits that her master's thesis did not go as well as it could have, though she attributes that to a mismatch between her advisor's interests and her own. In talking with other students, however, Helen discovered that the graduate studies director had recommended that two other Asian-American women leave the program. This suggests that the professor probably had a bias, but whether it was conscious or unconscious is unclear.

Unconscious schemas and subtle biases can disadvantage women in many ways. For example, first impressions are crucial, but because many people do not expect women to be scientists or engineers, they will often assume that a woman in a technical situation must hold some other, generally lower-status position. "I've had people think that I was someone's secretary," says Rachel, an engineer in her twenties.

"For half my medical school career, people thought I was a nurse," says Jane, who graduated from medical school in the 1980s.

Men are not the only ones who make such assumptions. As an undergraduate in engineering in the 1990s, Tanya attended a technical job fair. She asked a woman at one company's booth if the company offered internships. "And [the woman] replied, without even looking at my resume or anything, 'I'm sorry; we don't have business internships,'" Tanya says. "She wasn't mean—the assumption was just that you're a girl, so you must be a business major."

People will sometimes also attribute lower status to women by how they are referred to. Research has shown that students see professors addressed by title rather than first name as having higher status, and, as expected, more students address male professors by title than female ones.[6] It happens in other situations too. During an interview for a faculty position a few years ago, Kathryn was introduced to "Dr. Male Professor" as "Ms. Postdoc"—though of course she also had a PhD.

Even when men know that a woman is a scientist or engineer like them, they may try to push her into nontechnical roles. During group work in college, for example, women are frequently expected to act as secretary for their teams, often with the excuse that women have better handwriting than men. In a lab situation, the note-taker usually has fewer opportunities to do hands-on work, which can mean she gains fewer technical skills from the project.

Men (and women) who are supportive of women in science and engineering may still find themselves making negative assumptions about a woman's competence because the skills needed for success have traditionally been regarded as masculine. For example, Rachel, an engineer in her twenties, recently drew up and had made "a drip pan, just a stainless steel pan, nothing complicated." Her boss was surprised and confused that she had been able to do this. "It's kind of strange, because he's one of the most supportive people in the company in terms of hiring women," she says.

Brianna worked as a teaching assistant (TA) for her university's geology field camp several times. "Even if I wasn't doing anything and the male TA was helping another group, I would see guys lining up to ask questions of the other TA and not coming over to ask me questions," Brianna says. "Usually by the end of the summer camp they were coming to both of us; we were both quite competent, and eventually they figured that out."

A common result of this assumption about women's competence is that a woman must outperform a man for others to rate her as his equal. In one often cited study, researchers in Sweden looked at evaluations of applications for postdoctoral fellowships.[7] The researchers found that women received lower average scores than men in all three areas on which they were graded: scientific competence, quality of proposed methodology, and relevance of research proposal. This was not because their work was of poorer quality. Using a measure of scientific productivity that included both quality and quantity of research papers, the researchers found that women received lower scores than men with the same productivity. In fact, the average female applicant had to be two and a half times as productive as the average male applicant to receive the same competence score.

Another form of subtle bias is women's exclusion from men's professional and social networks. Because people are more likely to associate with others who resemble them, whether based on gender, ethnicity, age, shared interests, or other characteristics, many times men will, intentionally or unintentionally, exclude women from their informal networks. On the surface, this may be a minor thing—a woman might not have wanted to play golf anyway, and a group of women can certainly exclude a man in a similar fashion. When men compose the higher ranks of a workforce, however, being shut out of networks can have a significant impact on a woman's career. Men use social settings to talk shop, often dividing up work assignments. Women who are not present may be left with less interesting or important things to work on, which can make them appear less qualified for promotions or for employment elsewhere.

Furthermore, although formal application processes exist for graduate programs, postdocs, and jobs, the chances of getting a good position increase if you know the right people. A graduate advisor can introduce students to potential postdoc advisors at conferences, or call up Joe and encourage him to consider a particular candidate. Or the advisor can simply write a standard recommendation letter. Women have developed their own networks and mentoring relationships, which have helped to overcome some of these hurdles, but since men are still more likely to be in power, women's attempts to circumvent men's networks can accomplish only so much.

Women have also attempted to gain acceptance into men's networks and male fields in general by acting more masculine. Stereotypes still persist that women who look and act traditionally feminine are less committed or intelligent than their male counterparts. Janet described a woman in her chemistry graduate program in the 1990s: "Her makeup [and] her nails were done; she was also smart as all get-out. She ripped through her research and got a PhD in four years. And there were male [students] in the program who just could not take her seriously. Because she looked the way she did, they assumed that her research had to have been fluffy crap that didn't have any scientific merit."

As a result, women in male-dominated science and engineering programs sometimes wear baggy sweatshirts and jeans, avoid makeup, and try to look and act like "one of the guys." While not an ideal option, and one that certainly shouldn't be necessary, blending in like this can have the advantage of avoiding unwanted sexual attention from male colleagues and being more easily accepted into male networks. Samantha, an assistant professor of engineering, never consciously decided to portray herself as tomboyish to fellow students and colleagues, but playing sports with the guys has definitely benefited her. "When I was looking for an academic job [a few years ago], I think I gained a lot of credibility because I played ice hockey. . . . I was serious. I was strong," she says. "I do have this more stereotypically feminine side. I've always kept a few sewing projects on the side. . . . But I never talk about those things in front of my colleagues." On the other hand, women who act too masculine in certain ways, such as being highly competitive or aggressive, can experience negative repercussions, because they are acting so far outside the traditional gender schemas of the people around them. "Where's the line between assertive woman and bitch?" asks Tanya.

Whether a woman is perceived to be too feminine or too aggressive, or otherwise encounters bias, past discrimination can affect her during the hiring process. A sexist supervisor is unlikely to give a glowing reference, for example. But even when previous supervisors are not overtly discriminatory, bias can sneak in. Researchers at Wayne State University analyzed more than three hundred letters of recommendation written in the 1990s for successful candidates to medical school faculty positions.[8] The researchers found that letters for women were shorter on average and were twice as likely to contain phrases that raise doubt about the applicant's competence. Furthermore, possessive phrases in letters for women referred most to "her teaching," "her training," and "her application," while letters for men referred most to "his research," "his skills and abilities," and "his career."

"People will tend to write a [recommendation] letter for a woman emphasizing great team player, really hard working, really nice person, [and so on]," says Lauren, an academic physicist who has sat on many search committees. "For the male candidate of identical talents, they will say he's a real innovative scientist, a scientific leader, has good ideas, et cetera. Even though the woman may be innovative and have good ideas and the man may be a good team player and a really nice guy, people will emphasize different things in the letters."

Lauren once discussed this difference in recommendation style at a meeting with other science faculty at her university. After the meeting, a male professor whom Lauren describes as "absolutely right-minded on this issue, and definitely thinks we need to work harder to increase the number of women in the sciences," examined the letters he had written for his two most recent grad students, one woman and one man. "He held them side by side and said, 'Oh my God, I do it, too.'"

Seeing the effects of bias during hiring and promotion is often as easy as looking around an office to see how many women are there and what they're doing. "The way to tell whether a man is really sexist or not is [to] look at who they hire," says Theresa, a computer scientist who saw this in action at a government lab. "In my group, we had about twenty-five programmers, and twelve of them were women. It's because my boss there was not sexist. He really hired the best people there were. But there was another group that was right there in the same building, and there were ten technical people, and they were all men. Not a single woman. And the boss there was very sexist. Neither of them discussed it, neither of them said anything, but you could just tell by their actions."

Although a large gender disparity may be present among employees, because deliberations about hiring and promotion generally occur behind closed doors, it can be difficult to determine why and how it's happening. Even when one is on a search committee, it's difficult to ask Joe if he's rating Jim higher than Tina because he really thinks Jim is a stronger candidate or if he's giving him a bonus for being male.

Unfortunately, affirmative action and other programs intended to increase diversity in fields traditionally dominated by white males can create a backlash that harms the employees it brought into the institution. In particular, colleagues may assume that a woman gained admission to the school or was hired only because of a need to diversify and not because of her qualifications or competence. This can lead to discrimination.

In one study, college students received information about the performance of a work group that included both men and women and then rated the performance of some of its members. When told that the group had been brought together to ensure diversity, they rated a female team member less favorably than a male member. When the students were told that the group was formed because of previous excellence, ratings did not vary by gender. This occurred even though all students received the same information about the team's performance.[9]

Programs to increase diversity can also cause women to question their abilities. "Grad school was the first place where someone said, 'Oh, you only got in and you only got your NSF [fellowship] because you're a woman.' And that was horrible to hear," says Linda, a computer scientist who earned her PhD in the 2000s. "Even if you think it's not true, it eats at you a little bit. You start questioning: Did I get that because I deserved it, or were they bringing in extra things? Is this extra thing of my gender weighing too heavily?"

Questions and assumptions about the role of diversity programs in a woman's achievements are amplified when she is also a member of a minority group. Alicia is half Hispanic and half white. Her peers in high school told her, "You're a Hispanic woman; of course colleges are going to want you." Some implied that she would get in only because of that and/or tried to convince her to tell colleges she was white. On the other hand, her father insisted that she use her minority status to her advantage.

"I was a really strong applicant," says Alicia, who was valedictorian at her high school in the 2000s. "I don't know how strong. I don't know what admissions officers looked at. There are so many nuances to the admissions process that it's very possible that I received preference over some of my friends because of my background. And that made me feel kind of guilty."

Although it's less likely for a female faculty member or a

woman in industry to directly hear that she got something only because she's female, her coworkers may certainly think it or make such comments when the woman is not around. Those beliefs can impact how they interact with her and create serious obstacles to her achieving respect (if it is even possible) in such an environment.

Although overcoming the backlash against affirmative action is frustrating, being a token can be worse. Tokenism occurs when a department, laboratory, or other group hires one woman or minority to give the impression that the group is working toward increased diversity. But the group is often so hostile that the token cannot work productively. If the token leaves, the others in the group use this to reinforce their bias that women aren't cut out for jobs in that field. If the token stays, the stress and lost productivity of the negative environment, not to mention the hostile people around her, will make it difficult to impossible for her to be promoted. In the meantime, of course, the group will not seriously try to hire more women or minorities.

Sometimes people will set up tokenism situations to specifically reinforce their biases. As Theresa, a computer scientist, explains, "I've seen this nasty technique many times. The sexist man in charge finds a woman who's not very talented but who has some connection, and he hires her. And then all the men in the department say, 'See, it's really easy for women to get hired. So-and-so isn't very smart, has no qualifications, but she got hired just because she's a woman.'"

While hiring multiple women simultaneously is theoretically possible, it rarely happens due to the low numbers of open positions. Thus, almost every all-male group starts to increase its gender diversity by hiring one woman, so some women will continue to experience being the only female in a group of men. But there's a big difference between being a trailblazer and being a token. While a trailblazer has a supportive environment and is able to accomplish things that will advance her career and open doors for other women, a token must constantly fight bias and discrimination, and success is next to impossible.

Hiring decisions are not the only ones made behind closed doors; salaries are also a private matter. As such, when women are paid less than the men around them, they often don't know. Salary surveys often show that women's salaries are less than men's, with gaps approaching 20 percent.[10] As bias contributes to men being offered promotions at a faster rate than women, women are more likely to be in lower positions that pay lower wages. Women also take a hit in potential salary if they decide to work part time or to stop work for a while when they have children. Part-time wages are often less than half of those offered to full-time workers, and part-time workers are rarely eligible for benefits.

CAROLYN, 49

Carolyn earned a fine arts bachelor's degree but needed a more dependable source of income than her art. In the early 1980s she took a few computer science classes at a local university and then landed a programming job at a small startup. One of the founders of the company became infatuated with her. He called her a "sex kitten," invited her to social events, and literally chased her around her desk. "The whole company saw this, and unbeknownst to me, many thought I was sleeping with him and believed that was how I got my job," she says. The stress caused health problems that landed her in the hospital.

Carolyn moved to another state and to a different company, where the atmosphere was much more welcoming, despite a dearth of women. After a few years a large technology company recruited her, and she found herself facing gender bias yet again—more subtly this time. "They did not give me a starting bonus. Not once was I given stock options. About six years into it I realized that the men—I'm usually the only woman in these groups—were getting stock options all along."

During part of her time at this company, Carolyn worked for a sexist boss. "I was told before I got in his group that he hated women, but I didn't believe it. . . . They always make him have a woman in his group to be the token female, and then he runs them off. I was so arrogant. I thought, I'm gonna be different; I'm so good."

This boss focused on Carolyn's marital status, repeatedly asking her—in front of coworkers—what was wrong with her that she wasn't married. He would hardly talk to her about anything else. "I look back on this and [think], why didn't I do something, but I was just so floored when he would say things like that."

Her male coworkers also left her out of their networks. "I wasn't one of the boys. I wasn't using their restrooms or drinking with them at night. And so when a new project would come down, the guys divided up all the pieces, who would do what, and I would get what was left over. They had it all figured out because they talked to each other socially."

In the early 2000s, Carolyn decided to go back to school to earn a PhD in computer science. "[I thought] that if I was with people who were really educated, they would be more refined and they wouldn't be prejudiced." But she soon learned otherwise.

Her research group was led by her advisor and another professor, Dr. Q. The problems began almost immediately. "[In group meetings,] whenever I would try to say something, [Dr. Q] would just run me over and humiliate me in some way," she says. He also prevented her from talking to people in industry at meetings and conferences, sometimes literally putting himself between her and the other person. "I found two journal papers where [Dr. Q] basically takes my ideas and uses them as his own. Ideas that he, in front of everyone, pooh-poohed me about." Dr. Q's students also let Carolyn know that he was using his clout to make sure that conferences where he served on committees rejected her papers. "It sounds unbelievable, but these things happened."

Carolyn's advisor did very little to change the situation, however, and she didn't think that registering a formal complaint with the university would make a difference. "They're not going to dismiss the professors who pull in tons of money and grants. They're going to take the side of the person they're invested in."

Carolyn was not invited to contribute to any of the group's research papers, so her publication record was on the short side. This made it harder for her to obtain a research position after earning her PhD. She is now working in industry as a research scientist, but in a different area of computer science than her dissertation focus. Her current work group is very supportive and has done a lot to repair the self-confidence that her graduate school experience tore to shreds.

Carolyn is careful to emphasize that the discrimination she's experienced has been a small part of her career. She's had lots of great experiences and worked with many wonderful people. Still, the sexism has left its scars.

In the midst of the more common subtle and hidden gender bias, overt bias still occurs. Even though this country has come a long way since Carolyn's experience with it more than twenty years ago, sexual harassment is still widespread. Women in male-dominated fields such as many science and engineering disciplines are particularly vulnerable.

In a 2005 survey of more than 2,000 college students by the American Association of University Women, 62 percent of women reported having been sexually harassed on campus. Most of this harassment is from other students, but 7 percent of students (male and female) reported being sexually harassed by a professor.[11]

Many women I interviewed talked about being subject to lewd comments or lewd pictures. Tara's male colleagues at one job in the 2000s watched *The Howard Stern Show* during work. Michelle took an undergraduate physics class on vibrations and waves in the 1990s in which "the professor had a belly dancer gyrating on stage and was making sexual comments about how her breasts wiggled—vibrated."

Several times during Bridget's career, starting in the 1980s, men in positions of power, including a professor and a mentor in industry, hit on her. They generally made their interest widely known; one married man even left flowers at her desk.

"It undermined my accomplishments because I felt that if I did well, then people would assume it's because he's interested in me, not because I actually did a good job," she says.

Although awareness of and seminars on sexual harassment have decreased its incidence, sensitivity training can also have unintended consequences that are detrimental to women. In particular, it may make men more likely to exclude women from their networks because they fear being accused of harassment.

Catherine, an engineer, described a government internship in the 2000s where she worked with many older men. "They were very open with other guys . . . they would joke and talk about their families. They didn't treat me the same way," she says. Eventually Catherine learned that her coworkers had all been to sensitivity training right before she arrived. "I think they were all just really on edge and didn't want anything they said to be misconstrued, and so they just tried to talk to me as little as possible, which [is] really hard when you're in a working environment."

Catherine now has a permanent position at the same institution, and her relationships with her male coworkers are more collegial. "But I think that it definitely takes constant work on my part to subconsciously reassure them that I'm not just waiting for them to mess up, waiting for them to say the wrong thing. . . . I have to work harder at engaging them as opposed to them engaging me."

No one knows exactly how often sexual harassment in the sciences turns into sexual violence, but it does happen. In the 1970s, Madeleine worked her way up through a high-tech corporation to become its only female executive. She found the atmosphere among the other executives to be very sexually charged. During one company retreat she was asked what sort of prostitute she wanted for the night—all the men were getting them. At a subsequent annual sales meeting, the chairman of the board assaulted Madeleine while they were socializing with colleagues, aggressively groping and kissing her. "[He] just thought I was there for him. In that case there was another woman who poured a bottle of champagne over the two of us to distract him, because he was really mauling me, and I ran back to my room and locked myself in."

At a later retreat, one of the other executive officers followed her back to her room, forced himself inside, and raped her. She quit her job without reporting the rape. "I knew it was a culture in which I had no hope of getting any justice."

A few years later, Madeleine attended a conference at which she chaired a workshop for senior women. "We got to the subject of sexual harassment, and it turned out four of us had been raped in corporate settings, of the six of us senior women. We were stunned."

Intimate partner violence is also a problem. During graduate school in the 1970s, Gwen started having an affair with her PhD advisor, whose marriage was falling apart. About six months into the relationship, "[he] went crazy and almost killed me," she says. Over the next couple of years, he continued to beat her, often coupling the physical violence with threats that he would leave her and quit being her advisor. "He went to counseling, and it would be better for a while, and then I would get him upset and there would be an explosion and I would get beaten up again." It took a few years, but Gwen eventually switched PhD advisors and then found the courage to end her relationship, even though her former advisor threatened to kill her if she did.

At a recent conference she was part of a group of women talking to a female scientist who was being abused by her husband. "The women standing around talking with her, one after another, we said, 'Yeah, I've been there,'" Gwen says. No one tracks the incidence of rape or intimate partner violence among scientists and engineers, so it's unclear whether it is more of a problem for these women than for those in other settings, particularly very male-dominated ones, but this is obviously a serious issue that demands much more attention.

In too many places, some or all of these forms of overt and subtle discrimination combine to create an atmosphere that is hostile toward women. Being in such an environment not only inhibits a woman's career, it can also be bad for her health. One survey of college students indicated that overall, women had greater incidences of anxiety, depression, and stress-related physical symptoms than men, but women who experienced little or no sexism did not differ significantly from men on these measures. The differences occurred only among women who had experienced gender discrimination.[12]

Sadly, women who experience discrimination often do not report it. In the survey of harassment on college campuses, only 9 percent of the women who had been harassed told someone at their university about the incident. Many more—27 percent—didn't tell anyone at all.[13] The thought of confronting a harasser is understandably terrifying to many women. In one study, researchers arranged for a man to make three sexist remarks during a group activity in a psychology laboratory. Only 45 percent of the women confronted the man about at least one remark, and the most frequent response was a rhetorical question, such as "What did you say?" Only 16 percent of the confrontations involved a direct verbal comment, such as indicating that such remarks were inappropriate.[14] Of those who did not confront the man, 91 percent indicated after the activity that they had negative thoughts and emotions regarding him. Although these women noticed the sexist behavior and were in a situation in which retaliation was unlikely, most of them did not confront the speaker. It's no wonder that so few women speak up in situations in which negative consequences are more likely, particularly if they work in an unsupportive environment and fear that speaking up will jeopardize their career or academic standing.

Men who are supportive in other situations will sometimes allow discrimination to happen because they don't know how to stop it or fear for their own reputations if they take a stand for someone else. "Sometimes people make inappropriate jokes that involve women, and nobody ever says that these things are inappropriate," says Martha, a graduate student in physics. "They either laugh, or nobody says anything and they all look awkward, but nobody says anything. It's always the women who say, 'That's not funny; I'm offended by that.' After a while you think, why do I have to defend myself all the time?"

Making a formal complaint to a university or company isn't easy either. Although most institutions have a formal policy on harassment, many women have found that getting people to listen to their complaints is difficult. For example, two professors in Martha's graduate department at a private university have made inappropriate sexual comments and jokes to female graduate students and postdocs. The complaints about one professor went to the department chair. "He said that he took care of it. But apparently [the professor] was promoted right after that," Martha says. She and other students believe that the department has a climate problem, not only for women but also for minorities, but the faculty and administration have refused to admit that any problem exists. "[The students] deal with these problems, [but] nobody else in the department really seems to be aware of them," Martha says.

Discriminatory or harassing faculty members who have tenure are particularly a problem, as once a professor has tenure, the university cannot fire him/her except in the direst circumstances. And if the faculty member has other positive qualities—such as the ability to bring in lots of research money—then the administration often sees no reason to remove the professor.

Sometimes the powers that be will make a show of trying to improve the climate. When Janet was head TA for a chemistry course in the 1990s, it fell to her to speak with a male TA who appeared to be sexually harassing undergrads. "Not [to] the professor of the class, not [to] the head of undergraduate labs who also coordinated all the TAs, but to me, who had exactly zero authority over him in the real world," Janet says. "I'm still now trying to figure out if they really legitimately thought that my talking to him would be enough to stop it, or if this was just something to have done on paper in case there was a lawsuit later."

Some women have pursued lawsuits for sexual harassment, sexual violence, and gender discrimination and won, but these suits require enormous amounts of time, energy, and money, as well as more unpleasant, if not hostile, exposure than many women want to subject themselves to. Until we have a system that makes it easier for a woman to speak up, and more likely that she will receive justice, the majority of women are unlikely to report abuses.

Although these stories of bias and discrimination can be horrifying, overt discrimination has become less frequent due to both legal action and changing attitudes. The women I spoke with reported far more problems with older men than with younger ones. Men who have grown up around women with successful careers are more likely to see them as equals; certainly men who were born after the feminist movement got into full swing have had much more exposure to these dynamics.

Some women also reported that men who have daughters— especially adult daughters who are pursuing careers—tend to be more supportive of women. Gretchen saw this sort of transformation occur in her own father, a physician. "When I said that going to medical school is what I wanted to do, my father did a complete about-face in terms of his feelings about whether women should be in medicine," she says. "And it wasn't just for me. It made him think, wait a minute, why shouldn't medicine be open to any young woman who had enough education, intelligence, drive, and interest to do it? He became a great supporter of many young women."

Although the reports of bias-free environments are encouraging, the question arises: Have these women truly experienced no discrimination, or did they not see bias as such?

Women who succeed in male-dominated professions such as science and engineering may do so by wearing blinders—by ignoring all the injustices they encounter.

A person can characterize discrimination against his/her group, and particularly against him/her, as pervasive or isolated. Psychologist Mindi Foster and colleagues found that female college students' definitions of discrimination, and whether they saw it as pervasive or isolated, varied depending on whether they were envisioning discrimination (using written scenarios) or confronting discrimination (in a laboratory setting).[15] Various studies have shown that the belief that discrimination is pervasive can impair one's well-being, and so many people tend to minimize the bias they encounter.

Minimizing discrimination makes women individually feel better and thus helps them to continue working on their goals even in the face of adversity. But this minimization can hinder social change. Because women sometimes wear blinders and much of the bias going on nowadays occurs behind closed doors, it's difficult to know just how much of it exists, but one can safely say that no environment is completely bias-free.

In his 2005 speech, Larry Summers explained why he thought that discrimination was not as large a barrier to women's entry into the sciences as other factors. He talked about a well-known economic argument that states that if discrimination is occurring in a particular setting, such as science and engineering departments at universities, then an institution that does not discriminate should be able to easily recruit highly qualified candidates from the group that is being discriminated against. He said he did not see evidence of this happening.

Let's take a step back for a moment. What would an environment that hired and promoted women without discrimination look like?

Having a partner and children, taking maternity or paternity leave, and handling other issues related to family would not be positive or negative factors. In meetings, ideas would be heard and valued based on their quality and not the gender of the person proposing them. Neither men nor women would make decisions in social or other situations to which the other gender was not invited. Salaries, start-up funds, lab space, and other resources would be provided to new hires without regard to gender. Everyone would have equal access to mentors. Supervisors would not make assumptions about what someone is capable of based on gender; all workers would have similar opportunities to prove themselves. No one would be expected to act a certain way based on his or her gender. If this environment was a college or university, then the students would evaluate their professors based on quality of teaching and not on expectations based on gender. Graduate students and postdocs would be open to working with a male or female advisor and interact with both similarly. In other words, every single person at the institution would be completely free of gender bias. Given what we know about human nature and gender schemas, this scenario is highly unlikely.

In fact, eliminating all bias internal to the institution is not sufficient. Discrimination from outside sources would need to be tackled as well, since bias from outside the institution can also put obstacles in a woman's path. Reviewers of grant applications, journal articles, and conference papers can hold tremendous power over a woman's career, particularly as she works toward tenure. In a corporate setting, clients may prefer to work with one gender or the other. Bias that a woman encountered as a student or in previous positions may mean her resume is not quite as good as that of a man who didn't have to put up with such discrimination. Or that brilliant woman may have gotten sick of putting up with bias and decided to turn her talents elsewhere long before she applied to a university or industrial research lab. The world needs talented women in all fields, and sexism should not be a deterrent to any career choice.

A
DEGREE OF BS

WOMEN

IN

UNDERGRADUATE

SCIENCE

Although the experiences a woman has as a child are important to developing an interest in science and engineering, the path to a career in these fields really begins when she starts college. In the technology field, a strong programmer may not need a college degree, but in most disciplines one is necessary for work beyond washing glassware. Undergraduate classes in science or engineering provide a woman with skills and knowledge, not only about concepts but about experimental techniques. In college, a woman also begins to experience firsthand how science and engineering fields are set up on a male model to which she is expected to conform.

The number of women receiving bachelor's degrees in science and engineering has increased overall during the past two decades, but in some disciplines it's still pretty small. In 2002, women received 21 percent of the bachelor's degrees in engineering and 46 percent in science. The percentage varies according to field, however. Women earned more than 60 percent of bachelor's degrees in biology but less than 25 percent in physics. Over time, the percentage of women earning degrees in the computer sciences has actually been dropping; women earned more than 35 percent of these degrees in the early 1980s but earn less than 30 percent now.[1]

The increasing number of female undergrads in science and engineering has helped with some of the problems that women face in male-dominated environments. Women aren't as likely to be isolated and alone, for instance, and sexual harassment is generally less pervasive in environments with more women. But the increasing number of women in science and engineering has done little to change the overall culture of these fields, which remains quite masculine and competitive.

A textual analysis of the mission statements of the top twenty engineering schools in 2005 (as determined by *U.S. News and World Report*) showed that even those short statements of purpose provided evidence of engineering's independent, competitive culture. Compared to the mission statements of the top twenty liberal arts colleges, the engineering schools' statements contained more "strong" and "power" words. "Community" was the fifth most common word in mission statements from liberal arts colleges but did not appear in the top ten for engineering schools.[2]

University of Colorado sociologist Elaine Seymour and colleagues have studied various aspects of the undergraduate science and engineering experience through in-depth interviews with students, among other methods. She suggests that women are more likely than men to enter college expecting personal relationships with professors. Women "are raised to work more for the approval of others than for intrinsic satisfactions and goals," she writes. "For many women entering college, engaging the teacher in a personal dialogue appears to be critical to the ease with which they can learn, and to their level of confidence in the adequacy of their performance."[3] The early semesters of science and engineering classes at most universities, however, do not foster a bond between professor and student and may even throw up barriers to the formation of such a bond. This has been linked to the slide in confidence that many women experience—and from which some do not recover.

But many female students do not consider whether a college or department is supportive toward women when choosing it. More immediate concerns, such as availability of financial aid and proximity to home, often loom larger in decisions. Especially for students who are undecided about their majors, more general college characteristics are important. Some universities are huge, with tens of thousands of students and a wide array of course offerings. Teaching assistants (TAs), who are graduate students, or non-tenure-track faculty may do much of the teaching. Undergraduate-only liberal arts colleges generally have lower student/faculty ratios and smaller classes than universities. Some universities are more selective than others, of course, and the quality of students varies widely.

Two subcategories of colleges and universities are particularly relevant to female science and engineering students:

women's colleges, which are liberal arts schools, and schools that focus on science and engineering (the words "institute of technology" or "polytechnic" are a good tip-off). Some of these are universities; others are undergraduate-only, but because of their focus on science and engineering they are not necessarily considered liberal arts schools. All of these types of schools have the potential to offer a supportive environment to women in science and engineering, but among individual colleges, some support women better than others.

Once a woman has chosen a college, she must select a major, usually in her sophomore year, which sets her on a path toward a particular area of study. Women usually choose their major because of an interest in the subject and a desire for a career in that discipline. But when a woman has interests in many areas, other factors, such as challenge, come into play. "The premier reason why I went toward math and engineering was because they weren't easy. English classes were always so much easier," says Rachel, who earned an engineering degree in the 1990s.

Some women also choose to go into science or engineering because few women are in those fields. As a high school senior in the 2000s, Ariane attended an engineering day for prospective freshmen at the university she eventually attended. "I remember looking around and thinking, where are all the girls? I toured around with a group of thirty, and there was maybe one other girl in the group," she says. "I knew at that point that women must be rare in engineering but that I was up for that kind of challenge."

But women who choose science or engineering for these reasons may find that their path is more difficult than expected.

Going to college is a huge change in lifestyle and responsibilities for most students: Unless they're still living at home, suddenly their parents aren't around to make sure they're doing their homework or going to sleep at a reasonable hour. Plus, in a 300-person lecture, taking attendance is impossible. The freedom can be overwhelming. But so can the competition. During freshman orientation at Cathy's science and engineering school in the 1990s, a motivational speaker asked all the students who were valedictorians or salutatorians at their high schools to stand up. About 80 percent of the students in the room rose.

Big fish from a small pond, meet hundreds of other big fish. Now you're all in a pond together, and some of you are going to be average—or worse. "It's kind of like four years of mental abuse, you know: you're stupid, you're stupid, you're stupid—because your classmates are going to be Nobel laureates in three years," says Janessa, who attended a science and engineering school in the 2000s.

Many students aren't prepared for this sort of academic intensity. "It's hard to go from being the top of the class to one of a crowd," says Kristin, who attended a private university in the 1980s. "My identity at that point was so linked with my prowess in math and science that I had to rethink some of my assumptions."

Some classes and programs exacerbate the competitive atmosphere created by putting so many talented students together in one place. The well-known competition among premeds often raises the stakes for their colleagues (regardless of major) in science classes, for example. Engineering programs at some universities accept only a limited number of students, often based on grades in core science and math classes. As a result of this competitive atmosphere, some students try to intimidate or even sabotage others. Helen's mathematics classmates at her public university in the 1990s repeatedly asked her what her scores on quizzes and exams were. Kim found that students at her science and engineering school in the 1990s changed the answers on review material to be inaccurate so that other students were more likely to perform poorly on exams.

Although both men and women are affected by competition, women may be more likely to lose confidence because of it. Studies suggest that women tend to underestimate their abilities while men overestimate theirs.[4] In an academically intense situation, this may mean that women are more likely to doubt their ability to succeed in a major that challenges them or to feel like impostors—and more likely to decide to leave.

Insufficient academic preparation can make things even more difficult. Kelsey graduated from a small, rural high school before attending a private university in the 1990s. "I hadn't had any advanced placement courses, and most of the people I went to school with had had many, especially in math and science," she says. "So I struggled quite a bit with calculus because I'd had a great teacher beforehand, but we'd only gotten to the end of precalculus, whereas most of the people in my intro class had had a year of AP calculus."

The way that science and engineering are taught, particularly in the first two years, can also disadvantage women and turn them off to these disciplines. At most universities, science and engineering students need to take the same introductory courses, such as calculus, chemistry, and physics, before moving on to more specialized classes in their particular major. The typical solution is to stick all of them in a large lecture hall so that one professor teaches hundreds of students at once. These initial courses are commonly known as "weed-out" classes. Tara, a physics major, described the weed-out classes at her large public university in the 1990s: "The classes were about proving that you can stick it out, not about learning the material. These classes don't teach you academic skills, but rather skills of survival."

Other women have likened taking weed-out courses to drinking from a fire hose: To succeed or even just get by, a student must soak up as much material as fast as possible. Such courses can affect women more negatively than men in two ways. First, it's quite difficult to establish a personal relationship with a professor when you're in a class with three hundred other students. Second, since women are more likely to underestimate their abilities, they may be more likely to weed themselves out even if their grades are good. Even those women who stay in science and engineering majors take a confidence hit. One study of female science and engineering majors at a large public university showed that while later in their college careers women recover some of the confidence lost in weed-out courses, they never return to the levels they had as entering freshmen.[5] As a student advances through an undergraduate career, classes usually do become smaller, though the exact size depends on the number of majors in the department. Tara found that her last two years of undergrad featured smaller classes that were less about simply enduring and more about learning the material.

Although some universities are trying to make their science and engineering classes more active, most classes revolve around a professor lecturing and students taking notes. Some professors give dry, boring lectures; are unprepared and disorganized; or are set in their ways about how they explain concepts. "His idea of teaching was basically to just read to you from the textbook," says Rose of one of her professors in the 2000s. Other faculty are dynamic teachers who engage the class and teach to a variety of learning styles.

Since universities put more emphasis on research when making decisions about promotion and tenure, faculty there often don't work as much on developing their teaching skills. At liberal arts colleges, where tenure depends on teaching as much as or more than on doing research, professors are more likely to be good educators. Courses at liberal arts colleges are generally smaller simply because there are fewer students, although large lectures for introductory courses do occur. Even at large universities, discussion groups and/or laboratory sections of twenty to thirty students usually supplement large lectures. But TAs rather than faculty generally lead these, and the TAs may also receive little or no instruction on how to teach before they get up in front of a class.

Given the fire-hose method of teaching and the general difficulty of the material covered in science and engineering classes, students are naturally going to need help understanding concepts sometimes. Students can ask questions in class or during office hours, when professors and TAs make themselves available to students who need extra help. Studies suggest that in most situations men spend more time than women trying to figure out things they don't understand on their own, asking for help only as a last resort. Women, on the other hand, are more likely to ask for help when they don't understand something, and they ask for help sooner.[6] But when surrounded by men who aren't asking questions—or only asking complex technical questions that indicate an understanding of the material—many women clam up, feeling that asking for help signals weakness and stupidity.[7]

"I'm pretty outgoing. Sometimes I have a hard time keeping my mouth shut!" says Tara. "But I don't think I said anything in class during my four years as an undergraduate. For the first time ever, I felt intimidated in a classroom. During office hours I might have spoken up a few times."

Attending professors' office hours can be much less intimidating than asking questions in class. Helen did this a lot when she was a mathematics undergrad at a public university in the 1990s. "I think that the professors really appreciated that I went to office hours, because I asked them some questions they thought were pretty intuitive, but it turns out that they didn't explain the concepts well enough in lecture," she says.

But many women will avoid such extra help if they think their instructor is unapproachable or if they think that the instructor will look down on them for needing assistance. "To me, professors were intimidating," Ariane says. "Walking into their office hours alone wasn't too appealing."

Women who fear asking professors for help are often more comfortable going to classmates, particularly other women, with problems. Many schools promote study groups and collaborative work. Janessa's science and engineering school had more men than women, but all the geology majors in her class were women. They formed a close-knit group that would do homework and attend professors' office hours together. Finding a study group that feels comfortable isn't always easy, however, especially if most classmates are men. The tendency of men to leave women out of their networks due to conscious or subconscious bias often begins with study-group dynamics in school.

Although some science and engineering fields have achieved equity at the undergraduate level, many have not. One of the biggest struggles for women in male-dominated majors is the isolation they feel. Of course, most women count men among their friends, and some—especially those who were tomboys as children or grew up with brothers—may feel more comfortable with men than with women. But some women in science and engineering classes constantly feel out of place or somehow "different."

Ariane found that the male students in her engineering program in the 2000s cliqued together. "In our lab classes they would become partners," she says. "I was the only girl in those classes. It's a real gamble whether or not some guy's going to walk up to you and say, 'Do you want to be my partner?' or whether you're going to sit there until the teacher assigns you the weirdo in the back that no one's signed up with, which implies that you're the other weirdo who should be matched up with him."

Eventually some of the male students expressed interest in Ariane—as a date. "Whereas before I was ignored, now it was, whew, that's the only girl—fresh meat. That's not where I wanted to be." Other male students gradually became her close friends. "I kind of became one of the guys. We could talk about whatever we wanted, do whatever we wanted."

This isolation and sometimes outright hostile climate can prompt a woman to change her major, either to a discipline outside science and engineering or to one with a better male/female ratio. Changes in major can also occur due to new opportunities and knowledge; most high schools don't offer courses in astronomy or other specialized fields, for example. Furthermore, the chemistry that a poor teacher bored a girl with in high school may become fascinating when taught by a dynamic professor. Or, some women want very much to be in a career in which they are able to help people and make a difference in society. Not all disciplines offer that, at least in an obvious way.

Rose, who attended a private university in the 2000s, changed her major from physics to biology. "I even thought about switching over to a humanities or social sciences major. But considering the classes I had taken up until then and what really interested me, I realized I did want to stick to a science," she says. "And I wanted to go the biology route because I could see the most direct applications to eventually helping people."

But others may not see a change from physics to biology in this light. Science disciplines have a definite hierarchy, with physics at the top, chemistry a couple rungs down the ladder, and biology and geology lower still. The ordering comes from the perceived difficulty of the subject, which correlates highly with the perceived amount of mathematics it requires. In reality, some parts of biology and geology are highly mathematical, and they're not easy in any case. But as Liz, who majored in biology at a science and engineering school in the 2000s, explains, "There was a perception that biology was much easier. And so [a biology major] wasn't looked at as a manly thing to do because you never want to take the easy way." The increasing number of women in fields such as biology and geology reinforces the perception that they are easy disciplines, as female-dominated areas are generally considered to be lower status than male-dominated ones.

Regardless of the number of female students in a department, there will probably be fewer women faculty members who can serve as role models and mentors. When I asked the women I interviewed how many female professors they had in technical subjects as an undergrad, some couldn't come up with any, and few remembered more than two or three—even recent graduates. At a small college like the one Phoebe attended in the 1990s, a couple can be enough. "Only two faculty members [in the chemistry department] were women, but that was out of five or six," she says. "I had both of them for courses, and I worked with one for my research." Because of this, she never felt a lack of female role models. But when a faculty of thirty includes only two women, it's potentially more problematic.

Research on the influence of female faculty is mixed, with some studies suggesting that the presence of female faculty encourages women to choose and remain in a major and others finding no effect. In a study of more than 50,000 students who began as freshmen in one of the public colleges and universities in Ohio during the late 1990s, women who had a female instructor in their first course in geology or mathematics and statistics were more likely to take additional courses in those subjects. In physics and biology, however, women were more likely to take additional courses if their first instructor was male. The study found no effect, positive or negative, on choice of major.[8]

My interviews with women present a similarly mixed picture. Kim, who majored in mathematics at a science and engineering school, says that the lack of female role models didn't affect her as an undergraduate. "I was in such a male-dominated field that I expected it. It's kind of the story of my life." On the other hand, Miranda, who attended a large private university in the 1990s, felt the absence of women professors keenly. "There were no female faculty in [my] department," she says. "It was a barrier for a long time because it was hard for me to see myself as a professor since I didn't have any role models."

Furthermore, some women didn't see the female faculty who were around as people they wanted to imitate. At her small public university in the 2000s, Lynn had one female professor, and she wasn't in Lynn's engineering department. "She just seemed like a workaholic, and I don't think she had any kids," Lynn says. "There wasn't anybody I could really relate to. That was another reason why I was thinking about grad school—if I got my PhD then I could come back to the university and be the woman professor."

Although some universities have developed formal programs to provide mentoring to female undergrads in engineering and science, mentoring is still informal in many departments. The population of female undergrads far outstrips the number of female faculty. A single female professor in a department cannot effectively mentor forty or even twenty female undergrads, especially on top of mentoring graduate students, teaching classes, writing grants, and performing all the other tasks that faculty members must carry out.

One way for a female student to obtain mentoring, though not necessarily from a professor, is through research. As an undergrad in engineering in the 2000s, Ayyana interned at a national laboratory. "At that job I had a female boss, who had a female boss," she says. "She was the first woman I saw who made me think, 'I have got to be like her,' as far as being a scientist goes. She was so dynamic."

Although scientific, laboratory-based research is expected from graduate students, undergraduates increasingly have opportunities to perform research in a faculty member's lab or to intern at a company. Laboratory sections can offer hands-on experience, but depending on the university, labs may be cookbook-style, with the answer already known. By contrast, in research experiences and internships, students work on real problems that no one knows the answer to and so have far greater exposure to what being a scientist or engineer is truly like than a lecture class could ever teach them.

In the 2000s Sarah spent a year and a half researching her senior thesis, which involved characterizing sediment samples she obtained herself. "It ended up taking me to a national geological conference, giving me a chance to create a poster and present my work with a bunch of graduate students." Undergraduate research may also lead to students' first academic publications or to graduate school. Carmen, for example, hadn't been planning to go to grad school, but her undergraduate research advisor invited her to stay for a master's, and she ultimately ended up doing a PhD with him.

Multiple studies suggest that students, particularly women, who have an undergraduate research experience are more likely to attend graduate school and/or to pursue a career in science and engineering fields.[9] In a 2003 survey of more than 1,100 undergraduates who had completed a summer research program, nearly 91 percent said that the experience had sustained or increased their interest in postgraduate education.[10] Amber loved the two summer research programs she participated in. "They are definitely what kept me going enough to go to grad school," she says. "I learned so much working there for the summer. Being able to ask people who really knew what they were doing and really loved their subject lots of questions was great. Meeting other serious science majors helped too."

Given the challenges and obstacles that female students encounter because a science and engineering undergraduate education is set up on a male model, one might wonder if a particular sort of college is best for women. When considering universities, science and engineering majors are likely to gravitate toward schools that focus on those fields. While such institutions provide an excellent education, they can have their downside for some students, demanding an intense focus that is certainly not for everyone, particularly for women with diverse interests.

VALERIE, 22

Valerie loved mathematics. During high school she took accelerated classes, competed on the math and robotics teams, and attended summer programs focused on math and science. Her parents supported her interests however they could. Valerie's goal was to become a college professor. "I was really attracted to the idea that I could just do math all day," she says.

Valerie chose a college focused on science and engineering because she wanted to be in a "hard-core" math and science environment with lots of other bright students. Her classes were very difficult from the start. "It was the first time that I was in a place where if

I didn't do the homework, I wouldn't understand the concepts, and I would fail the test," Valerie says. "That hit me really hard."

She had been one of the top students in her high school. At her highly selective college, however, she wasn't the smartest person by a long shot. "I was uncomfortable being in the middle of the pack. I felt stupid sometimes for not understanding things and having to go to other people for help," Valerie says.

The male/female ratio among the students was about 2:1, and Valerie sometimes wished more women were around. But she had hung out with a lot of boys in high school, so she was used to having male friends. Despite the male-dominated environment—the male/female ratio among the faculty was about 3:1—she doesn't remember ever experiencing any discrimination.

Valerie declared a double major in math and physics with a concentration in astrophysics after she discovered an interest in astronomy. Even though she was excited about the material she was learning, Valerie didn't have very good study habits, and her grades reflected that.

Her advisor, a female physics professor, was very supportive. "I was able to talk to her about a lot of things: about school, about my academic issues, about personal issues. She was always ready to hear whatever I had to say. She gave me advice on what classes to take and what I should do with my life and how I might figure those things out."

After four semesters of gradually decreasing grades, her advisor suggested that Valerie take a semester off to regroup. Valerie didn't want to leave, afraid that she would never come back. She ultimately decided that her advisor was right, though, and took a leave.

Two years later, Valerie hasn't returned to her science and engineering college, and she doesn't plan to. It was a difficult decision. "I had all these dreams to be a great mathematician, a great scientist," Valerie says. "I felt that if I didn't have that really high-level education and a degree from such an exclusive school, then I wasn't this amazing mathematician anymore. I was just average and ordinary."

Valerie is now taking classes at the university in her hometown, which has allowed her to explore interests outside of science and math. She's currently trying to decide between majors in physics, math, classical studies, and linguistics. She also has more personal time and a more balanced life overall. "I don't feel as intellectually fulfilled, but I'm also not spending four hours every night doing my math homework," she says. "I don't have to concentrate all of my effort and all of my brain power on [it]. I have time to have a life and do other things."

With many science and engineering schools still so male-dominated, women's colleges could appear to be the perfect solution for female students. All-female colleges generally have more female professors than do other schools, and they can provide very supportive environments. Sarah attended a women's college in the 2000s. If she hadn't been there, she says, "I might not have been as outspoken or as easy with my questioning as I was. I think I would have had less of a chance to explore those wrong but good answers if I had been in classes with men."

But women's colleges also have their drawbacks. Janet majored in chemistry at a women's college in the 1980s. As she explains, "There was more of an assumption that you could do whatever you wanted to do, and it didn't matter if you were looking at going into a traditionally male field. In some ways I think that made for culture shock in graduate school. I almost wish there had been a little sit-down with those of us who were going on to graduate school to say, by the way, there are people out there who don't think that some of these things are within your grasp, and you have to be prepared to deal with them."

Attending a liberal arts college can also present problems when a woman moves on to graduate school. Both unfamiliarity with the large, more impersonal university environment and the different preparation that liberal arts colleges and universities provide can be issues. "I wasn't badly prepared. I knew how to learn really well," says Linda, who earned a computer science degree from a liberal arts college in the 1990s. "But these people who came out of engineering schools—they weren't taking English literature, they were taking four other engineering classes. I had no hardware experience at all."

Despite this, a liberal arts college where a woman is able to have more personal interaction with both faculty and classmates may be a better choice than a large university. Classes are smaller, so students receive more personal attention. It's also easier to be the only woman in a class of ten than one of fifty, which may reduce the likelihood that a woman drops out of a major. In a small college, majors in a particular discipline have most of their classes together and get to know each other well. This means that being in a class full of men may be less intimidating.

In fact, a liberal arts education appears to lead to graduate school for men and women both. Nobel laureate in chemistry

Thomas R. Cech used data from the National Science Foundation to determine how many graduates of different colleges and universities went on to earn PhD degrees in science and engineering. Calculating PhD recipients per one hundred students enrolled to control for size differences in the institutions, he found that eleven of the top twenty-five schools for producing future science and engineering PhDs were liberal arts colleges.[11]

Of course, graduate school is not the only option after one completes a bachelor's degree. Most technical fields offer many job opportunities for those with bachelor's degrees. Indeed, in engineering and computer science, a higher degree is often not necessary at all. (The technology industry includes several notable figures who never graduated from college but have made important contributions to the field.) But the number of positions available to those with bachelor's degrees in some fields is low. Bachelor physicists, for example, are likely to find themselves working in positions that are more related to engineering or computer science than physics.

Furthermore, in disciplines such as biology and chemistry, the lack of a higher degree usually means performing only routine experiments. PhD scientists run laboratories both in and out of academia, doing the creative work of designing experiments and developing research programs. A scientist with only a bachelor's degree is likely to obtain a position as a technician and have few opportunities to advance without a higher degree. Because of this, graduate school becomes attractive to many women.

But graduate school presents its own set of challenges. Because a smaller percentage of female scientists and engineers go on to grad school than their male counterparts, isolation and a male-dominated atmosphere are even more likely to be problems. The next chapter explores the unique challenges of the graduate and postdoc world, crucial stepping-stones on the way to a faculty or senior scientist position.

DOCTOR,
POST-DOCTOR

BEFORE

AND

AFTER

THE PHD

Although many women and men decide that their education is complete after earning a bachelor's degree, some go on to graduate school. This chapter looks at the experiences of female graduate students in science and engineering. It also examines what it's like to be a postdoctoral fellow, or postdoc. These positions, which follow graduate school, provide additional training as well as a transition from being a student to an independent researcher. Grad students and postdocs experience many of the same problems as do undergraduates, only magnified. For example, since a smaller percentage of female science and engineering students opt to attend grad school than do male students, even fewer women are around, so female grad students may feel more isolated as a result. But graduate students and postdocs differ from undergrads in that most of their time is spent not in class but in the laboratory of a faculty member. A woman's relationship with her advisor and lab mates is crucial to her success—and too often causes intense frustration or even failure. And because the graduate and postdoctoral experience is so decentralized, programs intended to support women and change departmental climates often fall short.

So what factors influence a woman's likelihood of attending graduate school? The reasons are wide-ranging. In some cases, a PhD is a prerequisite for the kind of work they want to do, or might want to do. "I was working and realized that I wouldn't ever get challenging work without a graduate degree," says Nicole, a current graduate student. Others just want to learn more or to become better prepared for work. "I really didn't feel like I knew enough to be done with school. It was like, but I've only scratched the surface here," says Linda, who graduated from college in the 1990s. As Seema, who graduated from college in the 2000s, explains, "I felt like I could go on to get a PhD, but I certainly didn't feel prepared to enter the job world, the industrial world."

As with science and engineering undergraduate degrees, fewer women than men earn graduate degrees. In 2002, women earned 14.8 percent of the PhDs and 21.2 percent of the master's degrees in engineering. The numbers were better for science: 35.4 percent of the PhDs and 41.1 percent of the master's degrees. But women did much better in some science fields than others. For example, they earned 42.9 percent of the PhDs in biology but only 12.6 percent of the PhDs in physics.[1]

Linda Sax, an education professor at UCLA, examined the

grad school choices of a sample of more than 2,500 students who enrolled in college in 1985 and majored in a science or engineering field.[2] Her findings help explain why fewer women pursue graduate school in technical disciplines. Five years after graduation, 25.9 percent of the women and 32.6 percent of the men were enrolled in or had completed a science or engineering graduate program (master's or PhD). She found that for women, attending a four-year college rather than a university increased the likelihood of graduate school enrollment. This is likely a result of the increased attention that women receive at such colleges. For both men and women, college grades and interaction with faculty also increased graduate enrollment. Women were less likely to pursue graduate studies in science, however, if they put a high priority on raising children or if their career decisions were based on their ability to make a contribution to society. This last finding can be understood in light of the fact that many of the women in the survey went on to graduate studies in fields such as medicine and education, which have a more straightforward service-to-others aspect.

Universities offer many different types of postbaccalaureate degrees, only a couple of which are relevant to science and engineering. A master's degree can usually be completed in a year or two. Many companies, particularly in engineering and technology, will pay for their employees to work on a master's degree part time in exchange for a commitment to work at the company for a certain number of years. Classes may be held at night, online, or even at the company so that employees can participate more easily. This flexibility makes it much more common for people to earn master's degrees in engineering and computer science, which is often the highest degree needed in these disciplines, in contrast to many other areas in science or mathematics. Master's degrees are also more appropriate for women who aren't sure what they want to do afterward. "I wasn't entirely convinced that I wanted to go into academia. So I figured getting the master's was a good way to try out graduate school," says Miranda, who went on to earn a PhD in computer science.

The doctoral or PhD degree is not something to go into lightly, particularly in technical fields. A PhD usually requires a student to perform original research, to pass certain exams, to write a dissertation, and to defend her work to a committee of faculty members. Part-time PhD students are extremely rare in science and engineering, although some students do consulting or other work part time while enrolled as full-time students. The National Science Foundation tracks how long it takes graduate students to earn their degrees. For 2003 graduates, the median enrollment time ranged from six to eight years, depending on field.[3]

Many students go to grad school in a different field than the one in which they earned their bachelor's degree. After working for a few years, they may find that their interests have changed. A gradual progression from electrical engineering to computer science or biochemistry to molecular biology, for example, is relatively common. Many women move from more abstract fields to more applied ones, which makes sense if women are more interested in making a difference in society. Kim earned a bachelor's degree in mathematics, but as she explains, "I lost interest in the field. I didn't see how I could make an impact. It just seemed too large." She went to graduate school in computer science.

Changing fields between undergrad and graduate school

may make it more difficult to get into graduate school. Students who switch fields may need to take additional undergraduate courses either before or during graduate school to make sure they have the appropriate foundation for their graduate work. This can increase time to receipt of graduate degree, which can be more problematic for women if they wish to have children after establishing their careers. It's not a step to take lightly, but the women who do change fields are generally happy with their decision.

Obtaining adequate funding is another important aspect of choosing a graduate program. Graduate degrees, like any other college education, are expensive. But grad students have resources available to them that are not open to undergraduates. For one, universities use graduate students as cheap labor. They are paid to be teaching assistants (TAs) and research assistants (RAs). TAs assist with or teach courses. RAs work in a faculty member's laboratory; this research eventually becomes the basis for a student's thesis or dissertation. Money for RAs usually comes from the professor's grants and can restrict the student's choice of research topic or cause problems if the researcher runs out of grant money. This funding scheme can also cause problems with maternity or other leave time, and if a woman must change labs for whatever reason, she must usually start a new project, thus lengthening time to graduation.

In 1990–1994, men in mathematics doctoral programs were 10 percent more likely than women to be supported by RAs. In the same time frame, the difference for life scientists was 7 percent; men also had a slight advantage in the physical sciences. On the other hand, women were 7 percent more likely to have TAs in engineering and also had more TAs in mathematics and the physical sciences.[4] This suggests that women are more likely to work for advisors who do not have money to support them, and thus they spend more time as TAs as a result. It's possible that women may value working on research they really love over having financial support, but in other labs or institutions men may be more likely to receive funding simply for being male.

Students can also apply for a wide variety of fellowships to help support their education. The NSF graduate research fellowship, for example, currently provides a $30,000 stipend and $10,500 for tuition per year for up to three years.[5] Jocelyn, a physicist, found her NSF fellowship to be a big help when she began graduate school in the 1990s. "It meant I had my own money. I was free to choose an advisor because they didn't have to pay me. They just had to have time to talk to me," she says. In 2006, women received about 56 percent of the fellowships.[6] This figure is higher than that for women graduating with PhDs in science and engineering, both because this figure includes awards in the social sciences and because some fellowships are specifically set aside for women in computer science and engineering.

The best way for a woman to learn about a graduate program is to visit it. The biggest advantage of seeing a university firsthand is being able to meet current grad students, see how many women are in the program, and determine how happy they are. Often students are eager to share this information. "One of the female postdocs—the only woman I spoke to the entire time I was visiting the university—pulled me aside at one point and said, 'Don't come here. I hate it,'" says Julia, who did her graduate work in chemistry in the 1990s. Many other women received similar warnings, particularly about certain advisors.

The advisor is by far the most important person in a woman's graduate career. Usually the advisor is the faculty member in charge of the laboratory where she does research. In addition to supervising the student's project, a graduate advisor may also help the student learn how to write scientific papers and present at conferences as well as provide information about ethics and best practices in the field. He or she may also assist the student in networking with colleagues, which can lead to postdoctoral fellowships or jobs. In general, a good recommendation from one's advisor is crucial to success after grad school. On the other hand, a biased or otherwise bad advisor has the potential to sabotage an entire career.

TANYA, 29

Tanya obtained a bachelor's degree in engineering from a small private college. After graduation she worked for three different technology companies over four years, during which time she decided she wanted to go to graduate school in computer science.

Tanya had been the only female electrical engineer in her class during her last two years of undergrad. She was also the only woman engineer in her department, and sometimes in her company, during much of her time in industry. As such, her first-choice graduate school was one where the dean of engineering and many computer science faculty members and students were women. Unfortunately, she didn't get in. She decided to attend the highest ranked graduate school where she was accepted. Tanya describes it as "a gigantic state school, the Home Depot of education."

Tanya's first research advisor never let her finish a sentence. "All of my ideas were crap, but he would later repeat my own ideas back to me as genius, as his ideas," she says. "It was not so much him saying, 'You, Tanya, do not belong here' as a matter of 'I'm going to regard you, graduate student, as nothing.'" Although her advisor treated all his students this way, she felt more disregarded, as the only woman, than her male counterparts. "The guys in my group were good," she says. "But they really didn't know what to do or how to handle it, because it was clear he was silencing me more."

One day, Tanya attended a meeting with her advisor, another professor, and his student. After the two students each described their projects, the two advisors announced that they had decided to switch who they were advising. "It was as if they were baseball team managers and we were free agents, and they just decided to swap us," Tanya says. She doesn't know if her first advisor complained about her, if her current advisor realized she was in a bad situation and decided to get her out, or if something else entirely occurred. "I did feel like I was getting fired by my group, but it was also something I wanted," she says.

After a crossover period of a year, she began to work exclusively with her new advisor. "Now that I have an advisor who values my opinion, it's clear, one, how much happier I am and, two, how much more successful I'm going to be because he's teaching me to be an independent researcher rather than a technician," says Tanya. Unfortunately, switching advisors has set back her research, as she had to start a new project with her new advisor. There's no way she's going to finish graduate school in her goal of five years.

In Tanya's department, graduate students generally work by themselves. However, one student in her current research group, a man two years ahead of her, has been a valuable source of information and support. Tanya does a lot of informal mentoring as well. "I know who all the female grad students are, and I invite them to my house," she says. She's also working to set up a more formal mentoring system for women graduate students in her department.

"Grad school is very homogeneous," Tanya says. "I feel like I see one type of guy that you see over and over again. And that's the very nerdy, very dedicated guy who's always doing his work and loves it, loves every second of it. . . . All I ever feel is that I'm failing. I don't have the long list of publications. I don't have the internship at IBM. I'm just average. And I've never been average before."

Graduate education is quite decentralized because the advisor–student relationship is at its core. Although the university administration or a college dean may provide some leadership, for the most part departments are able to set their own requirements for degree programs. Furthermore, each advisor generally runs her own laboratory as a private fiefdom. Many departments have guidelines about when the student should have completed qualifying exams and other preliminary work, but the graduate advisor determines when the student has done enough research and written enough papers to warrant a PhD degree. This gives advisors tremendous power over their students and also makes it quite difficult to effect changes in the departmental or campus culture. A professor who has tenure and has run his lab the same way for twenty years is unlikely to change in major ways. As such, selection of advisor is crucial, especially for women, because of the potential for bias.

The process of choosing a graduate advisor varies from university to university and from discipline to discipline. Sometimes departments admit students with the expectation that they will work in a particular faculty member's laboratory. In such cases, faculty members hand-select the students admitted to the program, and networking—of the kind that women often lack—can be essential to securing a spot. But other methods of advisor selection also occur. Particularly in the life sciences, students may rotate through several labs, working in each for a quarter or semester, before choosing one to join. In other cases, students must ask professors if they have open positions; faculty may also recruit students after seeing their performance in classes and on projects.

Women choose their advisors for many reasons, the foremost one being interest in the faculty member's research. Certainly, if you're going to be working on a project for the next six years, it had better be a fascinating one. But an equally important factor, often ignored in the decision-making process, is the quality of the student-advisor relationship. Women who are warned that a faculty member is sexist or generally difficult to get along with will often assume that they won't be affected. Many of my interview subjects shared this opinion, only to find they experienced the same problems as the women who had come before them. Of course, a good role model or mentor need not be of the same gender. One might expect that a female advisor would be more sensitive to the concerns of women graduate students and thus be more welcoming, but this is by no means universal. At least one study has suggested that the gender of one's mentor is unrelated to students' experiences being positive or negative.[7]

Regardless of gender, advisors come in many varieties: Some are very hands-on, dictating students' exact projects, meeting with them frequently, and sometimes micromanaging. Others are very hands-off, allowing students to choose their own projects and providing input only when specifically requested. More experienced graduate students or postdoctoral fellows in the lab may do most of the mentoring in a hands-off advisor's lab. Other advisors walk a middle course between these extremes.

Different people—male and female alike—want and need varying amounts of guidance and support. Tara, a graduate student in astronomy, found that her advisor offered different levels of support at different times. "It reminds me of parenting. I don't have kids, but I think that at the beginning you hold the hand a little bit tighter, and then at the end you let it go," she says. "And I'm starting to hear [my advisor] say, 'What do you think? You decide what you should do.' In the beginning there was a lot more, 'Try this, and don't wander too far from this plan.'"

On the other hand, Brianna, a recent graduate student in geology, had an advisor who was quite hands-off. "He was very clear from the very beginning that he was extraordinarily busy," she says. "It was very much a situation where I was completely self-motivated throughout my graduate school career. There was never any encouragement. There were never any deadlines."

This hands-off relationship worked for Brianna, although she admits that the lack of direction likely lengthened her time in graduate school. Most female grad students, however, want more hands-on mentoring from their advisors and are more likely to become frustrated when they don't receive it. Women are less likely to receive the mentoring they need if a male advisor creates a network only with the male students in the lab. A female advisor may also deny a female student mentoring because the advisor never received any as a student or feels that the advisee needs to toughen up.

Advisors often model their lab groups and advising on what they experienced as graduate students. There can be a sense of, "I went through hell and survived, so you ought to be able to get through hell too." In addition, assistant professors who need to show a certain level of research productivity to obtain tenure may particularly push their students. In accordance with science and engineering being greedy disciplines, high expectations, including long hours and single-minded dedication, are common.

Women with children and those who are looking for a more balanced life often find such expectations unreasonable. For example, Phoebe, who attended graduate school in chemistry in the 2000s, found that her advisor wanted his students to work sixty or more hours a week and to be completely focused on science. She wanted to have time for a life outside the laboratory, which included pursuing a master's degree in education. "We clashed over this many times. I made it clear that I wasn't that type of person. He's a very thoughtful person and was very concerned for my education, but we had very different philosophies about what the experience should be like," Phoebe says. She and her advisor ultimately worked out a plan through which she was able to finish her PhD with him and earn a master's degree in education.

Some advisors move beyond simply having high expectations or being too busy for mentoring students to openly belittling students, calling them names, making sexist or otherwise offensive remarks, and even making threats. Students may also find themselves shut out, unable to speak in meetings; their ideas unheard, their voices silenced. In some laboratories this behavior is equal opportunity: Men as well as women are subject to it. It's all part of a masculine trial by fire that has been passed down through the scientific community, advisor to advisee, for decades. Many women have no interest in participating in such a ritual, but others perpetuate it.

Seema, a recent graduate student in computer science, received a link to an online quiz from a lab mate that was meant to determine signs of being in an abusive relationship. "The questions were, Does your boyfriend do this? Does your boyfriend say that? Does your boyfriend put you in this situation?" Seema explains. "So I take this quiz and instead of 'boyfriend' read 'advisor.' I answered seven of the ten questions yes, and apparently if you answered more than three yes, you were in an abusive relationship." The advisor in this case was a woman, and she was abusive to all her students. Seema left the lab not long after.

Some advisors reserve their hostility for their female graduate students. The harassment may not be explicitly sexual in nature, but it's certainly gender-based. When Kathryn was a graduate student in geology in the 1990s, she found her first advisor difficult to work with. "He told me when I first came in that it wasn't worth his time talking to me because I wouldn't understand anything until I had taken a year's worth of anatomy," she says. After six months she got a new advisor. "That, likewise, was a difficult relationship, only this time it was made much worse by the fact that I was female. This is a person who was threatened by having women ask him questions, question his intelligence," Kathryn explains. He simply did not answer any of her questions, although he discussed scientific work with male students. Kathryn received very little support from him right down to seemingly small things. "When I got up to defend [my master's thesis], I had a dress on. My advisor's introduction consisted of a joke. He said, 'Oh, I didn't recognize her in a dress,' and he sat down. So I had to start my master's defense with the whole room laughing at me," says Kathryn. "It's really easy for people to dismiss that, but it's a real uphill battle to ignore the emotional consequences." Rather than try to change advisors again, Kathryn left with a master's degree. She eventually earned a PhD at another university.

If a woman finds herself with an abusive advisor or other negative lab group situation, she can change advisors, as Kathryn did at first. It's usually not easy, though. The student often must start on a completely new research project in the new lab, which can lengthen time to graduation. Other faculty members can also be reluctant to take on a student who is having problems with another professor for fear that they will have difficulty working with the student as well.

Although the relationship with one's advisor is important, a woman's interactions with other members of her lab group are also crucial. Labs differ widely in size. A well-known scientist at a top institution may have thirty graduate students, postdoctoral fellows, technicians, and others working in her lab. A new assistant professor or researcher at a more teaching-focused institution may have only two or three students.

"In biology, there's a lot of money to do research, so people want big labs. A professor's career depends on getting good grad students and postdocs. And so the more the better," explains Michelle, who earned a PhD in biology in the 2000s. She likens a lab group to a polygamous marriage. "While you're rotating, it's the courtship phase, and you are the cutest thing around. You get all this attention, and it's all so nice. Then you get married, and things go well for a while, but then you get unhappy. From the advisor's point of view, though, there's all these other wives. You're kind of a downer, but this one here is so much more fun right now."

Surveys of PhD students and studies of doctoral programs have suggested that smaller lab groups would improve the graduate school experience, as professors would have more time to support their students.[8] Other lab members may provide mentoring when the advisor is unavailable; Brianna relied heavily on others in her lab, for instance. But there are no guarantees that a woman will receive such support. Postdocs and other graduate students have their own work to do and may feel that they are in competition with others in the lab. Advisors have been known to set two students on the same project, with a reward for whoever finishes first. In other labs, students hoard chemicals or other supplies and fight for time on shared equipment.

In some departments, the majority of graduate students come from foreign nations. Overall, the number of Americans wishing to earn advanced degrees in science and engineering fields has not kept pace with the growing need for workers in these disciplines, in part because of the intense educational and work demands. In 2003, only 53 percent of grad students in engineering and 75 percent in science were U.S. citizens or permanent residents.[9] Foreign students make up the balance. This adds diversity to a lab group but can also give rise to cultural and language barriers. Students may cluster according to race or culture, shutting out others with different backgrounds. Furthermore, in some countries, prevailing cultural norms do not give equal rights and equal status to women.

Julia, a chemistry grad student in the 1990s, worked with a foreign male postdoc who didn't like women. "I would see something in my data and I would say, 'Oh, you know I saw this and I researched it and I was thinking that it might be due to this,' because I was really seeing some things that we didn't expect," she says. "And he would say, 'No, no, it's not that,' and if I asked him why, he'd just say, 'Because it isn't, you don't know what you're talking about, you don't understand that.' And my advisor would just sit there and nod, like, yes, yes that's right, you don't know what you're talking about. And then a few weeks later the postdoc would come up and say, when I mentioned something about my data, 'Well, you know, I've been thinking about it, and I think it's this,' and it would be exactly the same thing I had said."

After this happened several times, Julia began to write up everything she presented in detail in her lab book and date it. "At one point I shoved my lab book in front of the postdoc and said, 'Here is what I said and when I said it,' and he said, 'No, no, when you said it, it was different because you didn't know what you were talking about.'" Julia's advisor was less than sympathetic, telling her that this was her problem because she didn't understand the postdoc's culture.

An even more important factor than the number of foreign students, however, is the number of male versus female students and faculty. Graduate programs in science and engineering are usually more male dominated than undergraduate programs. Even if the ratio overall is pretty good, it may vary wildly between subdisciplines and between individual laboratories. A woman in a male-dominated laboratory may be left out of the network among her lab mates whether or not they are overtly sexist. In Wayne State education professor Maria Ferreira's study of a chemistry department with only male faculty, she found that female students were less likely to feel that others took them seriously, that men asked them for help, or that they could ask men for help.[10]

Although the gender of one's mentor is not correlated with better or worse experiences in graduate school, the presence of female faculty appears to be important. Beril Ulku-Steiner and colleagues at the University of North Carolina surveyed PhD students in fourteen departments, seven with gender-balanced faculties and seven with male-dominated faculties (including biology, chemistry, and mathematics). All departments were gender-balanced in their student populations. Women in male-dominated departments reported lower academic confidence and lower career commitment than both women in balanced departments and men in either type of department. They also felt that their departments were less sensitive to family issues.[11]

Confidence is crucial to success but in short supply among many female students in science and engineering. Studies have found that men and women enter graduate school with similar confidence levels but that women's confidence drops more steeply during a graduate program.[12] Many women end up feeling lost or frustrated during their graduate school careers, particularly if their mentors are not supportive.

When Kristin was a graduate student in physics in the 1990s, she initially worked on an extremely difficult project—one that an industrial group has only recently achieved. "It wasn't a realistic project for graduate students to stake their careers on," she says. Frustration with the research, lack of support from her advisor, and competition with another student in the lab destroyed Kristin's confidence and self-esteem. "I was weepy for quite a bit both before and after I left the project. I was not a happy person. I was in therapy for two years," she says.

This lack of confidence makes women both more likely to leave graduate school and more susceptible to mental health problems while graduate students. In a 2004 survey of graduate student health at the University of California, Berkeley, more than half the female respondents reported feeling overwhelmed or exhausted frequently or all the time. These emotions were more common among women than men, as were feelings of hopelessness, sadness, or depression.[13] A hostile climate is thought to be one factor contributing to the greater mental health problems among female grad students.

The hostile climate and lack of confidence can extend beyond the laboratory into the classroom, both for grad students taking courses and those acting as teaching assistants. Most graduate students take at least a few courses. PhD programs are generally structured so that the courses are all taken in the first year or two, after which the student focuses on research. Classes may be graded pass/fail, but anything less than a B is often considered failing, and the classes are often much more difficult than those at the undergraduate level. This is particularly true for those students who come to graduate school from liberal arts colleges where classes were small and professors quite accessible.

"Because you're at the graduate level, pretty much everything is taught by the professors themselves," says Jennifer, a recent graduate student in biology. Her classes incorporated a lot of guest lectures by professors who do research in the areas covered. "You're getting the material from the horse's mouth, so to speak, rather than having it digested through a textbook and a professor who may not exactly know what's going on. The bad element is that some of the faculty are better lecturers and teachers than others," she says. Just as some advisors belittle their advisees, some professors belittle students in their classes. Angie, who earned her PhD in physics in the 1990s, recalls one professor who insisted that they should have learned certain advanced mathematics concepts in kindergarten. Even in this highly refined university environment, professors may favor male students over the women in their classes, particularly if female students are few and far between, due to gender schemas or conscious bias.

Isolation is also a problem. Justine, a graduate student in mathematics in the 1990s, took many courses in which she was the only woman. "On one hand, there's part of you that's really focusing on the class, trying to take notes, trying to take questions, being really mentally involved, but then the more social part of me would not be there," she says. "This became more important in grad school also because it was 90 percent of what I was doing. . . . This was it. If I wasn't feeling really connected to the group of people I was working with, that would feel sad. . . . Sometimes I felt like it would be less stressful for me if there were more women around."

Graduate students often also work as teaching assistants for courses. This can mean running a discussion section of thirty or fewer students that is tied to a large lecture course taught by a professor, running a section of a laboratory course, or having primary teaching responsibilities for a class. Universities often require students to TA for a semester or two, but many schools prefer that students take care of this requirement in the first year or two and focus on research thereafter.

Some graduate students find themselves in front of a classroom without any substantive training in how to teach. More universities are providing TAs with some pedagogical instruction, although this is more likely to mean a one-afternoon seminar than a semester-long course. "My initial feelings about teaching were dominated by fear," says Brianna, a recent graduate student in geology who received no preparation for teaching. This lack of training and support can be more detrimental to women than men because some research suggests that students tend to evaluate female teachers more harshly than male ones.

Janet discovered this as a chemistry TA during the 1990s. "One of the undergraduates, after I had graded the problem sets and posted my solution set, came up to me and said, 'No, you got this one wrong because it doesn't agree with the answer I got.'

He essentially came out and said when pressed—I don't think he meant to; I think it just spilled out—'You're a girl; what could you know about physical chemistry?' Which was a little shocking," Janet says.

So what makes a graduate department a good place for a woman? In the early 1990s sociologist Mary Frank Fox conducted interviews with chairs and other faculty in twenty-two departments of chemistry, physics, electrical engineering, and computer science, in which the number of doctorates awarded to women was consistently low, consistently high, or had significantly improved. She found that improved departments had a history of leadership by the chair or dean on issues relating to the participation and performance of women. In particular, these leaders had taken a stance toward the harassment of female students and addressed claims, whereas in departments with consistently low numbers of female graduates, the chairs and faculty downplayed claims of sexist behavior.[14]

Furthermore, in chemistry, electrical engineering, and computer science departments with consistently high and improved numbers, chairs and faculty said that good environments for women had very strong faculty–student and advisor–advisee relationships, which were also good for men. In contrast, faculty in all physics departments described them as masculine environments that were unfamiliar or intimidating to women. The faculty in physics departments that graduated consistently low numbers of women felt that this environment was fixed and women needed to adapt to it (or get out). In the departments with high and improved numbers, faculty felt that the environment was more adaptable.

Researchers at the University of Washington followed ninety-nine graduate students, male and female, in a variety of disciplines, for four years in the late 1990s. Two years into the study, the researchers gave the students pencil and paper and asked them to write and/or draw about their graduate school experience for a few minutes. While the researchers were not expecting fields of flowers, they were surprised at the number of students who drew precipices, steep slopes, chasms, and traps. In many cases the students included no safety nets, ropes, or guides.[15] Graduate school was incredibly difficult, and the students felt as though they were on the journey alone.

Unfortunately, this feeling does not subside once women in math and science receive their graduate degrees, for then they must endure another treacherous experience: the postdoctoral fellowship. Women who want to become professors in science or mathematics will likely need to complete one or more post-docs, which are also a prerequisite for some positions outside academia. During a postdoc, a woman works in an academic, industrial, or government laboratory, usually doing research, sometimes teaching. On the one hand, postdocs are still learning how to be independent researchers. On the other hand, they already have PhDs, which in the past was enough to show they were ready to lead their own labs as faculty members (and still is in some disciplines). A postdoctoral position generally lasts only one to three years, much less time than a PhD program. Depending on the field and the job market, however, researchers can end up doing multiple postdocs before finding a permanent position, or staying in one postdoc position for an extended period of time. Five years as a postdoc is now common in some disciplines.

Because of the uncertainty about the length of a postdoctoral appointment and its scope, a postdoc is an odd, in-between sort of position. "When you're a postdoc, you're really nowhere. You're really in limbo at the university. . . . You're not a student, you're not a professor, so you don't really exist in the hierarchy," says Vera, a recent postdoc in physics. Postdoctoral associations have sprung up on some campuses to bring postdocs together and negotiate with the administration. But problems still exist, especially for women.

The number of postdoctoral positions has more than doubled in the past thirty years, but they are distributed unevenly across disciplines. In engineering and computer science, for example, it's still common to go directly from a PhD program to a faculty position. But in other fields, particularly the life sciences, postdoctoral fellowships have become a more important academic proving ground than grad school. According to the National Science Foundation, in 2003 about 10,000 people were doing postdocs in the life sciences, but only about 100 were in computer science. Overall, women were about 36 percent of the postdocs, although this varied considerably by field.[16] Research using data on postdocs who earned their PhDs between 1981 and 2000 suggests that women in biology and engineering are more likely to take a postdoc than men, while women in chemistry, physics, and math are less likely to take a postdoctoral position.[17] The reasons for these differences are unclear but are probably influenced by the availability of tenure-track faculty positions, the appeal of jobs outside academia, and gender bias. Another study found that female postdocs were only 83 percent as likely as male postdocs to obtain a tenure-track faculty position.[18]

In the 1970s, competitive fellowships supported most postdocs. This portable funding was limited to two or three years and allowed the postdoc to perform independent research with guidance from a mentor. Now research grants to principal investigators fund 80 percent of postdocs, restricting what the postdoc is able to work on and reducing independence.[19] "You have different goals than your advisor, if you think about it, as a postdoc," says Laurie, a recent postdoc in biology. "You want to do something different so that you can broaden your abilities from what you've been doing. But often an advisor who gets a big grant and wants a postdoc to run it, they want someone who knows what they're doing."

Postdocs can occur in academic, industrial, or government settings. An academic postdoc is similar in many ways to a grad student. A postdoc works under a professor on a research project, but usually with more independence and a larger role in lab leadership. This means that the hostile advisors who make some graduate students' lives hell can do the same for a postdoc, and female postdocs deal with similar issues as grad students, including being shut out of male-dominated networks. About three-fourths of postdoctoral positions are in academic institutions.

On the other hand, taking a postdoc position in an industrial or government lab can be a good way of deciding whether one would be happier in or out of academia. Although internships give students a taste of industry or government, those positions are often not representative of work in those sectors. Internships are short, interns are the bottom of the food chain, and expectations for interns vary widely. In contrast, a postdoc works as the equal or near-equal of her colleagues, and for enough time to take on major projects.

Miranda, a computer scientist, completed a postdoc at an industrial research lab in the early 2000s before returning to academia as a tenure-track professor. "I work in a field where we have a lot of contact with industry. A lot of what I do is very practically applied. So I knew that building up that network of contacts in industry would be very important for my future career," she says.

Postdocs outside academia have hazards and perks that those inside don't. For example, academic postdocs are usually hired on a specific grant that guarantees funding for several years. Industrial postdocs often don't have the same job security. On the other hand, postdocs can lead to permanent positions in government and industry. While this can happen in academia, the resulting job is not tenure-track faculty but rather a staff scientist or research associate—not the sort of academic job that most postdocs are aiming for.

Miranda's group at the industrial research lab became a casualty of the dot-com crash less than a year after she arrived. Because she was working on a side project, Miranda was transferred to another group rather than laid off. But the postdoc never turned into a staff position, even though she had been told this was likely when she was hired. "It turns out that this postdoc lasted for three years just because of the way that things went down and the hiring freeze and everything," she says. "This ended up being a postdoc that was extended and extended and extended until I was ready to leave."

One of the most common complaints of postdocs is lack of mentoring. In a 2004 survey of postdoctoral fellows conducted by *Science* magazine, mentoring was cited as the most important attribute of a principal investigator (PI).[20] But a survey of postdocs at the National Institutes of Health revealed that mentors there met with their female postdocs less often.[21]

Even before she arrived at the university in the early 2000s, Justine, a recent postdoc in mathematics, says, "[it] was clear that there would be no mentorship, that the faculty gave the postdocs zero mentorship. But I felt like the benefit of being in a place where there's so much activity would be worth it." Fortunately, her PhD advisor continued to give feedback on her papers during her postdoc.

Although most PhDs complete postdocs in labs other than the ones where they did their graduate work, Michelle remained in her graduate lab. She wanted to explore some additional aspects of her thesis work, and her advisor saw the usefulness of keeping around a skilled researcher who was familiar with the lab. "We had joked in my thesis lab that the PI was so hands-off that being a grad student was like being a postdoc and being a postdoc was like being a faculty member—you just didn't have any resources," she says.

In industry, Miranda discovered that male and female postdocs were mentored differently. "I didn't always feel supported in the lab. . . . I feel like in general the female postdocs were left to fend for themselves and the male postdocs were very much mentored and shepherded through the system. It seemed like they knew a whole bunch of things that we didn't." She found that working with and being mentored by women was thus crucial. "They could help me navigate this really weird environment because they had done so successfully."

The structure and timing of postdocs also disadvantage women. The lengthy postdocs that many women must complete before obtaining a permanent position have worsened the dilemma of when to have kids. This means that more women are having children during their postdoctoral fellowships, which has its perils. Most postdocs are eligible for dependent health insurance from their employers (although it may be costly), but they may not have access to on-site childcare. Especially for those supported by research grants, paid maternity leave may not be available or may be at the principal investigator's discretion.

Vera, who had her first child as a physics postdoc in the 2000s, experienced health problems during her pregnancy. "The professor I was working with was very understanding, and he let me work at home a lot when I was unable to go to the lab. So I had flexibility, but it was coming directly from him personally; the university itself didn't have any support system," she says. "I feel that if my professor had been less flexible, or more critically dependent on my productivity, I would have been in a very bad situation."

Salary is another issue. Although postdocs make more than graduate students, they make significantly less than PhDs in permanent positions. A survey of 7,600 postdocs conducted by Sigma Xi found their median salary to be $38,000, well below the median of $71,000 for all PhD holders.[22] This puts a significant dent in a woman's lifetime earnings if she spends five years in a postdoc position, making it difficult to support a family, especially since many research universities are located in cities where the cost of living is high.

Furthermore, multiple postdocs also have the potential to uproot families. A researcher may do two or even three postdocs, each lasting one to three years. If each position is at a different university in a different city, this means several moves. Partners need to find new jobs, and the kids must make new friends. Many couples, especially those in which both partners are postdocs, end up with long-distance relationships. And those who do obtain positions at the same institution often find themselves making compromises.

Julia, now a chemistry professor at a community college, and her husband looked for postdocs together in the 1990s; he got one first. A professor at the same university wanted Julia to postdoc in his lab but didn't have a lot of money, so the university offered Julia a lecturer position as well as a part-time postdoc in chemistry. "The first year was quite good. My advisor didn't tell me that he was going to be on leave," she says. "[Because he was gone,] I was forced right away to go and do a lot on my own and really be very, very independent. And teach the class without any help from anybody and do some research without any help from anyone. . . . I got to advise an undergraduate on my own too."

Then her advisor came back from sabbatical, and he wasn't happy that she was applying for assistant professor positions. "I think he decided the first year went so well that I should just stick around. Of course, he forgot that he didn't have any money to pay for me after two years," she says. "He actually didn't send references he told me he was going to send. So I didn't end up getting any callbacks from any schools."

The university assured Julia that she would receive a third-year teaching contract. "Around August 25th or so, they said to me, 'Oh, that fell through; we don't have anything for you, so really you're just paid through the end of August. That's it.' Which is not really the way to leave a postdoc. You don't usually get less than a week's notice to finish up and leave. So that pretty much ended at that point, as far as I was concerned, any chance I had of going into academics."

Although Julia's situation could have happened to a man, some discrimination is obviously gender-related. For example, there exist researchers who will not hire female postdocs if they are married or even in a serious relationship because they might become pregnant. If the postdoc cannot perform certain research duties during pregnancy (such as those that involve radiation or toxic chemicals) and then spends three months on maternity leave, she has not been a fully productive researcher for about a year. This is a significant portion of a three-year-long grant, and so some researchers decide just not to take the risk. Of course, many labs don't present hazards for pregnant women that would require them to scale back on their activities, and some advisors are willing to work with women to minimize risks. But others do discriminate in this way.

Graduate-school and postdoctoral positions aim to prepare scientists to be faculty members. But obviously this training system has major flaws. The centrality of the advisor–student relationship means that many women feel they have nowhere to go if the relationship goes sour. Their training also focuses on research far above teaching or any of the other skills necessary for success as a professor. And if a woman chooses to take a nonacademic route, she may also find her education lacking. The next chapter turns to women's experiences in academia.

The faculty position is supposedly the pinnacle of scientific work and a reward for all the education that aspiring professors go through. But many women find that being a faculty member presents a whole new set of challenges in addition to the ones they have faced for the last ten-plus years.

A LAB
OF HER OWN

WOMEN

SCIENTISTS

IN

ACADEMIA

After finishing a PhD and possibly one or more postdocs, many female scientists and engineers pursue a faculty position in academia. It's important to have women strongly represented in academia, because female faculty also serve as role models and mentors to students, and their scarcity can affect the choices of the next generation. The career can be a very rewarding one, but the challenges of being a female professor are numerous. Some women are able to overcome the obstacles and thrive, and many of them love the work they do, but much could be done to improve academia for women in science and engineering.

The first hurdle is finding a tenure-track job. Fewer positions exist than PhD holders who want them, so some women end up in contingent faculty positions off the tenure track instead, especially if their partners are looking for an academic job as well. Once a woman obtains a faculty position, she may find that some of the challenges are familiar from her education, such as isolation, exclusion from networks, a lack of mentoring, bias, or a generally chilly climate. These challenges are often magnified because the number of women has decreased yet again—many have had the experience of being the only female professor in their departments, for example. Other challenges are more particular to the life of an academic, including over-coming inadequate preparation for some aspects of faculty positions, obtaining funding for research, maintaining productivity, and in general doing everything necessary to obtain tenure if a woman is on the tenure track. Male faculty face these challenges as well, but women are usually more affected both because of bias and, if they're married, the unequal distribution of household and childcare responsibilities. As a result, women are more likely than men to be denied tenure or to leave a faculty position before being considered for tenure.

According to the National Science Foundation, in 2003 women represented less than 19 percent of full-time senior (tenured) faculty and 35 percent of junior faculty in science and engineering. These numbers vary a lot by discipline; women were less than 7 percent of the tenured faculty in engineering but about 29 percent in the life sciences.[1] These percentages are smaller than those for women earning either bachelor's degrees or PhDs in these disciplines, contributing to the lack of female role models and mentors discussed in previous chapters.

Many different factors have influenced women's slow entry

into academia's ivory tower. The tenure system is one problem. In industry, people generally do one job for a while and then move to another company or get promoted up the career ladder. But once a faculty member has tenure—granted or denied after about six years as an assistant professor—she does essentially the same job for the rest of her career unless she decides to move into administration or leave the university.

Until recently, the faculties at most campuses were almost entirely composed of white males. It takes a long time for these men to complete their careers and retire. Although a growing student population or expansion in a particular discipline can cause a university to add faculty positions, often jobs open only when a current faculty member retires or is denied tenure. And, of course, only a percentage of these open faculty positions go to women, and women are more likely than men to leave a university before receiving tenure. And thus change is slow. "Basically, we've hired one woman per decade," says Lauren, a tenured physics professor, of her department. "We need to hire more. I'm working on that."

As an illustration, sociologist Robyn Marschke and colleagues studied the hiring and retention of men and women at a public research university. In the 1990s, the hiring pool of PhDs was about 40 percent women (averaged over all disciplines, not just science and engineering). The university had about 20 percent female faculty. Using data on current hiring and retention rates (including at what age professors left) for men and women, they calculated how long it would take for the percentage of women faculty to equal the percentage in the PhD hiring pool. They found that if hiring and retention did not change, the university would never reach 40 percent women; it would stabilize at 34 percent instead. This was in large part because women were more likely to leave the university and did so earlier in their careers. Under a condition of equal hires for men and women as well as equal exits—improving retention so that women left at the same rate and age as men—the university would reach 40 percent women in twenty years.[2]

In a survey of more than 4,000 graduate students (male and female) in eleven fields, including ecology, molecular biology, mathematics, chemistry, and geology, 87 percent of respondents said they definitely or maybe wanted a faculty position at some point in the future.[3] But academic positions are scarce—no more than half of doctoral recipients will end up with a full-time tenure-track professorship, because there simply aren't enough positions available.[4] In 2003, nearly 1,200 students graduated with PhDs in physics, but there were only 679 open faculty positions (tenured, tenure-track, and contingent).[5] Furthermore, in some fields the options outside the professoriate are few. "The kind of math that I chose is really geared toward academic positions," says Justine, an assistant professor. "If I had known about this in college, I might have thought about making a change."

The shortage of tenure-track positions can appear even worse to an aspiring academic because the vast majority of faculty jobs are at less prestigious colleges and universities, including community colleges, whereas PhD recipients generally want to work at a well-known research university or a top liberal arts college.[6] "You only get a PhD from a research, PhD-granting institution, so the models you see in front of you are only those models. Also, most faculty, to be successful, [want to] place their students in the very best places because it brings glory to them," says Lily, a university administrator. Although some research universities have stepped up their recruitment of female faculty, women are still more likely to work in other types of academic settings.[7]

Paula, a physicist, applied to fifty jobs during the year she was on the academic market in the early 1990s—every open tenure-track position in her field at liberal arts schools and community colleges. Applying this widely is common, but even so, many aspiring academics will still be on the job market for several years before landing a permanent faculty job. This is one reason why the length of time spent as a postdoc is increasing. For example, Lena went on six interviews during the first year of her academic job search in the 2000s, but she didn't get any offers. Undeterred, she applied again the following year and received two offers.

Women must deal with bias in the hiring process as well. Some of the women I spoke with felt that they were interviewed simply because the university needed to show some attempt at diversity rather than because the college was truly interested in hiring a woman. On the other hand, Miranda doesn't think that affirmative action was a factor in her success rate—six interviews and five offers during a job search in the 2000s. "They went out of their way to make me feel like I was talented because of my background and not because of my gender. And I really appreciated that," she says.

Once a woman obtains a tenure-track position, she also starts a complex balancing act that is not only quite time-consuming but can be made more difficult by bias. The typical professor teaches, prepares grant proposals, does research, mentors graduate students, and performs service to the department and university, which generally means sitting on committees. According to the U.S. Department of Education's 2004 National Study of Postsecondary Faculty, full-time faculty in engineering worked an average of 56.1 hours per week; natural sciences faculty worked 53.4 hours.[8] And that's just an average; some faculty put in far more hours. Although professors in some disciplines have a lot of flexibility in when and where they do their work, some "face time" is always necessary, not only with other faculty but also graduate students and postdocs.

"Being a faculty member is like being the CEO of a small business. If you're not working, nobody's working. The business comes to a halt when you come to a halt unless you've got a really well–oiled machine and a team, and even then you need to be available to provide the direction," says Margaret, a former assistant professor in engineering. Putting together that well–oiled machine is a new faculty member's first priority. In addition to getting a salary, a newly hired assistant professor generally receives lab space and some start-up funds from the department, which may be used to buy equipment, pay students or technicians, or remodel a lab.

An equity study conducted at MIT in the 1990s revealed significant differences between male and female faculty in the School of Science in terms of salaries, start-up funds, and amount of lab space. Since then, many other universities have conducted similar studies and made attempts to rectify inequalities.[9] They still exist, however: Using data from two national surveys of faculty, University of Iowa education professor Paul Umbach found that women's salaries were, on average, 6.8 percent less than men's, even after controlling for discipline and rank.[10] With fewer resources available, female faculty are at a disadvantage from the very beginning

At most universities, a faculty member's first priority is her research, and that means writing grant proposals. Grants fund research; they pay the salaries of graduate students, technicians, postdocs, and even faculty members; they buy materials; and they help fund the department and university through indirect costs. An untenured professor who has difficulty obtaining funding for her research is much less likely to earn tenure. Although some postdoctoral fellows are involved in writing grants and some graduate programs now offer grant writing courses, grant writing is often not a skill that aspiring faculty learn.

Furthermore, money to support academic research is far from unlimited. The federal government is the primary source of funding in the United States, but grants are extremely competitive. In fiscal year 2006, the National Institutes of Health (NIH) funded only 20 percent of the grant proposals it received.[11] The National Science Foundation (NSF) estimates that it funds about 27 percent of the proposals it receives each year.[12] Some researchers obtain funding from industry, but this is usually reserved for research with obvious commercial applications.

A 2005 study, by the RAND Corporation, of three different government agencies that fund research in science and engineering found no significant gender differences in the amount of funding requested by or awarded to men and women by NSF and the Department of Agriculture. At the National Institutes of Health, however, women on average received only

63 percent as much funding as men. Eliminating very large award winners (where women are quite underrepresented) and controlling for other characteristics, such as age and grant type, still yielded a 17 percent funding gap between men and women.[13] Since women are best represented in the life sciences and thus more likely to apply to the NIH for funding, this is a serious disadvantage.

Focusing on research also means running a research group and advising students—more skills never formally covered in a future academic's training. Sometimes grad students and post-docs have opportunities to mentor more inexperienced people in the lab, but not always. "Learning how to manage graduate students was definitely challenging. I know how to mentor me, but I didn't necessarily know how to mentor people who are not like me . . . people who went at their work differently, who had different sets of talents and needs," says Lauren, a tenured professor of physics.

Every professor must decide how to advise students—hands on or hands off? Does the mentoring extend only to research or to other aspects of a career as well? New faculty members often follow the style in which they were mentored, but women who had poor advisors may adopt radically different styles with their own students.

Lena, an associate professor of biology, is a very hands-on advisor. In addition to guiding her students' research, she also helps them learn other skills. "I put a lot of time and effort into my graduate students, much more than other advisors," she says. "I don't want my students to have to repeat my mistakes, and I don't want them to go out there and not really know what's expected. They really have to know how to write a paper and how to write a grant."

Kelsey, an assistant professor of biology, doesn't see her graduate students very often. "Lab space here, as at any university, is rare and precious. And so my lab is actually at a different part of campus, in a different city, than my academic office," she says. "I have a lot more email conversations with some of my mentees than face-to-face ones."

Contrary to what we might expect, research for a faculty member often does not involve actually sitting at the lab bench performing experiments, writing computer code, or building new devices—those duties are what graduate students and postdocs spend most of their time doing. Professors at liberal arts colleges who have only undergrads in the lab are more likely to be hands-on, particularly in the summer, when they're not teaching. Faculty who work in more theoretical areas also do a lot of their own research, since much of it occurs in their heads. But many faculty members spend most or all of their time developing new research projects, getting them funded, meeting with students to discuss results, writing papers, and giving talks about their work. This can be quite a transition for someone who is used to running experiments most days.

"I actually haven't been able to spend as much time at the bench as I had either anticipated or I really want," says Kelsey. "But I guess that's the typical progression: You go from bench scientist most of the time to grant writer and lecturer and paper writer. It just came about a little sooner than I expected."

In addition to doing research, faculty are also expected to teach and perform service to the university. New faculty may receive little to no support for teaching, as the university assumes they learned how in graduate school. But, as discussed in the previous chapter, many graduate students receive little or no instruction in how to teach. Furthermore, those with fellowships or working in well-funded labs may not have been a TA at all. As Carmen, an assistant professor of engineering at a large university, explains, "I hadn't prepared lectures. I hadn't prepared homework. I hadn't prepared exams. I essentially hadn't learned how to teach, so I had to teach myself how to teach in a very immediate setting."

This lack of preparation for teaching is problematic because even though research is a faculty member's first priority, teaching evaluations are starting to play a larger role in tenure evaluations, especially at liberal arts colleges. And while some studies suggest that students evaluate male and female teachers equally, others do not. In one study, students described their best and worst teachers. The researchers found that students were more likely to look to female faculty to be nurturing and male faculty to be entertaining.[14] As the authors note, while a professor can use the same lecture notes with the same jokes year after year, helping students requires continual output of time and energy, potentially placing a larger burden on female faculty.

Margaret, who was an assistant professor of engineering at a large university in the 2000s, had her initial experience with gender bias from students in the first course she taught. "I look really young, and I'm a woman, and I'm small, and I'm Asian. All these sorts of different things led to disrespect. . . . It was a little bit of attitude [and] comments on course evaluations."

Female professors may also be expected to take on a heavier burden of service to the university simply because they are in environments with few women, and committees are supposed to be diverse. "I was immediately put on every search committee because every search committee had to have a woman, and I was the only one," says Lauren, who started as an assistant professor of physics in the 1980s. Lena, a biology professor, says, "A man emailed me and said, 'Could you please sit on this committee because we need a woman to be a member of it.' I was supposed to be the token woman. So I emailed back and said, 'No, not for that reason.'" She adds, "The next time he asked me for something, he asked me in a different way." Female professors are also more likely to be asked to participate in recruitment and student events in an attempt to attract and retain more female students.

Neither graduate school nor postdoctoral positions formally prepare aspiring faculty for committee work, although some may gain experience through student groups. Performing an adequate amount of service is supposed to be an important part of being a professor and thus in achieving tenure. But in reality, research usually counts for so much more in tenure decisions that an assistant professor who spends a significant amount of time on service is less likely to be tenured.

Many faculty members struggle with how to divide their time between these varied tasks, in particular between research and teaching. "The interesting thing about being a professor is that you're hired to teach, but what they really want you to do is research. So you're never actually taught how to teach. But that's really your job. But the emphasis is actually on doing research and bringing in money, so it's this weird, schizophrenic kind of job," says Claire, a tenured professor of biology. Many universities claim that teaching is their number one priority, and yet the pressure is on assistant professors to "publish or perish." Providing evidence of a certain level of research productivity is essential to obtaining tenure—but few departments have specific guidelines for the level needed.

The typical measure of research productivity is the number of papers published in scholarly journals. Many researchers have found a gap between the productivity of men and women, with women publishing fewer papers on average. In their book *Who Succeeds in Science? The Gender Dimension*, Gerhard Sonnert and Gerald Holton suggest that while women publish fewer papers, their publications are more thorough and comprehensive, as evidenced by the fact that they receive more citations.[15] In two more recent studies, researchers were able to sharply decrease or even eliminate differences in productivity by controlling for variables such as rank and type of institution. Women are more likely to be assistant professors as well as to work at less prestigious institutions where teaching and service demands are typically higher. A comparison of full professors at prestigious research universities yields a gender difference in productivity of only 5 percent, for example.[16] But an equal level of productivity can come at a high price. Women, particularly those with children, often end up with super-scheduled lives in which they devote few if any hours to leisure or interests outside career and family responsibilities.

A good relationship with one's colleagues is also essential to achieving tenure as well as to effectively contributing to the department. Every department has its own set of personalities and politics, some of which can pose hurdles for female faculty and for untenured faculty in general. Since colleagues eventually recommend a woman for tenure (or not), junior faculty often feel they must tread lightly and even censor themselves.

"I have to pick my battles very carefully and think about what I say. I'm less willing to bring things up and rock the boat during department meetings because I'm not sure how my colleagues are going to react," says Miranda, the only female professor in her computer science department. "I do actually feel quite a bit as if I'm not listened to in department meetings, as if I'm not given the benefit of the doubt as much as my male colleagues." This includes a male assistant professor who was hired after her. "There's nothing that my colleagues do to treat this person differently overtly. But he's given a lot more deference in department meetings."

A woman's marital status can also affect her relationships with colleagues. Some research suggests that men are more likely to collaborate with married women because they feel more comfortable with them. If a woman's husband works in the same department, he can also provide her with an entry into male networks. Collaboration between spouses can be quite fruitful, although other scientists may assume that the man is the driver of the research, the one who develops the ideas, while the woman does more of the grunt work.[17]

The number of women in a department can also have a significant effect on how accepted and supported female faculty feel. In a survey of more than six hundred faculty members, women perceived the climate of their department to be chillier than men did. But women in departments where the faculty was more than 60 percent female found the atmosphere to be more supportive than those with less than 60 percent women.[18]

Very few science and engineering departments have more than 60 percent women, but at some universities women are starting to reach a critical mass for truly useful networks and support. "There's more of a community now that we have maybe double the women than when I was first here," says Cecilia, a tenured engineering professor, of her university. "There are more senior women now, which is really great. And there are senior women who aren't those 'alpha female' types, you know, like 'I had it hard so I'm not going to help you.' They're very gracious, nice women who are really, genuinely supportive of the younger women. There are still a few alpha females, but there's enough of a critical mass of nonalpha females."

Women who wanted to be scientists or engineers thirty, forty, or more years ago had more visible and difficult obstacles to face than women do today. Men told them outright to leave. They had to fight and fight to get what they wanted, often making huge sacrifices, such as not having children or even a partner. Some of these women are reluctant to provide support to other women, feeling that the newcomers should be strong enough to overcome the same obstacles that they did. But since women are often left out of men's networks and mentoring relationships due to conscious or unconscious bias, developing supportive networks of women has proved crucial to female professors' success. Many departments now automatically assign new assistant professors to mentors; others must seek out people who are willing to show them the ropes.

Margaret, an assistant professor of engineering in the 2000s, received mentoring from two other female faculty. The first was a full professor. "She is the person in the department whose [research] area is most closely aligned with mine, so we started collaborating. . . . She was more my academic mentor. There was another junior faculty member several years senior to me, and she was my cultural mentor."

Aspiring professors are increasingly keeping networks in mind when they look for jobs. Indeed, Samantha, an assistant professor of engineering, chose her university in part, she says, because "[there] were more senior professors at [this university] who expressed interest in mentoring me, who expressed interest in writing me into their grants."

Mentoring continues to be important even after tenure is achieved. "I have a network of senior women where we co-mentor each other all the time," says Maria, a computer scientist who is now a university administrator. "Once you get to a certain point, especially if you mentor others, there's just [lots] of people who are willing to mentor you." Having a diverse circle of advisors who can mentor a woman on a wide variety of topics at many different stages of her career can be incredibly important to an academic career, as was the case for Claire.

CLAIRE, 52

Although some women know early on that they want to go into academia, Claire knew only that she wanted to do biological research in some setting. While she was a postdoc, Claire attended a lecture by a professor at another university. "[After the talk] I came up to ask her a question, and I said, 'Hi, I'm Claire Postdoc,' and she said, 'Claire Postdoc, I know who you are; I want you to apply for this job.'" It turned out that Claire had impressed a woman who was now a postdoc in this professor's lab. Claire applied for the job—a tenure-track faculty position at a public university—and got it.

Claire's postdoc advisor had encouraged her to write a grant proposal near the end of her postdoc. "That didn't get funded. But in writing that grant, I got ideas as to what I wanted to do next. And so when I got to my lab and started setting it up, I wasn't lost or confused or anything like that. I knew what I wanted to do, and I had ideas for what to do next, so I just kept working on it."

It wasn't always easy, of course. When Claire arrived on campus, construction of her lab hadn't even started. Her extremely supportive department chair became frustrated with the university's slowness. "I was in this room that was really, really small, and he came over one day and he was like, 'That's it!' He went to the room that I was supposed to have as a lab—it was a classroom—and he started throwing chairs out into the hallway."

As a woman and an African American, Claire was in high demand as a potential committee member. Her chair helped ensure that she wasn't too overloaded with service work to do well at her research and teaching. "He would meet with me periodically and go over my CV. He kept saying, 'You've got to publish more papers,' and he was right. He was on [the] promotions and tenure [committee], and I think that's why I got tenured, because looking back at my package, it was not that strong."

After she received tenure, Claire began collaborating with a researcher she knew from grad school. Eventually this researcher succeeded in recruiting Claire to her private university. "She introduced me to the man that I ended up marrying.

And I got pregnant. That caused me to come here. I didn't leave [my former university] because I was unhappy. I left because I had a different life here that I needed to attend to."

The marriage didn't work out, but Claire has been happy with her new university. Her colleagues are very supportive, although she finds that dealing with the administration and the scientific field at large can be frustrating sometimes.

"The competitive nature of research funding now and getting papers published has escalated in a way that is unbelievable. Submitting things to get funded, having them continually returned as not funded, and being evaluated on that basis is difficult." Women on funding panels have mentored Claire, however, helping her to tailor her proposals to the requests. This has helped her obtain grants and avoid some of the problems women often face when shut out of men's networks. "It's like the old boys' network, but it's the old girls' network."

Claire finds that both the best and worst aspect of being in academia is that she is her own boss. She loves the flexibility of her hours and the fact that no one tells her what to do. At the same time, she says, "I'm a terrible boss. I know I'm not working hard enough. . . . And I take on way too much because there's no one to tell me not to. . . . You have to be really honest with yourself about what you can and cannot do and when you can and cannot do it. And sometimes you have to learn that the hard way."

Overall, Claire is satisfied with her career. "I'm amazed that I get paid to do this every day. . . . I would really like to be able to just do [science] until I literally drop dead at the bench."

As was true for Claire, the biggest milestone for a tenure-track faculty member is receiving tenure. Women are concentrated in the rank of assistant professor in part because they are more likely than men to be denied tenure or to leave before going up for tenure. The recent *Beyond Bias and Barriers* report from the National Academy of Sciences found a 4 percent difference in tenure rates favoring men over women; other studies have found similar differentials.[19] On average, women also take longer than men to go up for tenure and to be promoted from associate to full professor. The reasons for this are complex and many, including bias, family responsibilities, lack of support from department and institution, and even lack of confidence.

Most of the assistant professors I spoke with were worried about whether or not they would be judged good enough for job security at their institution. "I know that this semester has not been good for me, productivity-wise. I don't know how much that will affect my tenure chances. That's certainly the next big hurdle, getting tenure and knowing whether I can stay here beyond my seven years and really establish roots or not," says Kelsey, an assistant professor of biology. "It's a place that I'd like to stay, but so much of that depends on granting me tenure and letting me stay."

Until her pretenure review, Miranda, an assistant professor of computer science, felt confident about her eventual tenure decision. Now she's not so sure. "One of my reservations [about taking this position] was that I would be the only female faculty. I think if I had done a little more digging I might not have chosen to come here, because apparently there have been women who have preceded me and have not succeeded. And now that I've gone through the pretenure review, I can completely see why," she says. Since teaching is very important at her institution, other faculty—all men—observed her in the classroom as part of her review. In discussions after these visits, they gave her only positive feedback. But in her review, much of the feedback was negative.

"Here I was, trusting that my department was going to do what was in my best interest, which was help me improve as a teacher, or at least prepare me for what I was going to be hearing about in my pretenure review. And instead they went the easy route of, 'Just tell her everything's fine and we'll let this anonymous letter to the dean, which she's not supposed to see, but which I saw anyway; we'll just put all our concerns there.' That really shook my trust in the department. And it's really made me wonder if I'll get tenure here."

In contrast, Lena, an associate professor of biology, has a split appointment in two departments, each with about one-quarter female faculty. She was fairly sure that her upcoming tenure decision would go in her favor, and encountered no hurdles. "I don't think that it's a problem at this university. They're pretty clear what they expect from you, and I have a lot of support from my two departments."

Women who leave before a tenure decision or are denied tenure take a variety of career paths. Overall, studies have found that men are more likely to exit the tenure track for nonacademic jobs, whereas women are more likely to take contingent faculty positions.[20] While the exact reasons for this difference are not known, regardless of the job they switch to, female science and engineering faculty are more likely to cite working conditions, family, and job location as reasons for changing jobs.

Although Margaret, an engineer, thought a small college would be a better fit, she obtained a faculty position at a large university in the 2000s. "The general lore is that it's easier to go down in quality of institution than it is to go up in quality of institution, and this was at the upper levels. And so I [thought that I] may as well start here, and if I don't make it here, then I can try something else," she says. Within a couple of years, Margaret explains, "I started to realize, I don't think I'm in the right job. I don't think that I can be the driver for a research program. . . . I was able to be successful, but the activities that were of greatest interest to me were not going to get me tenure."

Lily also left her university before going up for tenure in the 1980s. "It was clear to me that this wasn't going to be a successful enterprise, and I started looking around for other things," she says. "In some sense I'm grateful it didn't work out, because I never would have moved. I talked to many women friends after that about how they felt trapped by a positive tenure decision. They couldn't leave it to go and do many other things that they had opportunities to do, because how could you give up tenure? . . . Most people have varied careers. They don't do the same things all their lives—except for faculty. Thank goodness that wasn't me."

After female faculty in science and engineering achieve tenure, some of the problems they face decrease, but others continue. Faculty must keep up their research productivity if they wish to be promoted to full professors, so maintaining a balance between career and personal life is still an issue. Similarly, isolation and exclusion from networks still occur. On the other hand, because they have job security, tenured faculty are more able to speak up and make changes in their departments that will improve the climate for both female students and faculty. One of the best ways to achieve this is to hold a position of leadership and have responsibility for making policy. Unfortunately, very few female scientists or engineers hold these crucial positions.

A 2000 survey of the institutions in the Association of American Universities, which includes 63 top research universities, found that a woman chaired only 4.2 percent of the 569 departments of engineering, math/statistics, earth sciences, chemistry, and physics/astronomy surveyed.[21] The number of female scientists and engineers among the ranks of deans, provosts, chancellors, presidents, and other leadership posts is also small, in part because so few women are associate or full professors in these fields; tenure is often a prerequisite for leadership positions. Even so, at many universities the number of women in leadership roles lags far behind those eligible for such positions, mirroring the lack of women at the top in corporations.

Although leadership positions allow women to make a larger impact on their institutions and the faculty and students there, such positions also reduce the amount of time spent on the activities that originally drew female professors into academia. Leadership positions take faculty members away from the laboratory; their research groups generally become smaller or cease to exist. Administrators also teach fewer or no courses. Some leadership positions are short term, allowing women to return to the laboratory after a few years. But in other cases, a woman must decide if she wants to give up the research program and scientific career she has worked so hard to build. Often, the answer is no. And even when it is yes, a woman may find it difficult to be successful as a leader because traditional gender schemas relegate women to supporting roles. Still, many women who have undertaken leadership positions have accomplished important things.

Lauren, a tenured physics professor, enjoys many aspects of being a department chair, a short-term leadership position. "It's being able to make things happen, good things, to be able to try to lead and push a department in a direction where it ought to go," she says. But she's frustrated that so much of her work is political. "There are moments when I find myself thinking that if I had wanted to be a marriage counselor, I would have sought a different occupation. I don't mean that literally, but when I have two colleagues sitting on the couch here in my office and one of them is saying to the other, 'Well, you should have known when you said that that it would hurt me,' I'm thinking, 'Oh, please.'"

Maria, a computer scientist, left industry to chair a struggling university department. There she worked hard to balance her administrative and research goals. "I had a rule that I would not be in the department on Tuesdays unless there was a donation of at least a million dollars at stake. And I also would go away for at least a couple weeks [a year] to visit collaborators," she says.

Although Maria loved being chair and had made a lot of improvements, she eventually felt she needed to move on. "Lots of people had said, 'You should be a university president. You have the personality to do that, and that would be a really good thing for you.' I was very uncertain about whether that was the right thing. I thought, well, if I got some high-level administrative experience—higher than being a department chair—then that would give me a sense of that's something I might want to do." And so Maria jumped on the administrative track and has been quite satisfied with her choice.

All the women I interviewed who held leadership positions had something in common: Others had sought them out and encouraged them to pursue such positions; they did not see themselves in a leadership role on their own. This reflects the results of a survey of female college presidents published in 2005 in which more than 70 percent of the respondents who had mentors reported that their mentors had sought them out.[22] Standard gender schemas make it easier for both men and women to see men as leaders, and this may be one reason why women are still underrepresented in such positions.

Although women in tenure-track and tenured faculty positions get much of the attention, many women are contingent faculty on short-term, renewable contracts, often working part time. Over the past couple of decades, universities have significantly increased their reliance on such faculty, who may be known as adjuncts, lecturers, research associates, or other titles. Although much of the increase in contingent faculty is in the humanities and social sciences, according to the U.S. Department of Education's 2004 National Study of Postsecondary Faculty, 13.6 percent of full-time engineering faculty and 19.3 percent of full-time natural sciences faculty were not tenured or on the tenure track. Furthermore, 21.2 percent of engineering faculty and 23.5 percent of natural sciences faculty were part time, the vast majority of these being contingent faculty.[23]

Hiring contingent faculty is a cost-cutting measure for universities. Not only are contingent faculty salaries generally lower than those of tenure-track faculty, but contingents hired to teach usually do not receive lab space, and they often must share offices. Students' education may also suffer. A study by University of Iowa professor Paul Umbach suggests that contingent faculty interact with students less frequently, use collaborative learning less often, and prepare for class less than their tenured or tenure-track peers.[24] This may be due to many reasons, including that contingent faculty have lower salaries and fewer resources.

According to the National Science Foundation, in 2003 women were about 27 percent of full-time non-tenure-track faculty and 31 percent of part-time faculty.[25] This is less than their representation among tenure-track faculty but more than that among tenured faculty, which suggests that women may not be more likely to end up in these lower-status positions due to bias, at least in some disciplines. But women with children and those with partners in academia are more likely to take contingent faculty positions. Part-time tenure-track positions are scarce, so a woman who wants or needs to work fewer hours due to family responsibilities will often take a contingent faculty job. Furthermore, since the chances of finding two tenure-track positions at the same or nearby institutions are small, one partner in a dual-career couple—more often the woman—frequently ends up taking a contingent faculty position so that they can stay in the same place.

While doing her second postdoc, Ashley began to apply to faculty positions, very few of which were open in her field.

"In grad school we were told to think about nontraditional careers," she says. "But I thought I was better than that." She and her partner had a pact that after five years of doing postdocs apart, they would both go to the place with the better job, no matter which one of them got it. "We both thought it would be me," she says. "My dissertation research, in my community, was really high-profile. . . . We thought that it would be a very short time before I got some kick-ass permanent job and he would move to be with me."

But Ashley's partner ended up with the better job offer instead. So she began making career sacrifices for the health of the relationship. She obtained another postdoc—not a permanent position—at a university ninety minutes from her partner's job. It wasn't even full time; two faculty members there cobbled together enough money to pay her half time. But considering how few people in the area work in Ashley's field, she took what she could get. Then Ashley got a grant funded, so the university converted her from a postdoc to a research scientist. Her salary is paid by whatever grants she can bring in. Having so little money has hampered her research progress, making it difficult to secure additional grants. Her partner is willing to move if Ashley receives an obviously superior job offer, but her slow research progress has made her a less attractive candidate to other universities. "I'm not happy where my career is," she says. "I feel like I've fallen into a trap." Since women are more likely than men to follow their partners and end up with contingent faculty positions, they are more likely to get trapped in this way.

Since contingent faculty positions are not paid as well as tenure-track ones, some part-time faculty have full-time jobs elsewhere. An engineer or scientist in industry may be invited to teach one class a year or semester, drawing on her experiences in the field. Indeed, hiring instructors with nonacademic experience can be useful in attracting students to programs. Other part-time faculty work part time at several different institutions, unable to make ends meet with what only one university offers them.

After working in the computer industry for many years, Julia began teaching chemistry, her PhD field, at a community college part time. She wishes that a full-time, permanent position would open at the school. "I think I have to wait for someone to retire or move on," Julia says. "They just don't have the budget to hire anybody else. And I know I've had very good reviews from the students. . . . I think they probably would consider me if they had a position open." She would also consider a lecturer position at a four-year institution but feels she's been away from chemical research too long to go after a tenure-track job.

Although for many women a contingent faculty position is extremely frustrating, some find it to be a good fit. After receiving her PhD, Mattie decided not to pursue a postdoc because it wasn't a good time for her husband to move. Doing research at a university as a staff member led to a non-tenure-track faculty position. "The position I have now is great. It's like a postdoc but with less stress. I do original research, I interact with students, I'm managing a couple of experimental trials. I also oversee a laboratory with a couple of employees underneath," Mattie says. And she works only forty hours a week, which she loves.

The only fly in the ointment is that Mattie is paid from a grant instead of having a regular salary. "It's never been a problem with these projects in the past to fund a research associate. But there is a possibility that funding dries up, and I may have to go and look elsewhere. That's a little scary."

Although many women assume while students that they are headed for an academic position, few realize the challenges that such jobs bring. When those become apparent—as well as the difficulty in obtaining academic positions—tough choices must be made. Brianna, a postdoc in geology, would like to go into academia. When we spoke, two positions were available in her field in the region where she would like to live. One position was at a community college; the other was tenure-track at a prestigious university.

"There are a lot of professional compromises I would make if I worked at a community college. If I did research it would be focused on teaching and learning, and I wouldn't be teaching the classes I want to teach. On the other hand, there are so many personal compromises that I'd have to make if I wanted to go work at the research university. I have absolutely no idea which way I want to go."

The climate for women in academic science and engineering is certainly improving. The increased focus both in scholarly literature and the media on the problems that academic women face has brought increased awareness as well as programs and policies to improve institutions, not only for women but for all faculty. Some women have found supportive environments in which they are able to succeed at doing work that they love. Other women, however, still struggle in male-dominated, biased environments or in positions that underutilize their skills.

Academia is a great option for some women, but many are looking at the obstacles it presents and deciding to pursue careers in industry, government, and other settings. The next chapter explores the possibilities and challenges that face a female scientist or engineer in nonacademic settings.

BEYOND THE
IVORY TOWER

WOMEN

SCIENTISTS IN

INDUSTRY AND

GOVERNMENT

In discussions of women in science and engineering, students and faculty members get most of the attention. The media reports on programs to attract and encourage girls and college students, as well as on the shortage of women in science and engineering faculty positions. But many women spend some or all of their careers outside the academy, and their experiences in these positions should not be discounted. In fact, they can point the way toward improvements for women in other scientific settings.

The primary alternatives to academia for science and engineering research are industry and government. Industry can include companies of all sizes, in a wide variety of different fields, such as biotechnology, chemicals, computers, electronics, and many others. Government includes national laboratories such as Lawrence Livermore and Los Alamos; military research facilities; and research centers associated with government institutes, such as the Centers for Disease Control. A smaller number of scientists do research at nonprofits, such as museums, independent research institutes, botanical gardens, and other noncommercial organizations.

Unfortunately, women in industry and government are not nearly as well studied as those in academia; I found very little research that specifically examined their experiences. Academic sociologists and psychologists naturally find it easiest to study women in academia, for they are nearby and access is generally straightforward. Gaining access to women in industry can be more difficult, especially if companies are worried that study results will reflect poorly on them. Furthermore, many consider academia to be of higher prestige than industry and thus contend that the representation and retention of women among faculty are more important to study.

For much of recent history, scientists have had two options, academic (basic) science or industrial (applied) science. Traditionally, academic science was seen as pure and noble, untainted by the prospect of profits, the realm of the true scientist. Industry, in contrast, was the refuge of the second-rate scientists, the ones who couldn't hack it in academia. In recent years industrial science, particularly in areas such as biotechnology, has become more highly regarded. But more importantly, with the number of PhDs awarded far outstripping the number of available academic positions, more and more scientists are working outside the university. According to the National Science Foundation, in 2003 only about one-half of PhD life scientists and one-third of

PhD physical scientists were working in academia.[1] Unlike science, engineering does not have basic and applied divisions; all engineering is applied by its nature, so graduates of engineering programs are expected to work in industry, as are computer scientists. Only about 2 percent of all computer scientists and engineers are faculty members.[2] Some scientists and engineers who end up as professors also spend time working in industry, either before or after earning their PhD. For all these reasons, examining the experiences of women in industry and government is important.

The experiences of women in academia and industry have many similarities, including chilly climates, barriers to balancing work and a personal life, and so forth. But some industry and government environments have a crucial element that academia lacks—flexibility, which appears to improve outcomes for women substantially. Many of the women I spoke with had considered going into academia or had been planning on it—until they got a taste of what it was like. After seeing, as students or postdocs, what their female professors, advisors, and others had to go through, they began to question their own goals. "I realized that I didn't really want to be an assistant professor in a physics department at all," says Vera, who earned a PhD in the 1990s and now works in the chemical industry. "I didn't want to go through the struggle of what I was seeing other women do. . . . I don't want to struggle for ten years to try to get tenure and then be totally exhausted and old."

Industry and government positions have many advantages over those in academia. For one, many industrial positions do not expect several (or any) years of postdoc experience from candidates. Engineers and computer scientists in particular can often make good salaries with only a bachelor's degree. In 2003, computer and mathematical scientists with a bachelor's degree and less than five years of experience had a median annual salary of $52,000; engineers made $53,000.[3] As a result, women in industry can start working for better salaries sooner, which helps their lifetime earnings and may also make it easier for them to work part time later if they so desire.

Although salaries in industry tend to be higher than those in academia, a pay gap still exists between men and women. A recent survey by the American Association of University Women (AAUW) found that one year out of college, women working full time across all occupations made only 80 percent of their male counterparts' salaries on average. This was not a result of women trading lower salary for increased flexibility or better benefits. Women who were employed in the "research, scientists, and technical" category made only 82 percent of their male counterparts' salaries, while women in computer science made 92 percent. In "engineering, software engineering, and architecture," women actually did better than men, earning 105 percent of their salaries, which may be a result of the scarcity of women in engineering combined with the drive to appear diverse in corporate America.[4]

As the years go by, female engineers lose their financial edge, while those in other fields gain some ground. Ten years out of college, women employed full time in engineering and architecture earn 93 percent of the salaries of their male colleagues; the corresponding figures are 94 percent in computer science and 89 percent in research, science, and technology. The pay gaps in these fields are actually smaller than those in many other areas. Ten years out, the average across all occupations in the AAUW study was 69 percent, in part because women are concentrated in fields that pay less than those more populated by men.[5] Since salaries are usually higher in science and engineering, the influx of women into those fields is helping to narrow the overall gender pay gap.

A woman may experience a larger or smaller pay gap depending on a variety of factors, including the environment in which she works. For example, a report that looked at the salaries and promotions of women and minorities at six national laboratories in 2001–2004 found that women were paid between 2 and 4 percent less at five of the labs. This study lumped technical and nontechnical employees together, so the salary differences specifically among scientists and engineers are unknown. The study also found that women were promoted at 80 percent or more of the rate of men at all the labs.[6]

While the results of this study are promising, gender equity is still an issue at some government laboratories. In 2003, the Regents of the University of California, who run Lawrence Livermore National Laboratory, settled a class-action gender discrimination lawsuit with more than 3,000 female employees of the lab. Employees alleged that they faced discrimination both in promotions and salary. As a result of the suit, the laboratory changed how it ranked some employees for salary increases and promotions, but this change did not affect scientists and engineers.[7] Furthermore, data collected by the women's group at Argonne National Laboratory in Chicago in 2002 showed that while the first four levels for PhD scientists (of six) each contained about the same number of male scientists, female scientists with PhDs were concentrated in the starting level, and their numbers fell off sharply after the third level. Many different factors may have caused this disparity, including more women hired at entry level because of a larger pool of recent female doctoral graduates, few women hired at higher levels, delays in promotions, and lack of retention.[8]

These findings reflect Eliane's experience as a PhD physicist at a government laboratory. "[The lab has] not been very successful at providing a lot of support for middle-career women," she says. "It's much easier to convince management to hire young women—especially since there are so many bright young women—to bring on postdocs and make them permanent staff, and coach and mentor them. When it comes to midcareer women, supporting them has proven to be a much more difficult thing to do."

According to the theory of "ghettoization," salary inequities result, in part, from women in a particular industry or field working in lower-paid, less prestigious specialties than do men. This is occurring to some extent in science, in that women are more likely to go into biology or geology, which some scientists consider to be less prestigious disciplines than, say, physics. For example, in 2005 women earned nearly 20 percent of all bachelor's degrees in engineering. When broken down by field, on the other hand, they earned more than 40 percent of the degrees in bioengineering and environmental engineering but less than 15 percent of the degrees in fields such as electrical and mechanical engineering.[9] Even within a particular discipline, women are often more likely to work in certain subfields or kinds of positions. Rachel, an engineer in her twenties, found that in the companies where she worked, quality control was a ghetto for female engineers.

Researchers have suggested several theories for how such ghettos form. The devaluation theory suggests that if more women fill a job, then employers see the job as less valuable and thus offer lower salaries. On the other hand, the job queues theory suggests that causality works the other way around, with employers offering low pay first. This causes men to seek other, better-paying jobs, and since employers can't find men to take lower-paid positions, they hire women instead. A third theory suggests that women choose less demanding (and thus more poorly paid) positions because they put lower priority on money and higher priority on parenting. Whatever the reason, women are concentrated in certain science and engineering fields and types of positions, and these often come with lower pay and lower prestige.[10]

Once a woman finds herself in a ghetto, it can be hard to get out. Ida, for example, was working as a technical writer at a computer company when she asked for opportunities to get involved in more technical work. "I faced resistance within the organization—ironically, because it's such an incredibly technical environment. I didn't face 100 percent resistance, but from the people that mattered, I did."

The theory of ghettos does not entirely explain the gender stratification in science, of course. For one thing, biology is hot. From the Human Genome Project to stem cells, cloning, and new methods for fighting disease, many of the most significant discoveries in the last twenty years have come out of the life sciences.

The field is growing and unlikely to stop. Based on the job queues theory above, men should dominate biology. The fact that they don't may be an indication of women's growing equality.

Another advantage of industry and government positions is that they are more likely than academia to offer family-friendly supports such as flexible schedules, part-time jobs, parental leave, and on-site or nearby childcare. *Working Mother* magazine annually ranks companies on the availability of such supports, and each year multiple companies that employ scientists and engineers make the list. Several are even on the magazine's Hall of Fame list, including DuPont and IBM.[11] But although *Working Mother* makes sure that the companies it honors actually allow employees to use the benefits offered, other companies only give lip service to these practices. Project ENHANCE, a study run by researchers at the University of Maryland, surveyed more than 1,700 women and 250 managers at twenty-five chemical companies. The survey found that while in many cases the companies had family-friendly policies such as flexible work schedules on the books, individual managers refused to allow employees to take advantage of them.[12] Similarly, a study of professional and technical workers in the biotechnology industry found that some employees considered family-friendly policies to be unusable even when they were available. As might be expected, the actual usability of such policies was more important to determining employees' productivity and commitment than their mere existence.[13]

Industry and government positions are also attractive to women because, on average, they require fewer work hours than do those in academia. For doctoral scientists and engineers who are in industry or self-employed, the average work week ranges from forty-five to fifty hours, depending on the discipline, whereas PhD scientists and engineers in government work an average of forty-three to forty-seven hours per week. These are averages, of course, and some women do end up working much longer hours. Ingrid, for example, worked at a technology company in the late 1990s, before the dot-com crash. "I worked from 10 AM to 2 AM. I slept under my desk when I needed to keep something running," she says. "I have no idea how I got through the last couple of years there. Actually, I do know, because I remember taking lots of ibuprofen and then stuffing bags of ice up my sleeves while typing, which is insane." Although most companies do not expect quite this level of dedication from their employees, many do expect, even require, more than forty hours per week if a woman wishes to move up the career ladder.

Women in industry and government are also more able to focus on scientific research than their counterparts in academia. "We're not teaching, and we don't have all these service committees, so we have more time in that sense. But the disadvantage is that here we don't have that many students and postdocs. . . . And so work that gets done has to be done by us personally," says Jocelyn, a physicist at a national lab. Positions outside academia can thus be a good fit for women who want to focus on research and aren't interested in teaching.

A disadvantage to working in industry, however, is that scientists must focus on whatever management thinks is important. Although some experimentation is encouraged and even required, at the end of the day the company needs products it can sell. Researchers in academia and government have more freedom in the research they do—if they can get it funded. Industry researchers may sometimes need to sell their research to management, but they do not need to write grant proposals constantly and hope that the money comes through. On the other hand, as Jocelyn explains, "At the national labs these days, we are constrained to work on projects that are specifically funded, either by internal lab programs or by us lab scientists writing proposals to internal or external funding sources. We're all fragmented. It's hard to get enough money to spend all your time on one project."

Another trade-off for women in industry and government is that they lack the job security that tenured professors have. While a university may push an older professor to retire if he or she isn't being very productive, such professors become "emeritus" and can usually keep an office and sometimes a lab so that they may continue to be active in their fields. But women outside of academia don't have this cushion. They can be laid off or fired at will.

Eliane, a PhD physicist, worked at government laboratories for more than two decades. Then, when the budget for the project she was working on was slashed as part of cuts across the lab, she was forced to retire in a reduction in force. Eliane used this early retirement as an opportunity to pursue a second career in science policy, but she wasn't intending to stop working in the lab yet.

Discrimination, bias, and isolation are also problems for women in industry and government, particularly in more male-dominated areas. The Project ENHANCE study of the chemical industry found that most women surveyed reported moderately high levels of sexist discrimination, and that the amount of discrimination experienced was highly correlated with job satisfaction. This was especially true of women of color and lesbians/bisexuals. Racial minority women also reported salaries, position levels, job satisfaction, and number of supervisees that were lower than those of white women.[14]

Sometimes the bias is subtle rather than overt. For example, Nicole, a geologist, worked in the 2000s at a small company in which only women were asked to answer the phone. "Normally it was the office manager, and the editor would take over for her on lunch breaks, but when one of them was out, people started pulling from the female [technical] staff to answer the phones," she says. "I eventually just started insisting that no, I can't, I'm busy today, I'm sorry."

Isolation is particularly a problem in some fields. Catherine, for example, works in a very male-dominated area of engineering, and while she has learned to handle the challenges, she worries about bringing other women into similar situations. "If I recruit people to work in my field, other women, then I just know that they're going to have to go through that six months of being uncomfortable, especially the forerunners. Do you really want to do that to other people? I kind of think of it as hoodwinking them into coming into the field," she explains. "The person who's in charge of recruiting [at my agency] always wants to send the women out to try and get more women. But [when we go out,] we have to tell people, 'We only have two women.'"

Women who end up supervising men may have an even more difficult time, because gender schemas cause incongruity between the roles of "woman" and "leader." In one study, researchers asked college students to mark whether 92 different adjectives were characteristic of successful managers, successful male managers, or successful female managers. They found that male and female students had similar perceptions of successful male managers and managers in general, but men had much more negative views of female managers than women did. Male students were much more likely to describe female managers as bitter, deceitful, easily influenced, passive, and quarrelsome, among other negative adjectives.[15] These results replicate those of researchers in the 1970s and 1980s; negative gender stereotypes have not changed significantly. Although women in science and engineering often don't have the title of manager, many aspire to and do run their own laboratories, managing the work of technicians and other scientists. Any time a woman is in power, she is more likely to be judged negatively than a man in a similar position, due to both conscious and unconscious bias.

Janessa is an engineer with an oil company in a remote area. She leads a crew that takes data and does maintenance on oil wells. Her current camp of fifty people has only four other women, one of whom is also an engineer. "I'm so used to working with guys, it doesn't bother me too much," Janessa says. "You certainly have to get used to how different guys react to your being female, fairly young, and also in charge." When she's on an oil rig, she's the boss not only of her crew but of everyone else on the rig. She has found that some men will go to the guys in her crew instead of to her. "I'm the one in charge. It's important to make that clear in a tactful way," she says.

Janessa has a good relationship with most of the men she works with. "Normally they're really receptive and nice. I've had a few instances where they've kind of been dicks; I'm not sure if that's the way they are or because it was me. Certainly that'll make it harder for me to do my job; I'll be a lot more reluctant to ask them questions . . . if they're cold and inhospitable."

Some women encounter different kinds of bias and discrimination, both subtle and overt, several times during their careers, as has been the case for Rachel.

RACHEL, 29

After graduating from college with a bachelor's degree in engineering, Rachel went to work for an automotive firm as a quality engineer. "It was made quite clear to me within a fairly short period of time that women were not welcome in any engineering department other than quality. None worked in any of the other departments. There was a very thick glass ceiling there," she says. Rachel did several internships as an undergraduate and found that most of the companies she worked for also had more women in quality than anywhere else.

After six months, Rachel got a job—not in quality control—with another automotive firm, one where she had interned and had a pretty good experience. She loved her first boss. "He mostly let me have the run of my area, didn't ask me a lot of questions, and let me do what I thought I needed to do, which was wonderful and extremely unusual for someone like me, so recently out of school."

Over the past several years, Rachel has transferred within the company several times. "I've been going from problem department to problem department, trying to get them stabilized. Because I understand all the technical stuff but I can help them pull it together with functional stuff, it seems to be that I can go between different areas pretty easily."

Rachel finds a lot to like about her job. It's mentally stimulating and fast paced, and, as she says, "Everyone I've worked for here has been of the small group of people who don't have a problem with women being in engineering." One of her bosses even went out of his way to recruit women into technical positions.

But not having a problem with women in engineering is different from treating them the same as men. After more than half a dozen years in the company, Rachel has yet to receive a promotion. "Most of the other people who have started since I did have had a couple promotions in a similar amount of time or less," she says. Overall, about 10 percent of the engineers in her company are women, and they are noticeably concentrated in the lower ranks. "There aren't any women in engineering management roles. There aren't any women in program management or project engineering roles."

In addition, Rachel worries about trying to have children while with this company. Most of her male coworkers have stay-at-home wives, so they are able to function as ideal workers. Plus, the company is not accustomed to its female engineers also being mothers. "One woman engineer is pregnant right now, but she is the first one that they've had," Rachel says. "I'm not exactly sure what I'm going to want to do once I have a baby. Right now I think that ideally I'd work part time doing engineering. I don't know if that's going to be an option."

She has thought about trying a different field but for now is sticking with engineering because it feeds both the creative and technical sides of her. "I don't feel like there are a lot of fields where I can use both. And in engineering you can. There are a lot of engineers who aren't creative, but they aren't very good engineers. They're very boring engineers."

As is evident throughout this book, in many organizations women receive promotions less often and rise through the ranks more slowly than men do. In a 2004 study of the careers of nearly four thousand life scientists with doctoral degrees, Laurel Smith-Doerr, a sociologist at Boston University, found that, keeping years since PhD and prestige of doctoral university constant, being female decreased the likelihood of holding a leadership position by 32 percent.[16] Many factors play into this, including lack of mentoring and access to networks, as Carmen discovered.

In the early 2000s, Carmen asked for a promotion after several years of working at a civil engineering consulting firm. Her boss refused, saying that she hadn't done enough in-depth technical work to warrant one. "I was furious, because the person who was in charge of giving me that type of task was my boss. . . . Part of me feels that he just made the basic assumption, and maybe it was not an intentional assumption, but made the assumption that I would be a support person, because I'm a woman, and [a male colleague] is going to be the expert, because he's the man. And so [a male colleague] was getting tutored and given the opportunities that he needed to grow as an expert, whereas I wasn't given the same opportunity."

On the other hand, some companies work hard to make sure that both men and women have opportunities to challenge and distinguish themselves. When Ayyana began her position as an engineer in a small company, she was on the lookout for gender bias, especially in regards to a male colleague hired at the same time. "I wondered if, both of my bosses and [my colleague] being male, there would be an issue, but there never has been," she says. "My bosses are really careful about either putting both of us on a project or giving each of us a different project, almost as if they're parents of twins."

Much of the research on gender and organizations suggests that women fare better in groups that have formal hiring and promotion practices. If the rules and standards are written out and available to all, then it becomes more difficult for search committees and managers to use subjective criteria in personnel decisions. Similarly, recruitment through networks often disadvantages women because they are more likely to be left out of such networks. One study of female engineers found that they were more likely to be promoted in hierarchical organizations, which have more formal policies regarding advancement.[17]

On the other hand, Smith-Doerr's research on female life scientists found that firms without a lot of formal policies were better for women. Organizations with clear rules are usually hierarchies, which often develop a hidden set of requirements that operate alongside formal policies. Network-based organizations are more flexible; centered on the connections between people and firms, they are more likely to run with what works best at a particular time or in a particular situation rather than by formalized policies. Although in Smith-Doerr's work, female life scientists were 32 percent less likely than men to hold a leadership position overall, a woman in a network-based biotechnology company was eight times as likely to have a leadership position than a woman in a hierarchical organization.[18] The key here appears to be flexibility. Whereas in a hierarchy there may be only one way up, a network-based organization offers many routes to running one's own lab.

Michelle, a PhD biologist, has worked at three different companies of varying sizes. She preferred the startup company. "The startup was a pretty masculine environment, but I felt very respected as a woman. I brought in a skill set that nobody else had, and so lots of different people wanted my input on things," she says. "You prove yourself, that you can do the work, and that's all you need to do." A couple of years ago, a much larger firm bought Michelle's startup. "There's so much more bureaucracy. It's so much more complicated to get anything done, to get a decision made."

In general, research in industry, particularly in network-based organizations, is more collaborative and interdisciplinary as well. Although more collaborative research is happening in academia, many faculty members still run their labs as private fiefdoms. This occurs in part because professors are competing with each other for individual glory: tenure, promotion, Nobel Prizes, and so on. In an industrial laboratory, however, the end target is a product that will be profitable for the company. Having this sort of collaborative goal means that scientists are more likely to work with each other and use each other's expertise. Considering what we know about women's reactions to the male competition rituals embedded in science education, this more collaborative atmosphere may be more welcoming.

And yet, this collaboration can also have detrimental effects for women. Research suggests that women on teams may be shortchanged when evaluation time rolls around. In one study, when evaluators did not receive specific information about the contributions of a man and a woman who had successfully completed a task together, the evaluators rated the man as more competent, more influential, and more likely to take a leadership role.[19]

The most flexible situation of all, and the one in which a woman has the most power, is working for herself. Research suggests that opening one's own business is becoming an increasingly common move for women who are frustrated with the barriers and rigidity they find in organizations.[20] It's not a complete panacea, of course, for a company needs clients, and a woman-owned company may have problems finding customers because of sexism and bias. Being self-employed is also financially unstable until the company becomes established, which may not be an option for a woman with a family to support.

Seema is CEO of a small technology company she founded with several classmates from graduate school. They're commercializing an idea that arose while they were students. "It's been extremely exciting and extremely terrifying at the same time," she says. As CEO, Seema finds that she spends a lot of her time doing business rather than science. "I often miss working directly on science and math, but in other ways I find being a CEO more rewarding. The nice part about being such a small company is that everyone really gets to do everything. In fact, everyone has to do everything." Again, flexibility is an asset to women.

Female scientists and engineers who opt to go into industry

or government positions often find a lot to like about their jobs. But they still face many of the challenges that frustrate women in academic settings, whether students or faculty. The next chapter looks at how women in medicine have faced some of the same issues. Although the practice of medicine differs considerably from that of science, the medical field offers a glimpse of what may be possible as more women enter scientific fields—and how much more still needs to be done.

THE FRONTIERS OF MEDICINE

WOMEN

DOCTORS

Women in medicine experience some of the same conditions that women in science and engineering do, but in other ways the professions differ enormously. At least in the United States, medicine was until recently a heavily male-dominated field, but since the 1970s women have flooded into medical school. In 2005–2006, women composed 49 percent of medical school graduates and 42 percent of medical residents and fellows.[1] Women are about 26 percent of nonstudent physicians overall.[2] But when the numbers are broken down by specialty, patterns like those overall in science and engineering emerge: Women are much better represented in some specialties than in others.

As undergraduates, aspiring physicians take many of the

same courses as do science majors, and more often than not, they major in a science discipline. But postgrad scientists and physicians take very different paths. Two years into medical school, students move on to clinical work. While graduate students in the sciences are in the laboratory performing experiments, medical students are in hospitals learning how to care for patients. Scientific inquiry is valuable to society in that it leads to new products and discoveries that benefit people, but this benefit is not immediate. A physician who saves a person's life, on the other hand, sees the results of her work firsthand. This more immediate sense of doing good in the world is one reason why women enter medicine and why it may be more attractive to some than science or engineering.

It has often been suggested that women are more suited to medicine than to science because medicine involves working closely with people. While this may be true in some specialties, particularly primary care, where doctors are able to form close relationships with patients, in other specialties, doctors spend most of their time with patients who are under anesthesia. Women are more likely to choose primary-care specialties and as a result have been described as the "housewives" of medicine: They take care of the grunt work while men are more likely to be in the better-paid, higher-status specialties. Primary-care physicians deal with routine illnesses and provide preventive care, work that is essential but often isn't recognized, much like the routine housework and childcare that women still do the bulk of. Specialists treat more serious illnesses and perform life-saving surgeries, and as such they receive more recognition and higher pay. One sees this sort of division in science as well, as women are more likely to be in lower-paid fields such as biology and geology, but the differences in pay and prestige are not quite as great as those in medicine.

Women in medicine also face many of the same challenges in balancing a career and a personal life as do their counterparts in science and engineering. Doctors not only work long hours, but since people can become sick and injured at any time, many physicians must work nontraditional hours or be on call. Medicine is doing better than science in regards to the availability of fulfilling part-time jobs, but much more could be done. Overall, medicine represents what could happen in science and engineering fields as more women continue to enter them, but we have a long way to go before equity will be truly reached.

JENNI, 46

Jenni comes from a family of physicians, including her father and both grandfathers. As a young girl, she wanted to be a nurse. Her father encouraged her to become a candy striper to learn more about nursing. "Within two months I decided I was not going to be a nurse. I was going to be a doctor. But it took me until I was fourteen to figure out that that was an option."

Jenni attended a private university where she could major in English while on the premed track. "The other passion in my life has always been books and language," she says. "I realized I was going to spend the next umpteen years of my life doing science, and this was my only shot to do something different." Although the English major made her less attractive to medical schools, she has found the training in narrative to be extremely beneficial in helping her communicate with patients. In addition, during her difficult first year in medical school, she knew that she had to get through it because she felt a career as a doctor would be more meaningful and satisfying than one as an English professor.

Medical school was difficult for Jenni because of the large classes and emphasis on exams. But when she finally started working with patients, Jenni found that she was both good at it and loved it. Starting in medical school in the 1980s, however, she experienced bias from male physicians toward both female physicians and female patients. During an obstetrics and gynecology rotation, for example, a male resident told her that female patients lie and not to trust them. But Jenni also found mentors and others to guide her, sometimes learning things that she didn't realize were necessary. For example, a female preceptor in a clinical skills course called the three women in the group aside to teach them how to carry the things they needed without carrying around a pocketbook.

Jenni had begun dating a geologist as a senior in college, and they married during her third year in medical school. When she chose internal medicine as her specialty, a male anesthesiologist she worked with was surprised that her husband was "letting" her become an internist. Jenni's response: "You know, my husband didn't consult me when he chose a field that requires him to live in a tent for four months out of the year, so I don't think he gets a vote."

Her husband attended graduate school across the country from her medical school. As such, they had a commuter engagement and then marriage until she started a residency at a community hospital near his university. The residency program she attended was constructed to allow residents to have lives outside the hospital and to take maternity and other leaves as needed. This made the program quite popular among women, and many stayed in the system to become attending physicians. But some doctors outside the program saw this flexibility as indicating a lack of commitment. One of her med-school classmates told Jenni: "That's a good residency for women, because they don't mind if you're not really serious about medicine."

During her first year of residency, Jenni received a lot of feedback that she was too aggressive. "I think that this is a gender issue. I think I got that feedback because I'm a large woman. People also find me intimidating because I am very articulate. If I want to get my point across, you're going to know about it," she says. "I get louder and pushier when I feel powerless. And internship is an experience of powerlessness at its very core." Fortunately, a couple of mentors were able to help her make choices about how she presented herself without feeling as if she had to change who she was.

When Jenni's husband received a faculty position in a different state, she moved with him. For several years in the 1990s, Jenni worked at a community hospital where she taught residents as well as cared for patients. But the residency program director was deeply hostile toward women. "This was a guy who had a very narrow vision of what it meant to be a physician and a very narrow vision of what it meant to be a woman, and the two just really did not coincide at all."

The hospital had no women in leadership who were not nurses, and some of Jenni's male colleagues were openly sexist, and not just to her. "I worked in that residency program for seven years, and there wasn't a woman who came through that program who didn't end up in my office in tears at one point or another," Jenni says.

After adopting a child, Jenni went into private practice with two other female physicians. Although she liked being in control, the financial insecurity was frustrating. They eventually sold the practice to a larger medical group, and Jenni is quite happy with working there. "I can possibly see myself moving to other positions in this group, but barring something truly odd happening, I think this is my job for quite a while."

Unlike in science or engineering, one cannot major in medicine as an undergraduate. Although some colleges have a premedicine major, most do not. Instead, premed students major in typical disciplinary concentrations, but they also complete a set of courses required by most American medical schools. These usually include biology, general and organic chemistry, physics, and calculus. Many premeds major in a science field; biology, chemistry, and bioengineering are common. But some women opt to major in something completely unrelated, as Jenni did, pursuing an interest or passion in another area before committing to a medical career path. This sort of exploration is more difficult for students interested in science or engineering.

Premeds are the bane of many science and engineering students. The stereotype is that premeds are uber-competitive, as they must have incredibly high grades to get into medical school. Women are less likely to fit this mold, however. "I actually called myself a closet premed," says Allison, a medical student who majored in physics. "I really wanted to go into medicine because I had this deep desire for service. I really didn't feel very competitive about it. I wanted to get into medical school somewhere, but I didn't feel like I was gunning to get into Harvard Med."

Unfortunately, the science and math requirements for premeds can be discouraging to women who are interested in medicine but have decided that they aren't good at math and science due to socialization pressures. In fact, the day-to-day work of being a doctor has very little to do with integrals or the molecular structure of benzene. "Premed is science, medical school is less science, and being a doctor is the least amount of science," says Betsy, who was premed and a political science major in the 1980s. "I knew that what I was learning in school, in organic chemistry, wasn't what it was to be a doctor. That wasn't what medicine was really about, at least the kind of medicine I want to practice."

For many women, the opportunity to work in a medical setting during high school or college cemented their desire to go into medicine. Like early exposure to research for scientists and engineers, these hands-on medical experiences, even if limited, were crucial in giving women a taste of the field and igniting their passion.

Allison spent a summer as a translator in an emergency room while an undergraduate in the 1990s. "I didn't know anything about medicine at the time, technically speaking. I knew that I was interested in it. I knew what I had learned in biology and chemistry. But to actually be the communicator in between the patient and the physician was a fascinating role, because I was really involved in what was going on," she says. As a translator, she worked with patients with a wide variety of ailments and was able to observe many different procedures. Allison particularly remembered one family in which the wife delivered premature triplets by C-section. The father was very shaken up. "I ended up realizing that I had a lot of power over whether or not this guy went home totally frightened for his children's lives or went home with a sense of comfort that the hospital was doing everything it could and that the children were going to live."

Getting into medical school is quite difficult; students need to earn top grades and high scores on the MCAT exam as well as to shine in interviews. Once they're in, however, it just becomes harder. The first two years of medical school focus on class work. Like the introductory science and math classes that provide a foundation for independent research later, med-school classes are supposed to provide a base of anatomy and physiology knowledge for later work with patients. Many women I spoke with felt that they did a poor job of this, however. "My first two years of medical school, as far as I'm concerned, were a waste of time," says Jenni, a physician in her forties. The last two years of medical school consist of clinical rotations in which students interact with patients and learn how to perform procedures while supervised by resident and attending physicians.

"When I started working with patients, I found what I really loved were the puzzles," says Gretchen, who attended medical school in the 1970s. "You had one clue: what the patient said was bothering them. Then you had to elicit information from them with your history, physical, and carefully chosen lab work in order to put together the pieces and come up with an answer. It was fun."

But while med students are improving others' health, they are often hurting their own. Sara and her fellow med students in the 2000s noticed large, negative changes in themselves. "By the second year, most of us had either gained twenty pounds or lost twenty—not on purpose. I think there were two people in the entire class that were not on some kind of [gastrointestinal] medicine, either for ulcers or reflux or something else. Better than half of us were on some kind of psychiatric drug. All of us had increased our alcohol consumption significantly. [Medical school] doesn't do good things to you." This stress is similar to that faced by graduate students in science, particularly those who must deal with a hostile climate.

Many women in medicine also experience hostility and harassment. Of the more than 4,500 respondents to the Women Physicians' Health Study conducted in the 1990s, 47.7 percent had experienced gender-based harassment, and 36.9 percent had experienced sexual harassment.[3] Harassment was more common during medical school or residency than in practice. Sadly, younger physicians reported experiencing more harassment than older ones. Although this likely reflects the increased awareness by younger physicians of what constitutes harassment, it also indicates that sexism is still alive and well in medical schools and hospitals. A study of fourteen medical schools conducted in 2002 found that 69 percent of the women surveyed had experienced gender discrimination or harassment.[4]

"I've always felt like becoming a doctor is half going to school and half fraternity hazing ritual," says Sara. "You have to learn things, you have to understand what's going on, but your professors are literally trying to berate you in order to quickly get you to answer questions."

Betsy had her first experience with gender-based harassment during her third-year surgical rotation in the early 1990s. "The [male residents] were sexist and vulgar. I'm not prudish, and they made me uncomfortable. I felt like I didn't belong there."

Physicians experience gender bias not only from other doctors but also from patients. It's understandable that a person may feel more comfortable with a doctor of the same sex, but this is not always possible, especially in a hospital or emergency situation where only certain doctors are on call. Gretchen recalls a young man admitted to the hospital one evening during her internship in the 1970s. "When I walked into his room, he said, 'You're not going to touch me. I'm not going to have a woman take care of me. I don't want any woman doctor.' And I said, 'Well, it's me or nobody, 'cause I'm the one on tonight, and that's it.' Within a few days, he thought I was terrific."

Harassment of women by other physicians is more likely to occur in male-dominated areas of medicine. During medical school, students must choose a specialty. The residency, the period of training after med school, and the physician's later career focus on that specialty. In 2005, more than half of the residents in obstetrics and gynecology, pediatrics, family medicine, psychiatry, pathology, and dermatology were women. However, the largest number of women was in internal medicine, where they made up 42.4 percent of the residents. The proportion of female residents in the various specialties has changed very little over the past several decades.[5]

In this way, medicine mirrors science, with some fields,

such as biology and pediatrics, becoming gender-balanced and others, such as physics and surgery, remaining male-dominated. A hierarchy exists in medicine just as in science, and the fields that have remained male-dominated are widely considered to be more difficult. Women are drawn to these specialties for a variety of reasons. A mid-1990s survey of physicians who graduated from medical school in the early 1980s showed that women's choice of specialty was more influenced by personal factors such as familial responsibilities, their marriage/spouse, personal social values, and clinical experience with the underserved.[6] The specialties women choose reflect this.

The specialties that women tend to pick mostly fall into two major categories. First, dermatology, psychiatry, and pathology are known as "controllable lifestyle" specialties. In these areas, physicians have personal time free of job requirements (such as being on call) and can control the total hours they spend working per week. Other controllable lifestyle specialties include anesthesiology, emergency medicine, and ophthalmology, which are also popular among women.

Allison, a medical student, was initially interested in surgery but is now considering other options, in part because she intends to have a family eventually. "I'm thinking about emergency medicine right now because you get to do small surgeries, you get do a lot of primary-care stuff, a lot of acute stuff," Allison says. "Lifestyle is a factor in that, because in emergency medicine you work shifts. You're on for so many hours, and when you're off you don't have a pager. You don't get called in to do an emergency surgery at 2:00 AM. . . . I'm also thinking about internal medicine because you can do the same sort of stuff as a hospitalist."

Another factor affecting women's specialty choice is the amount of contact doctors have with their patients. Pediatrics, general internal medicine, and family practice are known as "primary-care specialties" and make up the second category of specialty that women tend to choose. These specialties are the front lines of medicine, so to speak, these doctors are the ones who do basic and preventive care and refer patients to specialists as needed. Many women are drawn to these specialties because they are able to work one-on-one with patients over a long period of time (provided an insurance company doesn't get in the way). A surgeon, on the other hand, may see a patient awake and off the operating table only a few times.

Obstetrics and gynecology is a specialty with neither a controllable lifestyle nor close contact with patients. While the focus on women's health makes this an obvious field of interest for female physicians, because ob/gyn is a surgical specialty with an erratic schedule—women can go into labor at any time—some women find it a difficult choice.

J. E. did her residency in obstetrics and gynecology in the 1980s. "I liked the surgical subspecialties. I didn't want to do general surgery, because the residency was much longer, and it really was and still is a very male profession. And I liked having women as patients. But I probably didn't give as much thought as I should to my life thereafter and how difficult it would be to have such an irregular schedule. . . . If I had to replay that, I probably would have made a different decision."

Even women who choose surgical specialties may desire to work with underserved populations. Betsy chose her specialty during a fourth-year rotation in urology. "Women would come in, and nobody had any idea what to do for them. It was so clear that this was an underserved population in our country with women and their lower urinary tract problems. So I decided that I was going to go into urology."

So how do men choose their specialty? The study mentioned previously found that men were more influenced by income, parental preferences, and role models prior to medical school than were women.[7] This result is interesting, because studies of scientists suggest that women are more influenced in their decision to pursue a science career by early role models and personal encouragement than are men. Of course, in the 1980s boys were more likely to see male doctors who would be role models than women were to see female doctors. With the influx of women into the profession, particularly into pediatrics and other primary-care specialties, girls today are much more likely to encounter a female doctor while they're growing up. While a role model need not be same-sex—several of the women I spoke with described male physicians who acted as role models—the visibility of women in a profession is quite important to encouraging other women to enter it.

Regardless of the specialty chosen, residencies are generally a grueling ordeal. Until recently, residents could work thirty-six-hour shifts, separated by twelve hours of rest, and total one hundred-plus hours of work per week. In 2003, the Accreditation Council for Graduate Medical Education required that accredited residency programs limit residents' hours to no more than eighty per week. Individual shifts can now be no more than thirty hours and must be separated by ten hours of rest.[8] Despite these changes, the hours residents are expected to work are not conducive to a social or family life. "It was tremendously lonely," says J. E. of her residency in the 1980s. "I certainly felt that my time in the hospital and time working kept me away from other places where I could meet people."

Some residents continue to experience harassment. Betsy describes her residency in the 1990s as "horrible." The first two years of general surgery were okay, but the years of specific urology training were quite difficult. "The attendings I worked with were misogynists; they were hostile," she says. "They did not want me there. They found my presence intrusive. It had nothing to do with my personality."

Jane actually quit her residency in surgery in the 1980s. "I loved surgery. I absolutely loved it. It's like lab work. You use your hands to make something happen, and what you make happen is that you save somebody's life. And that's an amazing feeling," she says. But after a while, she got bored of it. "There are some changes in surgery and some new developments, but basically it's the same thing day in and day out, year in and year out." Jane also realized that a surgical career would make balancing work and family more difficult. She went on to do a residency in pathology.

In the Women Physicians' Health Study, women in anesthesiology, dermatology, ophthalmology, psychiatry, and surgery reported being highly satisfied with their specialty. Except for surgery, all of these highly satisfying specialties have a controllable lifestyle. General practitioners and general internists, who lack a controllable lifestyle, were most likely to want to change specialties.[9]

After completing a residency, physicians can then choose whether they want to go into private practice or academic medicine, or work at a hospital or medical center. Obviously, some specialties lend themselves more to private practice than others.

Gretchen, a recently retired internist, went into private practice with her husband in the 1980s. "It was the best in many ways because it was entirely mine, my own little world. That was something that I realized about myself: I needed to be in a profession where I really could call the shots, where I felt that I was the one to have the final say," she says. "I really enjoyed having a connection with my patients in private practice, and I enjoyed the power."

Betsy, a urologist in her forties, is the only woman in a practice with several men. "I've really found the perfect balance for me. It's close to my house, so my daughter is integrated; she's in and out of the office. The doctors I work with, my partners, have treated me well, as have the hospital and operating staff," she says. "But I found my own way. I'm not like the male doctors." She practices her specialty and draws a lot of female patients.

In academic medicine, the physician is a professor at a university medical school. This usually combines teaching med students, seeing patients at the university medical center, and doing medical research. Medical professors, like other academics, generally must achieve tenure within a certain time period if they wish to stay on the faculty, although some medical faculty are hired off the tenure track, and some medical schools have no tenure system at all. According to the Association of American Medical Colleges, in 2005–2006, women were 32 percent of medical school faculty members overall. As expected, the number of women faculty varies greatly by specialty. For example, women make up 22 percent of the faculty in pediatrics but just 2 percent of the faculty in orthopedic surgery. Furthermore, when broken down by rank, women are 38 percent of assistant professors, 28 percent of associate professors, and just 16 percent of full professors.[10] These numbers are similar to those for science and engineering, where women are 19 percent of tenured faculty and 35 percent of junior faculty.[11] The increasing number of women graduating from medical school has created a larger pool of potential female assistant professors. However, these women are not advancing to the senior ranks of medical school faculty at the same rate as men; researchers have suggested that family responsibilities, fewer resources, shorter work hours, and lower productivity due to the preceding three factors may all be problems, just as they are for female faculty in science and engineering.[12] Because few female medical faculty are in the senior ranks, even fewer are in positions of leadership. Although every medical school in the country currently has at least one female department chair or dean, the leadership of medical schools is definitely still male-dominated.

I talked with two women who had been medical faculty, but neither of them had stuck with it long enough to achieve tenure. Jane left her position to follow her husband to another state. Gretchen did not aspire to be a medical professor, but she was offered a faculty position specifically designated for a woman at the academic medical center where she was finishing her residency, so she took it. "The part where I was supposed to be a researcher just didn't make much sense to me," Gretchen says. She wanted to be focused on patients, not stuck working in a laboratory or writing grants, and so she left the position after a couple years. On the other hand, women who enjoy both research and patient care often find that a position in academic medicine provides a good balance between these activities.

Medical professors, like other academics, are expected to do research and publish in order to achieve tenure. Reshma Jagsi and colleagues at three Boston-area institutions looked at the authors of articles in six highly regarded medical journals in five different years from 1970 to 2004. In 2004, women were just 29.3 percent of the first authors and 19.3 percent of the senior authors. Over time, the number of female first and senior authors increased sharply in the obstetrics and pediatrics journals but remained low in the surgical journal. The unequal distribution of women in medical specialties, as well as the lack of tenured women in medical schools who are eligible to be senior authors, can partially explain this gap. Other reasons are likely similar to those for women's lack of advancement as faculty members: less time spent working, more of a focus on teaching rather than on doing research, and difficulty balancing work and family responsibilities.[13]

Institutional support may also be a factor: A survey of medical school faculty in the mid-1990s showed that women with children were less likely to receive research funding and secretarial support from their institution than were men with children. The survey also found that female med-school faculty were slightly younger, were less likely to be married and have children, and had fewer children than their male counterparts.[14] The latter differences may be related to the women's younger age, but they are also likely a function of the difficulties women in demanding careers have in balancing work and family.

Medicine has come a long way in terms of being family-friendly. Gretchen, who attended medical school in the 1970s, recalls being asked in her med-school interview what choice she would make between an ill patient and an ill child. "I said, 'Well, presumably I would have a husband who would also be in the formula there someplace in terms of either being able to help me take care of the patient or help me take care of the child.' And [the interviewer] was just appalled, absolutely appalled, that I would put this burden on a man who had a profession," she explains.

Such a question would never be asked in an interview today, and many medical schools and hospitals have instituted policies to help all physicians balance their work and personal lives. According to the Association of American Medical Colleges, in 2005, 43 percent of medical schools gave tenure-track faculty members eight or more years to achieve tenure, whereas six years is typical in science and engineering disciplines.[15] Parental-leave policies are common, and more and more physicians are opting to work reduced hours. A 2000 study found that 15 percent of all pediatricians were working part time; most of these were women.[16]

Part-time positions for physicians are often described as "good" part-time jobs in that the hourly pay rate is usually equal to that of full-time positions, benefits are provided, and employees are able to make full use of their skills and do interesting work. But many of these positions would not be considered part-time by much of the American population. In their recent study of female physicians, Rosalind Barnett and colleagues distinguished between full- and part-time positions based on how physicians' employers classified them. The researchers found that the reduced-hours physicians worked between twenty and sixty hours per week, while the full-time physicians worked between thirty-five and ninety hours per week.[17] Furthermore, finding a part-time position is not easy. In a 2000 survey of pediatric residents who were concluding their training, those interested in part-time employment were more than seven times as likely not to have a position at the time of the survey than those planning to work full time.[18]

Even if a woman is a full-time physician, she probably works fewer hours than her male colleagues. The difference varies according to specialty, setting (medical school, private practice, etc.), and year of the survey, but multiple studies have found that male physicians work five to ten hours more per week than their female colleagues.[19] The primary reason for the difference in working time is, of course, family responsibilities, which may include not only childcare and housework but also spouse and elder care. These duties fall disproportionately on women in general, but those with husbands in demanding careers are often particularly hard hit. Like female scientists, most married female physicians have another professional as a spouse; in the Women Physicians' Health Study, nearly half of the married respondents were married to another physician.[20] While two-physician households should have high enough incomes to hire others to perform some household tasks, and female doctors do spend much less time on cooking and cleaning than the average American woman,[21] female physicians, especially those with young kids, still spend significant hours on childcare.

Betsy has watched the women with whom she attended medical school decide to work in less demanding specialties and part time, while she works full time in an intense area. "If you need the money, that motivates you to work hard and create a business or practice that's hugely successful," she says. "But if you don't, by the time you have one, two, or three kids and have a successful husband, you think to yourself, 'What am I doing here? I don't want to be doing this. I want to go home to my children.' I don't know how you get around that. I don't know if our generation will pick up when we're fifty and create these much more intense careers or if we opt out so early that we can't. I'm divorced, and I have no choice. I have to support my daughter. You just get on this roller coaster and keep going and going and going, and now I have this successful and very surgical practice, but it's not the norm."

Some research suggests that many female physicians put off retirement until their sixties or later, so an increase in career intensity after child rearing is certainly possible.[22] This longer career may help counteract the suggestion that the profession receives less "bang for its buck" when educating a woman since female physicians are more likely to work reduced hours. It may also help with the problem that as more doctors choose to work fewer hours than have been traditional for physicians in the past, more doctors may be needed overall to adequately serve patients.

The increasing number of women in medicine is changing the profession in other ways as well. Women tend to focus more on the patient's emotional state and their own bedside manner, and the profession as a whole is starting to emphasize these factors as well. Many medical practices are moving toward a team approach to medical care, and women's skills in collaboration can be very important in such situations. Women are also more likely to choose to work with underserved populations, thus helping to increase access to medical care.[23] Female physicians continue to face obstacles and bias, but the profession is changing—and improving—in response to their presence, much more so than science or engineering disciplines have thus far.

Although the actual practice of medicine on a daily basis is quite different from that of science or engineering, women's experiences in medicine do illustrate several important points relevant to women in science and engineering careers. First, it's possible for part-time work to be well-paid and fulfilling, and the more often people request good part-time jobs, the more these opportunities will grow. Second, the traditional methods of teaching and practicing in a field are not necessarily the best ones, and experimentation with new techniques can benefit all practitioners, not only women. And third, although change is slow, it will continue to happen as more women not only enter the field but push for the career they want. These lessons are important to keep in mind as we examine ways to make science and engineering more welcoming to women.

HANGING UP
HER LAB COAT

WOMEN

LEAVING

SCIENCE

S o far, this book has focused on the experiences of women who have chosen to stay in science and engineering. But as the dwindling percentages show, women decide to leave these fields at every stage: before college, during college, after receiving a bachelor's degree, after working for a few years, during graduate school, after graduate school, after a postdoc, and after working for many years. Each woman has her own reasons for opting out of science, but common themes emerge. Studies of women who leave science and engineering focus predominantly on undergraduates who switch majors, since undergrads are an easy population to survey and a great deal of attrition does occur during the college years. But it's also essential to understand the motivations of women who leave at other times if we want to support career scientists rather than just science degree holders.

Multiple studies have shown that six central factors can reduce the likelihood of persistence in science and engineering: lack of early preparation, lack of parental encouragement, few role models and mentors, concerns about balancing career and a personal life, negative perceptions about the life of a scientist, and unwelcoming pedagogy.[1] The last three of these factors were most significant among the women I interviewed. Other studies of women at specific life stages have found additional factors in play in decisions to leave, such as a poor job market for grad students.[2]

Most women do not cite sexism or sexual harassment as the impetus for leaving science and engineering. Indeed, the women I interviewed generally described their leaving as a choice they made freely and not something they were forced into by a hostile climate. Some of these women may be minimizing their experiences of discrimination, however, and even if it was not a direct cause, bias certainly could have acted indirectly to "wear them down."[3] Elements of an uncomfortable environment, particularly a lack of support and a feeling of not belonging, came up in many discussions of women's choices.

Although discrimination and the challenges of balancing a career and personal life affect women more than men, many concerns that prompt women to leave science affect men as well. For example, the way science and engineering are typically taught at American universities can be as unwelcoming to men as it is to women, although men are less likely to leave technical fields for these reasons. Elaine Seymour and Nancy Hewitt, who have explored in depth the reasons why undergraduates leave science and engineering, suggest that it's easier for some women to follow their interests because they don't expect to be the sole or primary income earner for their families. Pressure on men to be a good provider keeps some of them in engineering and medicine—well-paid professions—even though they dislike them. Despite the fact that many women do become the primary provider for their families because of divorce, women seem to feel freer to follow their passions, even if doing so means a reduction in income.[4]

In their 1997 book, *Talking About Leaving: Why Undergraduates Leave the Sciences*, Seymour and Hewitt present the results of a three-year study of more than 450 science and engineering students at thirteen institutions. The researchers gathered data using interviews and focus groups with men and women both who chose to stay in science and engineering and who transferred into other fields. Many of their findings are relevant to women at other stages of their education and careers as well.

Seymour and Hewitt describe the weed-out classes and faculty inattention during the first couple years of undergraduate science and engineering education as a male competition ritual or rite of passage. "The nature of the challenge is as much moral as it is intellectual, in that it is intended to test the ability of young men to tolerate stress, pain, or humiliation with fortitude and self-control. . . . Young men must demonstrate by their demeanor that they have left behind their dependence on nurturing adults in order that the dominant males may acknowledge their worthiness to belong to the adult male community," they write. Because the men in science and engineering majors have grown up with the idea of such competitions and know that once they have proven themselves they will be welcomed and receive mentoring, they are more willing to stick it out. Women who do not have this background often find this process traumatic.

In the 1990s, Susan switched out of the physics major at her private university after only two semesters. "I needed someone to tell me that it was going to be okay. I also needed it not to be as hard as it was. There was no easing into anything. There was no cushion, even when you were having a really rough time," she explains. "And especially the second semester, my last one, there was no support of any kind. In the first semester, the professor was willing to go over things with us. And the TA that semester was perfectly happy to explain things. . . . The second semester, the TAs were not helpful, and the professor was not as accessible. I just was completely demoralized by the whole thing. I know a lot of other students were demoralized in the same way, men and women, but the men were more likely to stick with it."

Seymour and Hewitt suggest that men are socialized to develop an intrinsic sense of self-worth, that is, to depend on themselves and be independent. Women, on the other hand, are socialized to develop a more extrinsic sense of identity; they derive their confidence and self-worth from the approval of others. Of course, each individual experiences these socialization pressures to different degrees. But a woman who has spent most of her life looking outside herself for approval is not going to fare well in a competition in which all that support is withdrawn. This ties into the self-confidence problems that so many women in science and engineering have, both those who leave and those who stay. If one is self-confident because others are offering praise, and the praise goes away, then of course the confidence takes a dive.

Seymour and Hewitt write, "To be faced with the prospect of four years of isolation and hostility on one hand and the abrupt withdrawal of familiar sources of praise, encouragement, and reassurance by faculty on the other is, in our view, the most common reason for the loss of self-confidence that makes women particularly vulnerable to switching."

Although the researchers suggest that after the first couple years of undergraduate classes, faculty begin to offer support, this is not always the case, especially for women. Faculty at many large universities are just too busy to care about undergraduates, saving their mentoring for graduate students and postdocs instead. When mentoring is offered, male students may be more likely to receive it because of old boys' networks. Although women's networks can provide important support, these may not be enough to counteract neglect by male faculty.

Liberal arts colleges, with fewer weed-out classes and more accessible faculty, can provide more supportive environments for female science and engineering majors, without the competition rituals, but graduate school is still a whole new competition as students compete for an advisor's time and energy; too often, women are left out.

Although the atmosphere and lack of support are crucial to many women's decisions to leave science and engineering, other factors are also important. Like some men, women may get into science not because they truly love the subject, but because they (or their parents) think it will provide a stable career. Genevieve, for example, admits that she got into computer science in the 1980s entirely for mercenary reasons. "I asked my parents what would be a good thing to major in, because obviously I needed to be able to be employable after I graduated," she says. "Computer science was hot." But when she considered graduate school after working in industry for several years, computer science didn't even make the list of possibilities—Genevieve just didn't enjoy it.

Similarly, as an undergraduate in the 1990s, Nelly had to decide whether to major in writing or in engineering. "Math and science were concepts in which you have to be specifically trained. It seemed to make more sense to go to a technical school and learn as much as I could, and then I would have options open. Writing was a personal discipline that I could always develop on my own. I figured, I'll be a writer and an engineer on the side so I can make extra money and not be a poor artist. That was my little naïve dream." She found that engineering was too time-consuming for this to work, however, and eventually opted to write full time.

Even when women do have a true interest in science, they sometimes find that their interest does not correlate to what scientists and engineers actually do in their careers. Janet double majored in chemistry and philosophy as an undergraduate and then in the 1990s went on to graduate school in chemistry, a decision she calls "eminently practical." As she neared the end of graduate school, however, Janet became more and more unhappy. In writing a grant proposal for postdoctoral work, she discovered two things. "I didn't want to be on this whole cycle of always writing grant proposals just to keep the lights turned on," she says. "[Furthermore,] the kinds of research that people propose in sciences like chemistry nowadays are super-specialized. They're tiny little bits of scientific questions, and the questions that kept me awake at night actually had to do with larger issues, like why do we think that doing experiments tells us something about the deep structure of reality anyway?" Janet finished her PhD in chemistry but then immediately started a graduate program in philosophy.

For some women, the love of the subject and excitement of discovery compensate for the less pleasant aspects of science careers, such as writing grant proposals. But other women would rather find a way to use their love of science that doesn't involve the parts they don't like—or includes aspects they're not finding in standard science careers. This may include wanting to help people directly or spend more time with them, as well as be more creative, as was the case for Cathy.

CATHY, 33

Cathy majored in engineering at a science and engineering school in the 1990s. Her undergraduate advisor encouraged her to apply to graduate school, but her undergraduate experiences had, as she says, "stomped out my self-esteem," so she decided to work in industry. Cathy was interested in bioengineering, but since it wasn't her major field, she found it difficult to get biotechnology companies to consider her. So she took a job in research and development at a consumer products company, intending to make her way toward the healthcare industry.

She began working at a lab bench, designing her own experiments. Eventually the company switched Cathy to the engineering part of the project, where she took what she had worked on in the laboratory to a pilot plant and then a full-scale manufacturing plant. "I was a twenty-five-year-old female engineer . . . presenting my global engineering design to fifty-five-year-old heads of engineering from Europe, Asia, and South America," she says.

Although parts of her job were fulfilling and even exhilarating, Cathy wasn't completely satisfied. "Part of why I wanted to do bioengineering is that I feel like it saves the world a little bit. It's me being able to use my talents for good. And my project at [the company] was making soap. I didn't really feel like that was saving the world. It was making us cleaner, but not saving the world."

Then the company moved her from engineering to consumer research, a department that was almost all women; her supervisor said that it was the right next step for her career. "I didn't want to do it. It was almost like it was too girly. . . . It was 'What did a survey say' or 'How do I decide which perfume,' and I felt that was all really fluffy."

Throughout this time, Cathy had performed in theater productions as a hobby. After several years as an engineer in industry, she decided she needed to give acting a serious chance. And so Cathy quit her job, moved to New York City, took an intensive acting course, and began auditioning for theater productions, supporting herself by waiting tables and doing some consulting. While she did land roles in several productions, she realized that there was no way to know if she would ever become a Broadway star. Eventually, Cathy became frustrated with the theater and began to miss "using her brain." But she didn't want to return to engineering. "I really felt like I had gotten in touch with being creative. And that was part of my disgruntlement with engineering, that it was very dry."

A friend suggested sales, so Cathy got a job doing sales for a pharmaceutical company. "I get to understand the science and the drugs, but my job is to really communicate that and be a resource. . . . It was a creative challenge of really learning to think on my feet, of really learning to be a good listener, but at the same time I was psyched to have some biology to sink my teeth into."

Now, a few years later, Cathy feels as though she's learned what she can from sales and wants a position closer to technology. "I'm looking at getting into business development or something along those lines that requires me to understand science on a high level but where my role isn't in engineering. . . . For my personality, [engineering] just doesn't fit. It's just not as fun as something that has more to do with sales or client relations, where I can interface with people and I can be creative." Unfortunately, Cathy has found that positions that combine creativity and technical aptitude in the way that fits her are rare.

While some science and engineering fields are quite applied and provide opportunities to make a difference, and scientists and engineers do interact with other people frequently, the stereotype of a scientist as someone who works alone in a basement lab, shut away from everyone, persists. College classes are starting to include more group work, but it's not always clear that such interaction continues in scientific careers, which may turn off some women from these fields.

College classes also often don't feature the creative parts of science. Students memorize formulas and learn about basic principles in lectures, while labs are often cookbook-style, with a set of explicit directions to follow and the expected outcome already known. This work gives students tools to use to develop their own proofs, design their own experiments, build new technology, and so on, but it's not creative in itself. Some women are drawn to science and engineering because of the creative problem-solving aspects. But the sort of creativity involved in finding a way to synthesize a particular molecule can feel quite different from that used in painting a portrait.

"It felt more liberating, just being around other types of people and people who want to be creative," says Jan about her experience of taking art classes while a bioengineering major in the 2000s. Although she found science interesting, Jan had spent her free hours as a kid working on various art projects. "People around me wanted me to be a scientist. I felt pressured. It never really felt right when I went into science, because it wasn't something I did in my spare time."

Many of the women I spoke with identified someone from their childhood or adolescence who encouraged them to go into science. Indeed, many studies have found parental encouragement and the presence of role models and mentors to be important for persistence in science and engineering. Seymour and Hewitt found that women were more likely than men to cite a person as one of their reasons for entering science and engineering,[5] but if encouragement turns into pressure, a woman can end up going into a technical field to please others rather than to fulfill a genuine interest.

"I don't know that I had really made the decision to go to medical school because I wanted to go or because people told me it was a good thing to do," says Sara, who left medical school after two years in the early 2000s. "I definitely think that had I stuck with it, I probably would have ended up doing fine and coming out on top, but I don't know that I would necessarily be happy."

Women may also leave science in an effort to please others—namely, their romantic partners. Robin married a fellow computer scientist who was older and better established in his career than she. She loved working with computers but more than twenty years ago gave in to pressure from her husband to provide secretarial support for his consulting business instead. "He didn't really want me working with other people," Robin says. "I didn't know how to go out and look for a job, especially in the face of somebody who wanted me at home being a support system," she says.

Even if a partner doesn't pressure a woman to leave, she may decide to do so to achieve a better balance between her work and personal life, particularly if she has children. "I was working in intensely competitive corporate jobs that were extremely demanding," explains Chris, who stopped working as a materials scientist in the 1980s. "That kind of work was not really compatible with family life. . . . I was rethinking my priorities and decided to look for a kind of employment that would give me technical and business challenges and also be more compatible with family life."

Although most women who willingly choose to leave science and engineering are ultimately happy with their decision, many of them feel a tremendous amount of guilt. Every male-dominated class, every meeting of women's groups, and every sexist remark reinforces the need for more women in science and engineering. "I recovered from feeling incompetent pretty quickly," says Susan, who switched majors from physics to psychology in the 1990s. "But I was very aware that there are not a lot of women in science because women like me do things like I did. That was hard."

As Janet, who left chemistry after completing grad school, explains, "There was a way in which it almost felt like maybe I was being indulgent in following what was going to make me individually happy, because that meant there was going to be one fewer woman in chemistry to make it easier for the next batch of women who wanted to be in chemistry. And I tell people that and they look at me funny, like 'What are you talking about? How do you think that you have this kind of power to make things easier or harder for people?' But I know it made a difference to me to have women in the sciences visible and successful and having real lives outside of their work."

Women who don't feel guilt for letting down other women may feel that they have let themselves down. Sophia, for example, has a bachelor's degree in environmental science and is now in graduate school in a social science field. "I still have a hierarchy. If you're the smartest person ever, you should be an astrophysicist. The more mathy you are, the smarter you are and the higher rank you are. And so part of me still wonders, 'What am I doing, doing this social sciency stuff? That's not as good.'"

Some women escape the guilt, however, particularly those in fields where there are more women. "There were enough women that I knew going into the field that I had no doubt that the medical field, while it would continue to be a boys' club a little bit longer, was starting to even out," says Sara. "And I knew that I still wanted to do something with science. I mean, that was what my training was in. It was where my interests lay."

So after women leave science and engineering, what do they do? Very few studies have attempted to answer this question, as most researchers focus on why women leave. A woman who turns her back on chemistry after a particularly frustrating first semester weed-out course often takes a path different from the woman who throws up her hands after earning a PhD and working in the field for several years. Some women do end up in areas unrelated to science or engineering. But many women, like Cathy, find a position that uses their scientific training in some way—in her case, pharmaceutical sales. So what are other women doing?

The following examples do not constitute a representative sample, but they're interesting nonetheless. Many of my interviewees are pursuing careers that relate in some way to science. Part of this certainly stems from women wanting to use the education and experience they have in some way, particularly if they spent many years in graduate school. After all that work, it can be difficult to go in a completely different direction. But these women are also in science-related careers because they truly love science. Even the women who are doing things that don't appear on the surface to be related to science, such as writing novels and preaching sermons, are still putting the skills they learned in their science education to use.

Sara, who has a bachelor's degree in biology and dropped out of medical school, has held several positions in a science museum. "I really like museums. It's something I never understood was a career growing up. . . . I love learning new things all the time, and with special exhibits you get something new every six months."

Genevieve, whose bachelor's degree is in computer science, is a business professor. "It's certainly a lot more gender-balanced than my old math and science classes. [The department faculty are] about a third women; we're approaching balance. Our undergraduate population is about 60 percent female."

Nelly, who has a bachelor's degree in engineering and a master's of fine arts in writing, is a novelist. "I see literature, especially fiction, as a kind of engineering. You try to find solutions to the questions of the human condition. You test them and play with them in fiction, and see if they work. I don't see [engineering and writing] as very discrete disciplines."

Cate has a master's degree in geology. She teaches middle school science and dreams of opening a science summer camp for girls. "I like that I'm the one teaching science, because then the girls in my class, and the boys for that matter, know that women do science."

Chris has a PhD in materials science. After working in industry for many years, she moved into technology transfer, helping universities and other institutions to commercialize research. "In a way I'm a technical dilettante. The people who become faculty members really like depth in their technical understanding. . . . I'm really interested in the breadth of technology, and I'm really interested, as an engineer, in the application of technology. So it's really exciting to me to be able to look at an invention and try to figure out how it can be useful."

Liz has a bachelor's degree in biology and is currently in law school. "I'm not careful enough in the lab. I just wasn't made out to be a research scientist. . . . [Patent law] is a way to use what I've learned, this education, in a way that's not in a lab."

With PhDs in chemistry and philosophy, Janet is a philosophy professor who focuses on the ethics of science. "I do have this hope that I will be able to make some impact on the education of science majors here, and also nonscientists as well."

Jan, who has a bachelor's degree in bioengineering and a graduate certificate in science illustration, is working as a science illustrator. "Ultimately, what I want to do is make prostheses. That's something that I feel like I can do and be good at because of my science background."

Emma, who has a bachelor's degree in biology and a master's in mythology, is studying to become a minister. "I think that the divine is best known in looking at creation. And so science allows really excellent metaphors for talking about the numinous as well as practical representations of a creator. . . . I think it'll add a great dimension to my ministry to have a science background."

Susan switched majors in college; after earning a bachelor's degree in psychology and a PhD in history, she now studies the history of science. "I enjoy the research. I enjoy thinking about it. I enjoy writing about it. I have this long string of ideas for what I want to do next. I have my next five projects mapped out. I have enough stuff I want to do now that it could take me the next fifty years to address all of it."

Antonia enjoyed science as a child, especially biology. "I really expected to be going into science up until the middle of high school age," she says. But, as Antonia puts it, she was "seduced" by social science, which she majored in during college. Now she's taking the prerequisites for a master's in public health. "Public health is really how health and politics intermingle. It's sort of this hybridization of these interests that I've been continuing to have through the years. Despite not studying science much during college, it was still beneath the surface."

Have these women really dropped out? They are not doing science, in that they are not in a laboratory doing research; they are not engineers, in that they are not out there in industry designing products and building bridges; and they are not physicians, in that they are not caring for patients, but they are still using their science training in productive ways. Although this nation's universities and corporations certainly do need more female scientists and engineers in the lab, perhaps all of these "leavers" shouldn't be considered such a terrible loss.

Unfortunately, it's rare for a woman to return to science after a significant period away from it. Technology changes and new discoveries are made constantly, so time away from the field is particularly costly for those working in technical fields. "I didn't even think of trying to go back into computer science," says Robin, who recently rejoined the workforce after more than twenty years of working for her husband and raising children. "The field has changed phenomenally. . . . [And] I don't really want to work in the kind of world that most people who do computer stuff work in." Because of the rapid change in technical fields, few women return to being scientists or engineers in the strict senses of those titles; like Cathy, they are more likely to move into positions that require scientific knowledge rather than actual science or engineering research. But occasionally women do return to science after a time away.

After earning bachelor's degrees in math and English literature in the early 1980s, Theresa worked in writing jobs, because she was unable to find a position that used her mathematics skills. The job market was poor in general, and one interviewer told her flat out that he was looking for a man to fill the position. So Theresa went to graduate school in mathematics and computer science. She won several fellowships, did a summer research program at an industrial research lab, and had a really great idea. It wasn't, as Theresa explains, a Nobel-caliber idea, but it's still used today. However, a poor relationship with her first graduate advisor, a case of low confidence, and an interest outside graduate school came together such that she started to think about leaving.

"My [second advisor], who was a nice guy, I went to him and said that I wanted to drop out of the program. And he said, 'Why? You have a really good idea.' But I didn't believe him, because I thought, 'Oh, he's just saying that to be nice.' Because I didn't have the self-confidence to believe that my work was important. And I didn't realize I was so close to the PhD, either. If he'd said, 'Theresa, don't leave. You need to get this PhD. This is really important work. You're close to the PhD; I'll help you finish it,' then I would have stayed. But nobody said that to me. There was nobody in the department who said, 'Stay.'"

So she left.

After more than a decade of working outside science, Theresa returned to graduate school in computer science. Since she needed to finish her degree, she had an opportunity to catch up on the latest advances before jumping into a job search, which facilitated her return. "I always missed the intellectual challenge. It always seemed to me that there was something missing," she says. "G. H. Hardy said in *A Mathematician's Apology* that if you are good at something, you should do it. . . . And I am good at mathematical thinking and analytical thinking. I am good at scientific thinking. I felt that I really needed to be doing that." Theresa's self-confidence had also improved in the intervening years as she learned that the only limits she had were those within herself. Since finishing her PhD, she has worked at government laboratories performing research.

Emma also returned to science. A biology major, she dropped out of college in the 1970s when she married and became pregnant. But, as she explains, "When my second daughter was very young, I found myself starting to write poetry about missing my lab books." Several years after she left, Emma returned to finish her degree. After graduation, a budding interest in neuroscience eventually led her to a position as a research assistant in an academic lab. The principal investigator, impressed with her abilities, encouraged her to get a PhD in his laboratory during the 1990s. But Emma was a single mother by this point. "The only way you could get a PhD in neuroscience at [the university] was to do it full time. They didn't allow you to do it part time, and I knew I had to work. That just wasn't an option. My principal investigator kept going to the committee and saying, 'I want you to make an exception,' and they kept saying, 'We're not going to make an exception. It's a full-time program. She's just going to have to wait.'

When it got to the point where I might really seriously consider [the PhD] again, I didn't want to do it anymore. I didn't want to work in a lab. I didn't want to be isolated in a cubicle. My social nature was just begging for me to do something else." And so Emma left science again, setting out on a path that has led her to the ministry.

As the stories in this chapter illustrate, women take a wide variety of paths after leaving science and engineering fields. Some of these paths lead far away from research; others double back and bring women to science once again. Even if they end up in very different fields, most of these women are able to use some of the skills and knowledge gained from their time in science.

But science and engineering need not lose so many women. Many women find these fields interesting on an intellectual level but also find the environments in which scientists and engineers learn and work to be uncomfortable, unfriendly, uncreative, isolating, or even downright hostile. In many cases, the same changes that would increase women's likelihood of success in technical fields would also improve the retention of women who currently leave—as well as the retention of men. Major changes in undergraduate education, such as the elimination of weed-out classes and increased opportunities for hands-on projects similar to those in science and engineering careers, would be a good start. And even though women claim that sexism and sexual harassment are not why they leave, a hostile climate can wear down women until they use other problems as a reason to exit. Women should feel welcome and supported in all fields. Although many programs have been created to change institutional climates, much more work needs to be done.

The next two chapters examine ways to improve science and engineering education and careers so that women are more likely to succeed in, and stay with, them. Creating welcoming environments is not just about attracting new recruits, but about retaining the talent so crucial to these fields.

GET 'EM
YOUNG

ENCOURAGING

GIRLS

IN

SCIENCE

A lthough some women do become interested in science or engineering later in life, it's more likely that a girl interested in science and math at a young age will grow up to pursue those or related fields. The number of programs and resources designed to increase girls' interest in science has exploded in the last twenty years. These include summer camps, workshops, after-school programs, websites, computer software, and books. Programs for teachers, counselors, and parents have also been developed, either independently or in conjunction with student programs. Many of the programs have come out of universities and colleges that want to increase the number of female undergraduates in their science and engineering departments. Others have been developed by science museums or nonprofit organizations such as the Girl Scouts; companies have been partners in some endeavors as well.

I spent an afternoon with middle school girls participating in Techbridge, a program originally developed by the Chabot Space and Science Center in Oakland, California.[1] Techbridge partners with local elementary, middle, and high schools to run girls-only science clubs; it also hosts a summer program. In the clubs, students meet once a week after school with one or more teachers to do hands-on projects in a variety of engineering- and technology-related areas. Girls in the program have taken apart hairdryers and other small appliances, built their own telephones from kits, created "green" dollhouses from renewable and recyclable materials, and designed toys. When I visited, they were learning about forensic science, a unit designed to build on the popularity of television shows such as *CSI*. The hallway outside the classroom held a crime scene, complete with what looked like blood and vomit. The girls busily wrote observations before collecting the evidence for chemical testing to identify it. As I watched their excitement, it was hard to believe that some people don't think girls are interested in science.

One crucial aspect of the program is exposure to women in engineering and technology. At least once a semester, a role model visits each club or the students take a field trip to a local company. Role models talk about their careers and lives as well as lead the girls in a hands-on activity related to their work. During field trips, students tour the facility as well as engage in lab activities and ask employees questions.

Most Techbridge programs are in elementary and middle schools, so their effect on those students' career choices is not yet known, but 90 percent of the Techbridge participants who have graduated from high school have pursued college majors in engineering and technology. Other indications are also encouraging. At one middle school, the Techbridge program became so popular that a second section was opened, and both groups still have more girls than the twenty to twenty-five students that Techbridge considers ideal. Girls who were graduating requested that Techbridge organize a club at their high school so that they could continue with the program. They got it.

Techbridge is far from alone. Since 1993, the National Science Foundation has awarded more than $90 million in grants for programs that encourage K–12 girls and female college students to pursue careers in technical fields, programs that help parents and teachers to support girls, and the development of materials for girls to use.[2] Many private foundations and other organizations have also supported programs. The goals of science and engineering programs for girls can be grouped into three broad categories. The first is awareness of technical careers, gender equity, or both. The second is increased involvement in science and engineering. The third is improved skills and achievement in science and math. Programs come in many different formats, but summer camps, after-school science clubs, and Saturday academies are most common. These programs have taught educators a lot about how to get girls excited and more confident about science and engineering.

Structural problems prevent many programs from being as effective as they could, however. For one, programs usually begin by using funds from a grant, and unless someone steps up with additional money after the grant ends, programs are eventually scaled back or dropped entirely. Furthermore, while a two-week summer camp may get a girl excited about science, the positive messages and encouragement she receives there may conflict with what she hears from teachers, family, and peers the rest of the year. On the other hand, if her environment is nurturing, she may not be prepared to deal with the competitive culture of so many undergraduate science programs. To truly get girls interested in science and engineering and prepare them to pursue careers in those fields, systematic change needs to occur in the educational system and beyond. This is an ideal, however, and unlikely to happen soon. In the meantime, extracurricular programs will remain important ways for girls to gain confidence in and enthusiasm for science and engineering. Regardless of whether such programs are available, parents and teachers can incorporate the strategies that various programs have shown to be successful into their homes and classrooms.

The first key, of course, is to use learning strategies that work well with girls, such as hands-on activities. Science and engineering careers involve working on experiments and designing projects, so these activities give girls a better taste of what such jobs truly involve. Although boys may hog the equipment in mixed-gender groups, when girls get a chance to do experiments themselves, many will jump in. When girls are able to look at a problem, develop their own hypotheses, and test them, they learn the scientific method and problem-solving skills. By designing and building their own projects, they discover the creativity inherent in engineering, the perceived lack of which can draw them to other fields. The confidence that girls get from doing lab activities in some programs translates back to their regular classrooms, where they will protest if boys start hogging the equipment. Some programs place high school students in university laboratories so that they can be part of a team working on complex, ongoing research rather than on a problem constructed for a summer camp or one-day workshop. Studies suggest that such experiences are a powerful inspiration for these students.

In the 2000s, Valerie attended a coed summer program where she did original research under the guidance of a graduate student. "The six weeks that I spent at [the program] were the best six weeks of my life," she says. "It introduced me to what it's like to do math and science in college and in the real world. In high school, you take algebra classes, calculus classes, but I had no idea what a real mathematician did."

The experiments and activities used in programs are wide-ranging, but researchers have found that girls usually prefer doing things that relate to their lives in some way. "What is this good for?" is a common refrain in science classrooms, since the facts and formulas in textbooks and lectures are often disconnected from reality. Many programs thus use examples from girls' lives as a jumping-off point. In one program, girls played different sports and then learned about the science behind them. Girls in another program created their own shampoos and other personal care products, experimenting to find the best mix of ingredients.

Although girls want to connect science to their lives, they also want to see how what they are doing will improve the world. Some girls are also very interested in pursuing a career in which they can help others, and as such, they gravitate toward medicine, the social sciences, and biology. Science and engineering do provide many ways to help others, but these are often not as obvious as in some other fields. Programs that connect science to beneficial applications in society are thus good at encouraging girls to consider these careers. For example, programs have looked at how to make structures accessible to people with disabilities and developed hands-on museum exhibits that others can benefit from. The National Science Foundation has also funded the development of computer games and instructional software that set math and science in a societal context, such as the Animal Watch computer-based math tutor, in which girls complete word problems that relate to material they are learning about an endangered species.

An important component of many programs is collaborative learning, another strategy that increases girls' participation. Many boys prefer to work independently and compete against other students. Girls, on the other hand, often prefer to be on teams, sharing ideas and working together. Increasing group learning activities may appear on the surface to favor girls, but considering the increasing importance of teamwork and collaboration in science and engineering fields, improving all students' skills in these areas can make them more likely to be successful in their careers.

Most programs designed to get girls into science include some sort of contact with female scientists and engineers, whether these are graduate students, faculty members, or researchers in industry. Sometimes these women are program staff. Other times the program brings in speakers for an afternoon, as Techbridge does with its role model program. Some of the most successful programs, however, match girls with mentors who meet with them over an extended period of time.

Some mentoring programs have paired girls with mentors who are just a few years older, such as middle with high school girls, or high schoolers with college students. Although these mentors have little, if any, experience working in a technical field, they do have recent knowledge of the challenges a younger girl faces. A young girl may also find it easier to see herself just a few years older. These mentoring relationships can provide girls with confidence that they can get through the difficult adolescent years and be successful in math and science. Other mentoring programs pair students with women who have established careers in science and engineering. These relationships often focus on exploring possible careers and planning for life after high school.

In some cases, girls and their mentors meet regularly in facilitated sessions, completing activities together and sharing group discussions with other participants. In other cases, the pairs have a more informal relationship, communicating regularly but on their own schedule. Some mentoring programs have taken advantage of the Internet to pair girls and women who do not live near each other. While in-person exchanges can be more powerful, the email option provides mentoring opportunities for girls in rural areas who might not otherwise find a mentor.

Mentoring does not need to occur within a formal program, of course. During high school in the 2000s, Tess worked in a biology laboratory at a local university, where a female graduate student mentored her. "She was extremely encouraging and supportive," Tess says. "She also really let me do a lot of my work very independently, and she taught me a lot about good experimental technique but also just things like how to get yourself organized before you go in and have to carry out tons of experiments in a day, and just really practical stuff about how to survive in the lab."

One aim of programs that get girls doing science is to increase confidence in their abilities. After hearing that "girls can't do math or science" for many years, girls begin to believe it. Many also begin to fear being wrong, because being right is essential to good grades, high test scores, and achievement generally.

"The younger, elementary school kids don't have any issues around science. They just do it, because it is how they explore the world. . . . They have no problem asking questions," says Stephanie, who develops science programs for a nonprofit organization. "Something happens around fourth or fifth grade, and those are the kids that suddenly are really concerned about—I almost had tears in a workshop—worried about being right." Since a crucial part of science is experimentation—which may not lead to the correct answer—girls may begin to hang back. Extracurricular science programs in which grades and test scores are irrelevant show them that it's okay to come up with the wrong answer sometimes.

Many programs to encourage girls' interest in science and engineering also involve some of the most important people in their lives: Mom and Dad. The influence of family members on a girl's choice of career can be huge. Girls may receive encouragement from teachers and programs but still face discouraging messages at home. Many studies have found that due to either unconscious or conscious bias, parents are more likely to believe that their sons are interested in science, and less likely to think that they find the subject difficult, than are parents of daughters. These messages are powerful: Researchers have found that the more difficult a mother thinks that science is for her child, the lower the child's interest and self-efficacy in the subject.[3] Biases can definitely affect how a parent interacts with a child in a scientific setting. In one study, researchers videotaped families interacting with science exhibits at a children's museum. Even though boys did not ask significantly more questions than girls did, boys were three times as likely to hear explanations from their parents that connected the exhibits to general principles or related phenomena.[4]

A program with minimal family involvement might include a time at the end of the program for girls to share what they have learned with their parents. Programs with high family involvement get Mom and Dad (or the whole family) doing science and engineering projects with their daughter, setting the stage for exploring more science on their own. Parents do not need formal programs to do science experiments and other activities with their kids. Indeed, the connection between science and real life can be much more obvious at home than in a classroom or laboratory. Samantha helped her father, a carpenter, to measure and cut wood, learning about multiplication and fractions along the way. Brianna's father, an engineer, would bring home "cool technology" from work for Brianna and her sister to play with. Amber did experiments with her father in the kitchen using baking soda, acid, and other household chemicals.

The fact that all the examples above include fathers is, sadly, unlikely to be a coincidence. As girls, many mothers were discouraged from being interested in math and science, sometimes much more overtly than are their daughters. Dads are more likely to have science or engineering careers, and even if they don't, they are generally more comfortable with tools, machines, cars, and other technology due to experiences in high school shop class or with their own fathers. Mothers' discomfort with science and math can be a powerful, if unintended, message to girls, because moms are such strong role models and can be a girl's primary source of career advice. Programs such as the MAD (Mothers and Daughters) Scientists Club bring girls and moms together to do hands-on science activities and talk about gender-related issues.

Of course, fathers' involvement with their daughters' math and science experiences is also extremely important. In my admittedly nonrepresentative sample of interviewees, women who were only children or had only sisters were more likely to report having engaged in science- and engineering-related activities with their dads. As Tara, now a graduate student in astronomy, says, "I wonder if part of the reason I was comfortable with science is because my father didn't have a son to help him. If the car broke down, or something in the house needed to be fixed, he would ask me, 'Can you help with this?'" A few of my interviewees with brothers specifically noted that their dads invited the boys to do science-related activities, whereas the girls in the family were not included. Both parents should provide opportunities for all their children to explore interests with them, whether these are in or out of science and engineering.

Parents can also support their daughters by counteracting the bias girls experience in other contexts. Tess encountered gender bias both in the classroom and in extracurricular activities during high school in the 2000s. "Both of my parents made sure that I still felt supported in pursuing math and science, and they spent a long time trying to make it clear to me that those sorts of incidents were not as much a reflection on my abilities as on the other person's prejudices," she says.

In addition to focusing on girls and their parents, programs have also targeted K–12 teachers; these mainly take the form of workshops that discuss how to identify gender bias, how to create a gender-fair classroom, and how to integrate teaching strategies that work particularly well with girls. These programs work best if they extend beyond the workshop, with a mentor observing the teacher's classroom over the next several months and working with the teacher to change behavior. Bias is often so unconscious that it takes an outside observer who knows what to look for to identify it.

A workshop on gender-fair teaching, however, will only draw participants who are concerned about the topic and want to improve their teaching. Those who believe they have no bias, or who know they're sexist but believe that being so is appropriate, will not voluntarily try to improve their teaching. Ideally, all undergraduate education students would take a class that discusses gender-fair teaching and gives students an opportunity to practice it. Instituting such classes now, however, will not affect teachers who have already finished their education; school districts may need to require current teachers to attend professional development workshops that address gender bias to reach these educators.

Programs that target middle and high school counselors

would also be beneficial; only a very few do so now. Although parents, peers, and teachers are more frequent bearers of messages about science and engineering, counselors also often help students choose courses, learn about careers, and get ready for college. But counselors too may have gender biases they are unaware of, or lack information about how to prepare for careers in science and technology, so reaching these educators is very important.

Although many of these targeted science programs are successful, or at least appear to be, the success of others is negligible. Inadequate funding and disappearing programs mean that long-term outcomes are often not tracked. Participants in a summer camp for middle school girls may report on end-of-camp surveys that their interest in engineering has increased significantly. But does that translate into the girls' actually pursuing degrees in engineering when they reach college five years later? Programs that have been funded for many years by universities or other organizations have been able to track their participants to college, and these girls often do major in technical fields at higher rates, but this kind of information is available for a only a small percentage of the programs operating.

Furthermore, many programs are only a single intervention, for example a summer camp or a workshop. Although science clubs may meet weekly and mentors may communicate on a regular basis, few of these programs last longer than a year or two. A science club at a middle school, for example, is not often available to girls once they reach high school, so there is a lack of continued support to depend upon as they mature and face new challenges. One week of camp may provide girls with some valuable skills and raise their enthusiasm for science, but it is rarely enough to counteract years of gender-biased classrooms and other obstacles deeply embedded into their everyday experience. "Girls now may have lots of educational opportunities, but I don't think that society has caught up. Funds may be set aside for girls, social programs may be instituted, but it's the daily attitudes that inform what it is you feel entitlement to," says Nelly, a former engineering major who has a seven-year-old daughter.

The problem is that these programs are something extra, something special on top of the education girls are already receiving at school, rather than something integrated into it. To truly give girls the support and preparation necessary to succeed at careers in science and engineering, they need to learn in gender-fair classrooms with appropriate teaching strategies all the time. Teacher training is making a difference, one classroom at a time, but it will be a long time before all classrooms are providing the best education they can to both boys and girls. Although girls may be the focus, many educational strategies have the potential to benefit all genders of students.

Much still needs to be done, but a lot of positive changes have occurred in the past couple of decades. Certainly, after seeing girls in action, it's impossible to say that they universally don't like or are unsuited for science. "I'm optimistic," says Hilary, a middle school science teacher. "Even though the numbers of women in science fields are low now, I see girls wanting to do things. Especially when the girls are grouped by ability and with other girls, they will dig in and do things. It's usually the boys more than girls who say 'Eeew' when we do a dissection."

Fortunately for the young women whose precollege experiences have inspired them to enter science and engineering, many universities and companies are developing programs to support and nurture them. The next chapter looks at how this is happening—and what else needs to be done.

WELCOMING WOMEN

IMPROVING

SCIENCE

FOR

ALL

Most of the factors that will make science and engineering more welcoming to women are the same things that make any career better for women (and men), such as equal pay, the availability of good part-time jobs, reasonable hours for full-time work, schedule flexibility, on-site childcare, a workplace free of sexual harassment, and so on. And what provides a more welcoming atmosphere for female scientists also improves conditions for their male colleagues, including better teaching and advising at all educational levels, as well as clear guidelines for the achievement of PhDs, tenure, and other milestones. Science and engineering, as traditionally male-dominated fields that draw on skills that women are sometimes presumed not to have, also need changes at their cores. Engineers and scientists must let go of the idea that the only way to be successful is to be single-mindedly focused on one's work, especially in the early years of a career. Because these disciplines have been locked into this kind of thinking for so long, we have few examples of what kinds of achievements are possible on paths that take other routes.

If we are to learn, scientists and engineers must move beyond the mindset of "It's the way we've always done it, so it must be the best way." Nothing is the way we've always done it. The first PhD was not awarded until 1861.[1] Scientists used to work alone; now, collaborative research is common. The fields of computer science and molecular biology aren't even a hundred years old. In all the time that women have been in science and engineering, they have been told, "This is how it is; deal with it or get out." The sentiment may not have been explicitly stated, but the message was still clear. So many women bent themselves to conform to the masculine norms of these disciplines, sometimes losing other things they considered important in the process, including personal time, marriage, children, and well-roundedness. Enough women have entered science and engineering that it's time for the disciplines to start bending to them. It is possible to make these fields careers for people rather than careers for men.

So where do we start? Most of the research on women in science and engineering has focused on undergraduates. As such, it's probably clearer how to retain this population than any other. For example, a study of twenty-three coeducational academic computer science departments in Virginia found that departments with larger female enrollments were more likely to retain women. Other factors important to better retention of women included mentoring, good teaching, positive attitudes of faculty toward female students, and presence of female faculty.[2] Achieving some of this requires changing the departmental culture, which is not easy. Programs designed to support female undergraduates (and grad students) have generally been implemented on top of an existing departmental culture, leaving the core educational system unaffected. Programs for female students have included orientation sessions, tutoring, summer enrichment, scholarships, workshops, seminars, social events, dorms with other female science and engineering students, a women's advisor, and all-female classes, among others. Women's groups or centers usually run these programs, and they do provide support and opportunities to build a network to women in male-dominated science and engineering fields. The number of women earning bachelor's degrees in technical fields has increased, in part due to these efforts, but again, these programs are special, not routine. None of this has caused the faculty member who thinks that women don't belong in engineering to change his mind, or changed the masculine educational and work style of a department.

To improve the quality of teaching, professors and graduate students who act as teaching assistants need more instruction in how to teach. Just as in K–12 education, dry, boring, unorganized classes turn off undergraduate students, as do teachers who are never available or act as if a student is a waste of their time. Because men are more socialized to accept male competition rituals in which support is withdrawn, they are more likely to accept the existence of weed-out classes and faculty inattention, but these are by no means ideal conditions under which to learn; better teaching and support will improve their university experience as well.

"Why are undergraduate courses weed-out when everyone keeps talking about how badly we need scientists and people need to be more scientifically literate? Why don't we make them weed-in?" asks Stephanie, an informal science educator who earned a degree in environmental science in the 1990s. "That would pretty much change the science landscape, I think." Some universities are experimenting with smaller classes and more active learning in those courses, but such changes can be costly, and many faculty resist interference in their teaching techniques.

A teacher who wishes to instruct twelfth graders must complete a degree in education, including a student teaching experience, and pass exams to become certified, whereas a college professor who teaches students just a year older than those twelfth graders can step into a classroom without having taken any courses in education or having any teaching experience, not even a semester as a teaching assistant making sure that no one blew up anything in a lab. Learning how to teach should be an important component of graduate school, including courses on pedagogy and experience as a teaching assistant in different educational settings (large lecture, small group, and so on). Or, considering the number of students who earn PhDs with no intention of becoming professors, faculty positions could require a postdoctoral appointment focused on teaching. Regardless of the form that this training takes, it is clear that faculty members need to learn how to teach before stepping in front of a classroom. Scientists who do not want to teach and mentor students should not be professors but instead should be in research-only positions, which exist in universities as well as industrial and government labs.

Part of improving the teaching in science and engineering departments, of course, is incorporating new teaching methods that work well for both women and men. It's also doing the one-on-one teaching in office hours and in mentoring relationships with graduate students. This means that either graduate education needs to focus less on one-on-one mentoring with an advisor or that advisors need to be taught how to advise and then actually put time into doing so. A graduate student with a poor or absent advisor is in for a hell of a time. She may get through it and come out stronger, but she may also be crushed and leave. Although any change in the advisor–advisee relationship is likely to be met with resistance, clear guidelines about what constitutes advising and what is required for a graduate degree will help keep women—and men—from getting stuck.

Presence of female faculty also plays a role in female student success. Studies show that women in academic departments with predominantly male faculty have lower academic confidence.[3] Female faculty not only serve as role models for students but also, in large enough numbers, tend to change the climate of a department. A lone woman in a group of men is unlikely to be able to make many changes in the group's culture; even a few women can't accomplish much, especially if they are concentrated in the lower ranks and thus have less power. Once women reach a critical mass, however, they are able to effect more changes.

The goal of the ADVANCE program of the National Science Foundation is to increase the number of women in academic science and engineering and to help them advance through the ranks. Rather than provide grants to individual faculty members, the program offers grants to universities to help them transform their institutional climate, thus benefiting many women. Each university uses the funding in the ways that seem most appropriate to its campus and the resources and policies already in place. Most institutions implement multiple programs that address different needs. Because the NSF awarded the first ADVANCE grants several years ago, many of the original recipients have developed programs and materials that they are sharing with other universities.

A key component of most ADVANCE programs is mentoring and network building, which again and again have been shown to be crucial to success. In addition to creating a formal mentoring program within the university, some programs also provide female professors with funding to bring in speakers from other institutions who work in the same field and could be a useful part of the woman's network.

Various organizations already exist to connect women with mentors and networks more generally. MentorNet matches undergraduate and graduate students, postdocs, and untenured faculty with mentors from academia and industry; the pairs communicate via email weekly. In addition to organizations such as the Society of Women Engineers (SWE) and Association for Women in Science (AWIS), many professional societies have women's groups associated with them. These groups have online forums, programming at society conferences, and a variety of other resources and programs that help provide women with information and networks.

Although building networks can help fight some of the more insidious forms of bias, more overt bias also needs to be addressed. In her study of graduate science and engineering departments, Georgia Tech sociologist Mary Frank Fox found that those with consistently high or improved numbers of women graduating with PhDs also had leaders who took claims of bias and harassment seriously.[4] This is key, not only for students but for women in all settings. I heard stories of bias and harassment from a lot of women, and most of the incidents they discussed with me were never reported. And often when they did try to tell someone in power about the problem, they didn't get anywhere. Too many groups, particularly university departments, pay lip service to supporting women and not tolerating harassment but sweep anything of serious concern under the rug. Neither "He brings in a lot of research dollars," nor "He has tenure," nor "He'll retire soon," nor "Everyone knows he's a jerk," nor "He didn't touch you" is a viable excuse for bias and harassment.

It takes a strong woman to tell her department chair that a professor is making sexual comments to her. It takes an even stronger one to continue telling people higher in the administration, and to sue. This is one place where women's groups and networks can be crucial. Although every woman's individual experience is significant, there is more strength in numbers. If many women are saying the same thing, then people in power are more likely to take their claims seriously. Without women's groups and networks, however, women may not know that they are not the only ones who have been harassed or subject to bias.

Because women often do not report negative gender-related

experiences, human resources departments should look for statistical anomalies in the movements of their employees. They have a bird's-eye view and can see patterns that may not be apparent to others. For example, women consistently leaving or not getting promoted in a particular group can signal problems.

In the 1990s, Ingrid's group at a technology company on the West Coast got a new manager, a man from the South who called all the women in the group "little lady." She had already been thinking about transferring to another group in the company, and so she did rather than deal with him. About a month later, a woman from human resources asked to speak with Ingrid. "She said, 'All but one of the women in that department left within four weeks of when this guy came in, and it raised flags. We'd like to know why you transferred.' And I said, 'Well, it makes me nervous when I'm called 'little lady,' but he never did anything worse than that. So, if you talk to him, you should probably tell him that it means different things out here.'"

We do not know if this man was consciously sexist or simply using language he was accustomed to. Regardless, human resources was in a position to see the movement, identify the cause, and (we hope) deal with the problem. Ingrid adds, however, that "the people in HR need to be trustworthy. Employees have to believe that the company really wants to be fair before HR will get any honest information from people about why they do what they do at work."

In mid-1990s a committee investigating the status of female science faculty at MIT discovered serious differences in salary, space, and teaching assignments that favored men—and the number of tenured female faculty had hardly budged in the previous twenty years. Since the results were made public in 1999, other universities have also examined how they allocate resources, and made adjustments when they found significant disparities.[5] Universities and companies should conduct these surveys on a regular basis to help ensure equitable distribution of resources.

Universities and companies also need to make hiring and promotion processes more transparent, so that bias is less likely to be a factor. Many of the universities with ADVANCE grants have made increased transparency one of the goals of their programs, not only studying their processes but creating tools that can be used elsewhere. For example, the University of Arizona is developing management software for deans and department chairs to use in recruitment and retention. It's intended to help ensure that all candidates are judged on their actual merits and that women are not hurt by unconscious biases.[6]

Furthermore, in making decisions about hiring, promotion, and tenure, universities and companies need to focus more on the quality of candidates' research rather than simply the quantity, since by some accounts women publish fewer but better papers. Counting papers is easy, but it does not provide an accurate assessment of someone's research. Looking at where each paper is published, how often it has been cited, and who is doing the citing is a better determination, though this can also be problematic—a recent paper will obviously have been cited fewer times than one published longer ago, and a graduate student applying for a postdoc will likely have papers published only within the last few years.

To ensure bias-free assessments, peer review of grant proposals, journal articles, and other documents should be blinded so reviewers do not know the identity, and thus the gender, of the scientist being reviewed. In some cases a reviewer will be able to guess an author's identity based on the proposed research and whom she cites, especially if the field is small, but blind review can be particularly helpful to young scientists just getting started in a field.

One of the best examples of the power of blind review comes from a field quite removed from science and engineering, that of music. In the 1970s and 1980s, orchestras began to conduct some or all rounds of an audition with the musician playing behind a screen to hide his or her identity. Researchers found that these blind auditions could explain one third of the increase in the proportion of women among new hires in several major orchestras.[7] Although studies have revealed the existence of biases in peer review, as of yet no major effort has occurred in science or engineering to institute blind reviews.

Other ways institutions can make science and engineering more welcoming to women involve various aspects of balancing work and personal life. Most partnered women in science and engineering have partners who are also professionals, often in technical fields. As such, dual hires at universities, national laboratories, and other institutions are crucial. When departments begin a search, they need to recognize that a dual hire is a distinct possibility, and they should have plans for how to make it happen. Dual hires are often unsuccessful or detrimental to careers in part because one half of the couple—more likely the woman—receives a postdoc or adjunct position while the other becomes tenure-track faculty. High-quality, permanent positions are the goal and need to be more available.

Universities and companies also need to provide more childcare that is affordable, nearby, and flexible. Women also need access to private, comfortable spaces where they can express breastmilk for infants; if childcare centers are nearby, women may also be able to breastfeed at lunch or on breaks. Furthermore, institutions need to recognize that raising a child continues for years—not six weeks or a semester, or however long a woman's maternity leave is—and requires the time and energy of both parents.

Many institutions now allow women, and often men as well, to stop the tenure clock for a year after having a child, so that they are evaluated after seven rather than six years as an assistant professor. Although these extensions can help, they can also harm the careers of those who take them if the people on their tenure committee do not approve of tenure clock extensions, feel that taking time for family is an indication of a weaker commitment to science, or if they expect more work to be done because of the longer amount of time. Some men have taken parental leave or a tenure clock extension and then used the extra time to work, leaving most or all of the child-rearing responsibilities to their partners, thus disadvantaging those who actually use the time for childcare.

A better solution to the problem of the assistant professor and childbearing years coinciding is a part-time tenure track.[8] In this plan, any faculty member with care-giving responsibilities, whether for kids, elderly parents, or ill family members, can request part-time status (at least 50 percent) for between one and twelve years. Their entire workload decreases proportionally, as do salary and benefits. For untenured faculty, the tenure clock extends proportionately as well, with one year of half-time work equal to half a year of full-time work.

This may seem like an expensive proposal, but the university can use the portion of the professor's salary not paid to him or her to search for and hire contingent faculty to cover teaching responsibilities. More office space may be needed for these additional faculty, but considering that many adjuncts do not receive offices, this may not be a concern. This plan allows universities to attract and retain talented female faculty who otherwise would have taken jobs in industry or left science entirely. Searches to replace tenure-track faculty who leave (and provision of startup funds and appropriate laboratory equipment/space for new faculty) are costly, so the increased retention associated with a half-time tenure track has the potential to save universities money in the long run. A half-time tenure track also reduces the potential for abuse of the system, as pay is proportional to expected work, whereas with parental leaves and tenure clock extensions, faculty receive full pay for less work. It's also a good part-time job, as opposed to many part-time adjunct positions.

A number of universities already have provisions for part-time faculty on the books. Some of these apply only to tenured faculty, whereas others provide a part-time tenure track. Very few faculty know that part-time positions are possible, and even if they do, most do not feel comfortable taking advantage of them. It's still up to the faculty member's department chair to approve a part-time position, and this approval is not always given. More universities need to provide this as a viable option, so that taking it cannot harm a woman's chances at tenure or promotion. Companies and other institutions also need to make part-time jobs with interesting work, decent salaries, and benefits more widely available to employees.

A related option is to increase the number of opportunities for job sharing—in which two part-time employees share one position, and often an office and laboratory as well. This can provide a solution to the two-body problem if both partners work in the same field and wish to hold part-time positions.

Full-time employees should also be able to complete their job duties, and be considered successful, without working extra-long hours. "There is a technique of giving you a job that you can probably do in a forty-hour week, but you only get promoted, or indeed kept, if you do that job plus something else," says Ingrid, who worked at a technology company that used this strategy in the 1990s.

Making workplaces more flexible and better at offering employees a reasonable balance between work and personal life is not easy, of course. In the current system, working more (harder, faster) than the people around you is what gets you ahead; as long as everyone else is working a sixty-hour week, it's hard to make the decision to cut back. If, in an ideal world, everyone agreed to reduce hours, a stable situation with a more reasonable workweek could be achieved. For lasting change, this really must be everyone—not only in one department of one company, but throughout a company and throughout the industry.[9] Reasonable work weeks for all may sound like a utopian vision, but it's crucial that we work toward these improvements, which will ultimately benefit companies by generating strong employee loyalty and retention of talent.

It's also important to hire men who are aware of the barriers that women face and are interested in helping to remove them. A single woman or a small group working alone often receives little respect from colleagues; they're a special-interest group and easily disregarded. This is particularly true if the women are mostly in lower-ranking positions, as is often the case. But when women and men both start saying, "We need to do something different," those in power are more likely to listen. The ADVANCE program at the University of Washington recognized this and offered career development and leadership workshops to all faculty, male and female. The leadership development workshops have been institutionalized as part of the university's Leadership, Communities, and Values Initiative.[10] Many of the changes that would be good for women would benefit their male colleagues as well. For example, although it's only recently that fathers have become much more actively involved parents, more and more men want to have more than a few hours a week of quality time with their children.

Luckily, men do not have to wait for an invitation from women to help them break down barriers. Setting a good example in one's behavior and educating colleagues about bias can be helpful. At Case Western Reserve University, a group of male faculty known as the Grassroots Climate Change Committee is working to increase awareness of and involvement in reducing the barriers faced by women among male professors.[11]

Although much needs to be done at the institutional level, women can also individually take steps to improve their environment not only for themselves but also for other women. One of the most important things a woman can do is to learn about the culture of a university, company, department, advisor's laboratory, industry team, or any other group she's considering joining, before she says yes. As Rose, a graduate student in biology, says, "You can find the sort of research that you're so excited by, but if you go to that [principal investigator] and he or she just doesn't really take the time to teach you anything, your excitement for that research is not going to keep you there. I think it's far more important to find somebody that you can talk to."

Women may want to ask questions of the other employees, students, or faculty in private, without the boss around. Are they happy? Is the environment sexist or ultracompetitive? Do they receive support and mentoring? Would they join the group again? Gaining a range of perspectives, including the views of people who have left the group, can help a woman evaluate whether or not she would fit well with the team and help her discover whether problems are isolated personality conflicts or indications of larger issues. Faculty or others outside the group can also have useful knowledge, but they may speak in coded language too veiled to decipher because they hesitate to openly speak poorly of colleagues.

"No one told me that [my first postdoc advisor] was one of the three biggest assholes in my discipline ever to walk the face of the earth," says Ashley, who was a postdoc in the early 2000s. Although he had a reputation, she didn't know about it, and her advisor and other faculty in her graduate department didn't tell her directly. "They said he was difficult and that he was demanding, and to me that's okay. That's going to drive me and encourage me to do good things. [But] it was code for something they didn't want to say. They didn't want to be mean." Women need to be aware of such coded language and probe for more information as appropriate.

When one is considering a position, general questions about the retention and achievement of women are also important. What is the percentage of women in this group? How long do they stay? For a degree program, how many women start, and how many finish? How many women have been denied tenure or left before coming up for it? How often are women promoted? What reasons do the women give for leaving? If an advisor has never had a female graduate student finish a PhD in his twenty years on the faculty, something is probably wrong with that lab.

When red flags pop up, women should consider them seriously. For example, multiple women told me that they had ignored warnings about working with a particular professor or boss because the person was sexist or just generally hostile. These women believed that they were different or could handle it, and too often they were wrong. Even if a woman can handle being in a hostile or just unwelcoming environment, she is unlikely to do her best work there. Dealing with sexism takes time and energy away from the things that a woman actually wants and needs to be doing.

Institutions are more likely to address problems if they are not only aware of them but know that they are having a negative impact. Thus, when women turn down positions, particularly for reasons that are gender-related, they should let the administration or human resources know why. If the reason for going elsewhere is a lack of women in the department, or poor childcare facilities nearby, for example, and those in charge of hiring hear about the same issues again and again, they are more likely to realize that these factors are affecting recruitment and retention in a significant way and may take steps to improve the situation.

Women should also be aware what the going rate is in their field, as well as what is appropriate in terms of stock options, signing bonuses, startup packages, and other compensation outside of salary. In their book *Women Don't Ask: Negotiation and the Gender Divide*, Linda Babcock and Sara Laschever suggest that women have lower salaries in part because they do not negotiate for higher ones. Starting salary is particularly important, since future raises are often a percentage of current salary, so a woman who starts out behind often becomes further and further behind as the years pass. Women who know what others are being paid are more likely to ask for a higher salary than those with no information.[12]

Among my interviewees, the women who had a plan for the trajectory they wanted their careers to take and how they would balance that with their personal lives were more likely to be successful than those who expected that everything would fall into place somehow. Making the plan in concert with their partners, particularly if the couple wished to have children, was also important. Many men, even those who are very supportive of women's careers, still function as ideal workers and expect both that their careers will be more important than their wives' and that their wives will take on the bulk of parenting responsibilities. Discussing options and creating a plan to balance career and personal life for both partners can help prevent women from having to make hard choices and sacrifices down the line.

The women who were pioneers in science and engineering did not generally try to fight the underlying masculine culture of these fields. Instead, they tried to fit in. They acted like men as much as they could, sometimes forgoing marriage and children. They devoted their lives to scientific inquiry, often working harder than the men around them in an attempt to prove themselves and be accepted. At the same time, they did their best to ignore the harassment and obvious injustices they experienced on a daily basis. When one door slammed in their faces, they began knocking on other ones, intent on continuing their work and their careers, trying to find colleagues who were not afraid of a woman in science.

These women conducted significant research, and yet much of it was laughed at, passed over, or otherwise ignored simply because they were female. When women collaborated with men, including their husbands, these men often received all the recognition. Some of these women eventually stopped fighting and turned their attention to other fields. Others continued on in science or engineering but ended up bitter and hardened. A few began to agitate for changes that would benefit other women in these fields, often to the detriment of their own careers. Over time, the number of women in science and engineering has increased, and so has the volume of voices calling for change.

The generation of young women now entering technical fields has grown up with the feminist movement. The idea that a woman cannot pursue and succeed in a career simply because she is female is foreign to them. They are also questioning the idea that the only way for a woman to achieve is to act like a man and to fit herself into the structure of institutions that favor men. Unfortunately, changing a culture, even if the changes will be beneficial to those who currently dominate it, is not a simple feat.

As is evident throughout this book, changes are happening. Universities, companies, and other institutions are working to create environments that welcome and support women rather than simply tolerating or actively discouraging them. But it's not enough. We need to be aware of the inequalities and biases that women still face, and to celebrate women's successes. But we also need to make the deeper changes that will make science and engineering better fields for everyone to work in and for everyone to benefit from.

SO SHE WANTS TO BE A SCIENTIST

WHAT

NOW?

APPENDIX 1

*Does your seven-year-old daughter beg to go
to the aquarium every weekend?*

Is your ten-year-old collecting rocks? Or insects?

*Has your thirteen-year-old learned HTML
to create her own website?*

Does your sixteen-year-old steal your copies of Wired?

Y ou might have a potential scientist or engineer on your hands. Want to encourage her and give her opportunities, but not sure where to start? Here's a list of resources and ideas to get both of you going.

First off, ask your daughter what she does in science or

math class. Are hands-on or laboratory activities included? Is she excited and interested or bored out of her mind? Does she feel capable or incompetent? If you're worried—and even if you're not—you may want to ask your child's school if teachers there take continuing education on gender-fair teaching or if it is addressed in other ways. Also consider discussing the topic with your daughter's teacher at a parent–teacher night or, if the school permits, attending one of your daughter's classes to see the dynamics for yourself. Bring up any gender-biased behavior you noticed afterward; the teacher probably has no idea he or she is acting that way.

If your daughter is capable of learning faster than the class allows, consider whether moving her up a grade level or creating an independent study is appropriate. Some school districts now have science and mathematics magnet schools that offer advanced coursework and other opportunities in these areas. Conversely, if your daughter is struggling in or has anxiety about science or math, try to determine why. It may not be a lack of ability but rather a mismatch of teaching and learning styles. If you think that a single-sex classroom might be a better fit, the National Association for Single Sex Public Education (www.nasspe.org) and the National Coalition of Girls' Schools (www.ncgs.org) provide information about single-sex education, as well as links to schools.

Second, encourage the exploration of science and mathematics outside of the classroom. There are lots of different ways to do this. For example, many cities have a science center, aquarium, zoo, planetarium, and/or natural history museum. These can be a great way to spend a Saturday afternoon, and many also offer science camps, workshops, and other special events, some of which may be directed specifically at girls. Planetariums often allow the public to look through their telescopes, especially during meteor showers and other special astronomical events. Teens can volunteer or even get paying jobs at some museums doing a wide variety of different tasks. Many science centers also have websites with information about science topics related to exhibits, as well as suggestions for activities to do at home. Investigate what your local area has to offer, and keep science in mind as you plan vacations.

One good place to start is www.tryscience.org, which has links to science centers around the world. Parents can request a brochure called "A Family Guide to Science," which comes in a national version as well as versions specific to twenty-six different cities. The website also features experiments and other content for kids.

Is your daughter a Girl Scout? The Girl Scouts of America has a range of different resources and activities related to science and technology. If the kids in your daughter's troop are just tying knots and making crafts, suggest that they branch out. Even if your daughter isn't a scout, www.girlsgotech.org is a good site from the Girl Scouts, with information about careers, games, and a booklet for parents with activity suggestions.

Precollege summer camps and other programs are a great way to build skills and learn about different areas of science and engineering. Some programs focus on coursework and may earn your daughter high school credit; others are for enrichment only and may focus on research or other activities. A searchable directory of programs in science, mathematics, and engineering for precollege students is available at www.sciserv.org/stp/index.asp.

Many girls get their first taste of independent research from competing in a science fair. The Intel International Science and Engineering Fair (www.sciserv.org/isef) is the best known. This competition is fed by a series of science fairs at the local and regional levels. School districts and cities may also host science fairs that are not associated with the Intel fair. Check with your daughter's school to see what's available.

Intel also sponsors the Intel Science Talent Search (www .sciserv.org/sts/index.asp), which used to be known as the Westinghouse Science Talent Search. For this premier science competition for high school seniors, the grand prize is a four-year, $100,000 college scholarship. Students often begin the research for their projects years in advance, and they often work in research laboratories at universities.

Even if winning the Science Talent Search isn't your daughter's goal, working in a laboratory is one of the best ways to determine if a career in science is the right path for her. Some summer programs at universities offer students research experience. Or, if your daughter identifies a faculty member at a local university who is doing research that interests her, she may be able to directly apply to that laboratory. Keep in mind that some professors are more open to having precollege students in their labs than are others, so it may take a while to find someone receptive to the idea.

Summer programs and research experiences, in addition to increasing skills and knowledge, also bring a girl into contact with people who can act as mentors and role models. These people can be found among family members and friends as well. Especially since students often have stereotypical views of scientists, seeing scientists and engineers who are real people is important. And mentors and role models need not be female. Start asking around—you never know who may be lurking in your extended network.

Experimentation does not need to occur in a formal laboratory setting, of course. Chemistry sets, microscopes, binoculars, and telescopes can stimulate exploration at home. A field guide to local wildlife, plants, or rocks can help a girl learn more about her environment and encourage her to explore the outdoors even further. When a small appliance such as a toaster or hairdryer breaks and is replaced, allow your daughter to take the old one apart to see how it works. This sort of reverse engineering can be fascinating to girls, especially if they have not been encouraged to tinker before, and your daughter might figure out how to fix it. (A word of caution: Some appliances contain toxic materials. Do some research before letting your daughter at it.) Girls should be encouraged not just to take things apart, but to build things as well. Hobby stores sell kits for building robots, rockets, motorized vehicles, and other projects.

When she doesn't have her hands full of electronics, encourage your daughter to read widely about science topics. Make sure she has a library card and uses it. Biographies of women in science can be particularly inspiring. A subscription to an age-appropriate science magazine makes a great gift, because it will include articles on cutting-edge research and the latest discoveries, which are often more fascinating than the basic principles in textbooks. Some books to get you started are listed at the end of this appendix.

Another way for your daughter to learn about cutting-edge

research is to attend lectures at a local college or university that are open to the public (and usually free). These are intended for a general audience and thus should be appropriate for a high school student, although some lecturers do have a jargon-heavy style. These lectures often pertain to science-related topics in the news, which can also be fodder for discussion with your daughter. Many of the issues that are currently the subject of political debates are rooted in science, including stem cells, global warming, alternative fuels, funding for space missions, and genetically modified foods. Some studies suggest that girls are more interested in science when they are able to relate it to everyday life, so take opportunities to make connections.

Television programs and films can also spark a girl's interest in science. PBS shows many well-crafted programs on a wide variety of science and engineering topics, and various cable channels are devoted to science and nature. IMAX theaters are a great source of films about science. Girls' interest in science and engineering can also be fed by science fiction, whether in books, films, or TV programs. Keep in mind, however, that not all science fiction portrays women in a favorable light. Older sci-fi, in particular, often relegates women to supporting roles or love interests. Watch with your daughter, and talk about what you've seen. And don't forget the radio, which can be a great source of information about science. For example, National Public Radio broadcasts "Science Friday" every Friday afternoon. The show's companion website (www.sciencefriday.com/kids) has a variety of resources for parents and educators.

Although they may not be directly related to science, puzzles help develop problem-solving skills that are widely applicable. Puzzles include not only jigsaws but also crosswords, sudoku, and a wide variety of other brainteasers and bogglers. A book of puzzles or a subscription to *Games* magazine can make a great gift. Furthermore, some research suggests that playing video games can improve spatial abilities, which are crucial for success in many areas of math, science, and engineering. If your daughter is interested in such games, it may be worthwhile to let her play. Check the content of the games, however—some are quite violent and/or portray women negatively.

Computers are an essential part of much of the scientific work happening today. If your family can afford a computer, get one, and make sure that all your children have opportunities to work on it. Encourage your daughter to use the computer for more than instant messaging with her friends and typing up reports for school. Becoming familiar with a wide variety of programs, and even learning how to write computer code, can make many things easier later. Of course, the Internet is loaded with information about careers in science and engineering, games, activities to try, profiles of female scientists, and other useful information. Websites change constantly, so a comprehensive list is impossible, but the end of this appendix has a list to get you started.

Above all, encourage curiosity, whether it's science-related or not. Questions should always be okay. If you don't know the answer, don't feel embarrassed, brush off the question, or make up something. Make a project of finding out, and include your daughter in your sleuthing. Search the Internet, find a relevant book, ask a scientist, or conduct an experiment. Then go beyond the original question to learn even more.

SOME BOOKS FOR GIRLS:

The *Women's Adventures in Science* series: Ten biographies of female scientists in different fields. (The companion website, www.iwaswondering.org, has information about the scientists featured in the books, as well as a timeline of women in science, games, and more.)

Girls Think of Everything: Stories of Ingenious Inventions by Women. Thimmesh, C. 2002. Boston: Houghton Mifflin.

The Math Book for Girls and Other Beings Who Count. Wyatt, V. 1993. Toronto: Kids Can Press, Ltd.

The Science Book for Girls and Other Intelligent Beings. Wyatt, V. 1993. Toronto: Kids Can Press, Ltd.

The Sky's the Limit: Stories of Discovery by Women and Girls. Thimmesh, C. 2002. Boston: Houghton Mifflin.

The Technology Book for Girls and Other Advanced Beings. Romonek, T. 2001. Toronto: Kids Can Press, Ltd.

The Ultimate Girls' Guide to Science: From Backyard Experiments to Winning the Nobel Prize! Hoyt, B. C., and E. Ritter. 2003. Hillsboro, OR: Beyond Words Publishing.

SOME BOOKS FOR ADULTS:

How To Encourage Girls in Math & Science. Skolnick, J. 1997. Dale Seymour Publications.

Young Women of Achievement: A Resource for Girls in Science, Math, and Technology. Karnes, F. A., and K. R. Stephens. 2002. Amherst, N.Y.: Prometheus Books.

ONLINE RESOURCES:

www.discoverengineering.org is a site for kids from the National Engineers Week Foundation. It features information about engineering, games, and lots of links. Also check out www.eweek.org for information about Engineers Week, held annually in February, as well as many other resources.

www.tryengineering.org is a site for students, parents, and teachers with biographies of engineers, lesson plans, and experts who answer questions. It also includes lists of engineering-related summer camps and competitions, as well as a searchable database of universities with accredited engineering programs.

www.engineergirl.org, from the National Academy of Engineering, includes information about engineering careers and profiles of female engineers; the website also sponsors an annual essay contest on an engineering-related topic.

www.sciencenewsforkids.org includes articles about current science as well as science-fair project ideas, puzzles, and more.

www.kidsites.com/sites-edu/science.htm has links to lots of websites for kids that explore various aspects of science.

Many of the departments and centers in the federal government also have sections of their websites reserved for kids. For example, check out http://kids.earth.nasa.gov or www.ars.usda.gov/is/kids.

SO YOU'RE A
SCIENTIST

WHAT

NOW?

APPENDIX 2

Do you take (or teach) classes with titles like
"Macroepidemiology," "Electroweak Interactions,"
or "Probabilistic Systems Analysis"?

Do you put your kids to bed and then work until
2:00 AM writing journal articles and grant proposals?

Do you argue with your partner about algebraic
geometry and the "two-body problem"?

Do people call you "doctor"?

You might be a woman in science or engineering. While women are scarce in some disciplines, you are certainly not alone. Many programs and organizations bring together and support female scientists and engineers in college and beyond. Some also advocate for changes that will improve the experiences of all women; if you have time and energy to contribute to making solutions happen, these groups need volunteers.

Many universities have women-in-science (or -engineering) groups for undergraduate and graduate students, which may either be specific to the institution or local chapters of larger organizations, such as the Society of Women Engineers. Resource centers and women's advisors are also becoming more common, and they can help build a community of women and provide guidance, even if they are not strictly geared toward science and engineering. Groups specific to female postdocs are rare, but some universities have general associations for postdocs to network with each other and to advocate for change on campus.

Resources are also often available to women faculty on their campuses. Universities that have received National Science Foundation ADVANCE Institutional Transformation Awards have offices devoted to the needs of female faculty; some other universities have similar programs. Offerings vary widely but may include mentoring, career development workshops, and other support services. Many government labs and companies, particularly larger ones, also have formal women's groups. Even if your workplace doesn't have formal support programs, you can create an informal support network simply by regularly asking several female colleagues to lunch on a regular basis. These informal gatherings sometimes grow and mature into groups that receive formal institutional support.

Scientific organizations specifically for women, such as the Society of Women Engineers (SWE), can also provide support if a woman's institution does not have formal programs in place. SWE chapters at universities support students and provide opportunities for them to interact with women who are further advanced in their careers. SWE also hosts several conferences each year, offers an online career center, and does research on women in engineering. More information is available online at www.swe.org.

The Association for Women in Science (AWIS) has chapters in many cities around the country. Chapter events allow women to network with one another, and some match women with mentors. AWIS also lobbies Congress and publishes a magazine. The group's website is www.awis.org.

The Association for Women in Mathematics (AWM) has a mentor network, student chapters, workshops for grad students and postdocs, and other resources. The website is www .awm-math.org/.

The American Medical Women's Association (AMWA) publishes a newsletter and has created a set of online career development resources for physicians. It also hosts an annual meeting. AMWA is online at www.amwa-doc.org.

Although not specific to science, the American Association of University Women (AAUW) promotes education and equity for women and girls. It hosts an annual convention and other events, funds fellowships and grants, periodically publishes reports on various topics, and supports women fighting sex discrimination through its legal fund. AAUW is online at www .aauw.org. The American Association of University Professors (AAUP) is also not specific to science (or women), but it can be a useful resource for female faculty: www.aaup.org.

Many of the aforementioned organizations facilitate mentoring relationships for their members. Another option for online mentoring is MentorNet (www.mentornet.net), which has paired mentors and protégés for ten years. Its website also includes discussion forums and other resources.

Many general scientific organizations have committees or divisions that focus on issues of particular interest to women. These offer many different kinds of resources, such as sessions at conferences, newsletters, opportunities for networking and mentoring, and advocacy for change that benefits women. Below is a list of a few scientific societies, with links to their women's committees. It is not comprehensive. If you belong to scientific organizations not listed here, check with them to see if they have groups for women. Some organizations have diversity committees that address the problems of both women and underrepresented minorities.

AMERICAN ASSOCIATION OF IMMUNOLOGISTS
www.aai.org/committees/women/aai_wom.html

AMERICAN ASTRONOMICAL SOCIETY
www.aas.org/cswa

AMERICAN CHEMICAL SOCIETY
http://membership.acs.org/W/WCC

AMERICAN INSTITUTE OF CHEMICAL ENGINEERS
www.aichewic.org/pages/index.cfm?siteid=546

AMERICAN MEDICAL ASSOCIATION
www.ama-assn.org/ama/pub/category/172.html

AMERICAN PHYSICAL SOCIETY
www.aps.org/programs/women/index.cfm

AMERICAN PHYSIOLOGICAL SOCIETY
www.the-aps.org/committees/women/index.htm

AMERICAN SOCIETY FOR CELL BIOLOGY
www.ascb.org/index.cfm?navid=89

ASSOCIATION FOR COMPUTING MACHINERY
http://women.acm.org/

COMPUTING RESEARCH ASSOCIATION
www.cra.org/Activities/craw/index.php

INSTITUTE OF ELECTRICAL AND ELECTRONICS ENGINEERS
www.ieee.org/portal/pages/committee/women/index.html

MATHEMATICAL ASSOCIATION OF AMERICA
www.maa.org/wam/index.html

Some women in science and engineering are also creating informal support networks by blogging about their experiences online. Often using a pseudonym, these women share their personal triumphs and frustrations and discuss the challenges that women face more generally. A good place to start finding blogs by women in science and engineering is Scientiae (http://scientiae-carnival.blogspot.com), which collects posts by many bloggers on a particular topic that changes every month. Past themes have included balance, transitions, and inspiring women.

BOOKS

Many academic books on the issues facing women in science and engineering have been published. These often focus on female faculty. A few recent titles:

Athena Unbound: The Advancement of Women in Science and Technology. Etzkowitz, H., C. Kemelgor, and B. Uzzi. 2000. Cambridge University Press.

The Science Glass Ceiling: Academic Women Scientists and the Struggle to Succeed. Rosser, S. V. 2005. New York: Taylor & Francis.

Unlocking the Clubhouse: Women in Computing. Margolis, J., and A. Fisher. 2001. Cambridge: MIT Press.

Women in Science: Career Processes and Outcomes. Xie, Y., and K. A. Shauman. 2003. Cambridge: Harvard University Press.

For more personal accounts of what it's like to be a woman interested in science and technology, try the following:

She's Such a Geek: Women Write About Science, Technology, and Other Nerdy Stuff. Newitz, A., and C. Anders, eds. 2006. Emeryville, CA: Seal Press.

For specific strategies to use to achieve success, check these out:

Every Other Thursday: Stories and Strategies from Successful Women Scientists. Daniell, E. 2006. New Haven, CT: Yale University Press.

Success Strategies for Women in Science: A Portable Mentor. Pritchard, P. A., ed. 2005. Academic Press.

Some titles that more generally address challenges that women face in the workplace:

Why So Slow? The Advancement of Women. Valian, V. 1998. Cambridge: MIT Press.

Unbending Gender: Why Family and Work Conflict and What To Do About It. Williams, J. 1999. Oxford University Press.

NOTES

INTRODUCTION

1. A transcript of Summers's speech is available online at www.president.havard.edu/speeches/2005/nber.html.

CHAPTER ONE

A DIFFERENT EDUCATION
GIRLS IN THE SCIENCE CLASSROOM

1. Tindall, T., and B. Hamil. 2004. Gender disparity in science education: The causes, consequences, and solutions. *Education* 125 (2): 282–295. See also M. Sadker and D. Sadker. 1994. *Failing at fairness: How America's schools cheat girls.* New York: Simon and Schuster.
2. Sadker and Sadker, *Failing at fairness.*
3. Ibid.
4. Ibid.
5. Ibid.
6. Ibid.
7. Grigg, W., M. Lauko, and D. Bockway. 2006. The nation's report card: Science 2005 (NCES 2006-466). U.S. Department of Education, National Center for Education Statistics. Washington, D.C.: GPO.
8. Jovanovic, J., and S. S. King. 1998. Boys and girls in the performance-based science classroom: Who's doing the performing? *American Education Research Journal* 35: 477–496.
9. Sadker and Sadker, *Failing at fairness.*

10. Finson, K. D. 2002. Drawing a scientist: What we do and do not know after fifty years of drawings. *School Science and Mathematics* 102 (7): 335–345.

11. Barman, C. R. 1999. Students' views about scientists and school science: Engaging K–8 teachers in a national study. *Journal of Science Teacher Education* 10 (1): 43–54.

12. Dickson, J. M., C. F. Saylor, and A. J. Finch. 1990. Personality factors, family structure, and sex of drawn figure on the Draw-A-Person Test. *Journal of Personality Assessment* 55 (1 and 2): 362–366.

13. Moseley, C., and D. Norris. 1999. Preservice teachers' views of science. *Science and Children* 37 (6): 50–53.

14. National Science Board. 2006. Science and engineering indicators 2006. 2 vols. Arlington, Va.: National Science Foundation (vol. 1, NSB 0601; vol. 2, NSB 06-01A).

15. Ma, X., and J. Xu. 2004. The causal ordering of mathematics anxiety and mathematics achievement: A longitudinal panel analysis. *Journal of Adolescence* 27 (2): 165–179.

16. Pomerantz, E. M., E. R. Altermatt, and J. L. Saxon. 2002. Making the grade but feeling distressed: Gender differences in academic performance and internal distress. *Journal of Educational Psychology* 94 (2): 396–404.

17. Sadker and Sadker, *Failing at fairness*.

18. Frawley, T. 2005. Gender bias in the classroom: Current controversies and implications for teachers. *Childhood Education* 81 (4): 221–227.

19. National Council of Girls' Schools. 2005. The girls' school experience: A survey of young alumnae of single-sex schools. www.ncgs.org/public_pdf/2005_NCGS_Young_Alumnae_Survey.pdf.

20. National Science Board.

CHAPTER TWO

NATURE, NURTURE
WHAT'S BEHIND SCIENTIFIC ABILITY?

1. Caplan, J. B., and P. J. Caplan. 2005. The perseverative search for sex differences in mathematics ability. In *Gender Differences in Mathematics: An Integrative Psychological Approach*, edited by A. M. Gallagher and J. C. Kaufman. New York: Cambridge University Press.

2. Hyde, J. S. 2005. The gender similarities hypothesis. *American Psychologist* 60 (6): 581–592.

3. Ibid.

4. See references in Hyde, The gender similarities hypothesis. See also E. S. Spelke. 2005. Sex differences in intrinsic aptitude for mathematics and science? A critical review. *American Psychologist* 60 (9): 950–958.

5. See, for example, Spelke, Sex differences; also see C. J. Mills, K. E. Ablard, and H. Stumph. Gender differences in academically talented young students' mathematical reasoning: Patterns across age and subskills. *Journal of Educational Psychology* 85: 340–346.

6. College Board. 2006. 2006 college-bound seniors: total group profile report. www.collegeboard.com/prod_downloads/about/news_info/cbsenior/yr2006/national-report.pdf.

7. College Board. 2007. About the SAT. www.collegeboard.com/student/testing/sat/about.html.

8. Grigg, W., P. Donahue, and G. Dion. 2007. The nation's report card: 12th-grade reading and mathematics 2005 (NCES 2007-468). U.S. Department of Education, National Center for Education Statistics. Washington, D.C.: GPO.

9. Spelke, Sex differences, and Mills, Ablard, and Stumph, Gender differences.

10. Chipman, S. F. 2005. Research on the women and mathematics issue—A personal case history. In *Gender Differences in Mathematics: An Integrative Psychological Approach*, edited by A. M. Gallagher and J. C. Kaufman. New York: Cambridge University Press.

11. See, for example, L. Stricker, D. Rock, and N. Burton. 1993. Sex differences in predictions of college grades from Scholastic Aptitude Test scores. *Journal of Educational Psychology* 5: 710–718.

12. Chipman, Research on the women and mathematics issue. See also Stricker, Rock, and Burton, Sex differences.

13. See, for example, A. Feingold. 1988. Cognitive gender differences are disappearing. *American Psychologist* 43 (2): 95–103. See also A. Nowell and L. V. Hedges. 1998. Trends in gender differences in academic achievement from 1960 to 1994: an analysis of differences in mean, variance and extreme scores. *Sex Roles* 39 (1–2): 21–44.

14. Halpern, D. F., J. Wai, and A. Saw. 2005. A psychobiosocial model: why

females are sometimes greater than and sometimes less than males in math achievement. In *Gender Differences in Mathematics: An Integrative Psychological Approach,* edited by A. M. Gallagher and J. C. Kaufman. New York: Cambridge University Press.

15. Monastersky, R. 2005. Primed for numbers: Are boys better at math? Experts try to divide the influences of nature and nurture. *The Chronicle of Higher Education* 51 (26): A1.

16. Xie, Y., and K. A. Shauman. 2003. *Women in Science: Career Processes and Outcomes.* Cambridge: Harvard University Press.

17. Terlecki, M. S., and N. S. Newcombe. 2005. How important is the digital divide? The relation of computer and video game usage to gender differences in mental rotation ability. *Sex Roles* 53 (5–6): 433–442.

18. Levine, S. S., M. Vasilyeva, S. F. Lourenco, N. S. Newcombe, and J. Huttenlocher. 2005. Socioeconomic status modifies the sex difference in spatial skill. *Psychological Science* 16 (11): 841–845.

19. Spencer, S., C. M. Steele, and D. Quinn. 1999. Stereotype threat and women's math performance. *Journal of Experimental Social Psychology* 35 (4): 4–28.

20. Inzlicht, M., and T. Ben-Zeev. 2000. A threatening intellectual environment: Why females are susceptible to experiencing problem-solving deficits in the presence of males. *Psychological Science* 11 (5): 365–371.

21. Ambady, N., et al. 2001. Stereotype susceptibility in children: Effects of identity activation on quantitative performance. *Psychological Science* 12: 385–389.

22. Shih, M., et al. 1999. Stereotype susceptibility: Identity salience and shifts in quantitative performance. *Psychological Science* 10: 80–83.

23. Nuttal, R. L., M. B. Casey, and E. Pezaris. 2005. Spatial ability as a mediator of gender differences on mathematics tests: A biological-environmental framework. In *Gender Differences in Mathematics: An Integrative Psychological Approach,* edited by A. M. Gallagher and J. C. Kaufman. New York: Cambridge University Press.

24. See, for example, Caplan and Caplan, The perseverative search, and Chipman, Research on the women and mathematics issue. See also G. Becker. 1996. Bias in the assessment of gender differences. *American Psychologist* 51: 154–155.

25. Gurian, M. 2001. *Boys and Girls Learn Differently! A Guide for Teachers and Parents.* San Francisco: Jossey-Bass.

26. Spence, J. T., and C. E. Buckner. 2000. Instrumental and expressive traits, trait stereotypes, and sexist attitudes. *Psychology of Women Quarterly* 24: 44–62.

27. Twenge, J. M. 1997. Changes in masculine and feminine traits over time: A meta-analysis. *Sex Roles* 36: 305–325.

28. Twenge, J. M. 2001. Changes in women's assertiveness in response to status and roles: A cross-temporal meta-analysis. *Journal of Personality and Social Psychology* 81: 133–145.

29. Collaer, M. L., and M. Hines. 1995. Human behavioral sex differences: A role for gonadal hormones during early development? *Psychological Bulletin* 118: 55–107.

30. Ibid.

31. Lubinski, D., and C. P. Benbow. 1992. Gender differences in abilities and preferences among the gifted: Implications for the math–science pipeline. *Current Directions in Psychological Science* 1: 61–66.

32. Haier, R. J., et al. 2005. The neuroanatomy of general intelligence: sex matters. *NeuroImage* 25: 320–327.

CHAPTER THREE

COMPETING CLOCKS
CAREER, PERSONAL TIME, AND SCIENCE

1. For a discussion of ideal workers, see J. Williams. 1999. *Unbending Gender: Why Family and Work Conflict and What to Do About It.* Oxford University Press.

2. Jacobs, J. A., and S. E. Winslow. 2004. Overworked faculty: Job stresses and family demands. *The Annals of the American Academy of Political and Social Science* 596: 104–128.

3. Ward, K., and L. Wolf-Wendel. Academic motherhood: Managing complex roles in research universities. *Review of Higher Education* 27(2) (2004): 233–257.

4. McNeil, L., and M. Sher. 1998. Dual-science-career couples: Survey results. http://physics.wm.edu/~sher/survey.pdf.

5. Heylin, M. Early careers: It's mostly good news from a poll that probes careers of ACS members under 40 years of age. *Chemical and Engineering News*, December 24, 2001. pubs.acs.org/cen/acsnews/7952/pdf/7952survey.pdf.

6. McNeil and Sher, Dual-science-career couples.

7. Armenti, C. May babies and posttenure babies: Maternal decisions of women professors. *Review of Higher Education* 27 (2) (2004): 211–231.

8. U.S. Department of Health and Human Services. 2006. Infertility. www.womens health.gov/faq/infertility.htm.

9. Heffner, L. J. 2004. Advanced maternal age—How old is too old? *New England Journal of Medicine* 351 (19): 1,927–1,929.

10. Centers for Disease Control and Prevention. 2006. Reproductive technology success rates: national summary and fertility clinic reports. http://ftp.cdc.gov/pub/Publications/art/2004ART508.pdf.

11. U.S. Department of Labor. 2007. Compliance assistance – Family and Medical Leave Act (FMLA). www.dol.gov/esa/whd/fmla/.

12. U.S. Census Bureau. 2006. Father's Day: June 18. www.census.gov/Press-Release/www/releases/archives/facts_for_features_special_editions/006794.html. Note that this figure includes only those men who have been out of the labor force for more than one year primarily so that they can care for children under the age of fifteen. Presumably, some stay-at-home-fathers do part-time work while remaining their children's primary caregiver, as do many stay-at-home moms.

13. Kreider, R. M. 2005. Number, timing, and duration of marriages and divorces: 2001. Current Population Reports, P70-97. U.S. Census Bureau, Washington, D.C.

14. Mason, M. A., and M. Goulden. 2004. Marriage and baby blues: Redefining gender equity in the academy. *The Annals of the American Academy of Political and Social Science* 596: 86–103.

CHAPTER FOUR

SWIMMING UPSTREAM
BIAS AGAINST WOMEN IN SCIENCE

1. Valian, V. 1998. *Why So Slow? The Advancement of Women*. Cambridge: MIT Press.

2. Skeptical? Take the gender-science or gender-career demonstration Implicit Association Tests at https://implicit.harvard.edu/implicit/.

3. National Science Board. 2006. Science and engineering indicators 2006. 2 vols. Arlington, VA: National Science Foundation (vol. 1, NSB 0601; vol. 2, NSB 06-01A).

4. Niemeier, D. A., and C. Gonzalez. Breaking into the guildmasters' club: What we know about women science and engineering department chairs at AAU universities. *NWSA Journal* 16 (1) (2004): 157–171.

5. Martell, R. F., et al. 1996. Male–female differences: A computer simulation. *American Psychologist* 51, 157–158.

6. Takiff, H., et al. What's in a name? The status implications of students' terms of address for male and female professors. *Psychology of Women Quarterly* 25 (2001): 134–144.

7. Wenneras, C., and A. Wold. 1997. Nepotism and sexism in peer review. *Nature* 387: 341–344.

8. Psenka, C., and F. Trix. 2003. Exploring the color of glass: Letters of recommendation for female and male medical faculty. *Discourse and Society* 14 (2): 191–220.

9. Heilman, M. E., and B. Welle. 2006. Disadvantaged by diversity? The effect of diversity goals on competence perceptions. *Journal of Applied Social Psychology* 36 (5): 1,291–1,319.

10. Dey, J. G., and C. Hill. 2007. Behind the pay gap. American Association of University Women Educational Foundation, Washington, D.C.

11. Hill, C., and E. Silva. 2005. Drawing the line: Sexual harassment on campus. American Association of University Women Educational Foundation, Washington, D.C.

12. Klonoff, E. A., et al. 2000. Sexist discrimination may account for well-known gender differences in psychiatric symptoms. *Psychology of Women Quarterly* 24: 93–99.

13. Hill and Silva, Drawing the line.

14. Swim, J. K., and L. L. Hyers. 1999. "Excuse me—what did you say?!": Women's public and private responses to sexist remarks. *Journal of Experimental Social Psychology* 35, 68–88.

15. Foster, M. D., et al. 2004. Minimizing the pervasiveness of women's personal experiences of gender discrimination. *Psychology of Women Quarterly*, 28 (3): 224–232.

CHAPTER FIVE
A DEGREE OF BS
WOMEN IN UNDERGRADUATE SCIENCE

1. National Science Board. 2006. Science and Engineering Indicators 2006. 2 vols. Arlington, VA: National Science Foundation (vol. 1, NSB 0601; vol. 2, NSB 06-01A).

2. de Pillis, E. G., and L. G. D. de Pillis. 2005. Masculinity themes in the stated missions of engineering and liberal arts colleges. Proceedings of the Decision Sciences Institute, 18,441–18,448.

3. Seymour, E. 1995. The loss of women from science, mathematics, and engineering undergraduate majors: An explanatory account. *Science Education* 79 (4): 437–473.

4. Pomerantz, E. M., E. R. Altermatt, and J. L. Saxon. 2002. Making the grade but feeling distressed: Gender differences in academic performance and internal distress. *Journal of Educational Psychology* 94 (2): 396–404.

5. Brainard, S. G., and L. Carlin. 1998. A six-year longitudinal study of undergraduate women in engineering and science. *Journal of Engineering Education* 87 (4): 369–375.

6. Sax, L. 2005. *Why Gender Matters: What Parents and Teachers Need to Know about the Emerging Science of Sex Differences.* New York: Doubleday.

7. Seymour, E., and N. Hewitt. 1997. *Talking about Leaving: Why Undergraduates Leave the Sciences.* Boulder, CO: Westview Press.

8. Bettinger, E. P., and B. T. Long. 2005. Do faculty serve as role models? The impact of instructor gender on female students. *American Economic Review* 95 (2): 152–157.

9. See, for example, B. Brett and P. Rayman. 1995. Women science majors: What makes a difference in persistence after graduation? *Journal of Higher Education* 66 (4): 388–414.

10. Lopatto, D. 2004. Survey of undergraduate research experiences (SURE): First findings. *Cell Biology Education* 3: 270–277.

11. Cech, T. R. 1999. Science at liberal arts colleges: A better education? *Daedalus* 128 (1): 195–216.

CHAPTER SIX

DOCTOR, POST-DOCTOR
BEFORE AND AFTER THE PHD

1. National Science Board. 2006. Science and Engineering Indicators 2006. 2 vols. Arlington, VA: National Science Foundation (vol. 1, NSB 06-01; vol. 2, NSB 06-01A).

2. Sax, L. J. 2000. Undergraduate science majors: Gender differences in who goes to graduate school. *Review of Higher Education* 24 (2): 153–172.

3. National Science Board.

4. National Research Council. 2001. From scarcity to visibility: Gender differences in the careers of doctoral scientists and engineers. Washington, D.C.: National Academy Press. www.nap.edu/catalog/5363.html.

5. Graduate Research Fellowship Program (GFRP): Program Solicitation NSF 06-592. (2006). www.nsf.gov/pubs/2006/nsf06592/nsf06592.htm.

6. Committee of Visitors (COV) Report for the National Science Foundation (NSF) Graduate Research Fellowship Program (GRFP). 2006. www.nsf.gov/od/oia/activities/cov/ehr/2006/GRFcov.pdf.

7. Ulku-Steiner, B., et al. 2000. Doctoral student experiences in gender-balanced and male-dominated graduate programs. *Journal of Educational Psychology* 92 (2): 296–307.

8. See, for example, C. M. Golde and T. M. Dore. 2001. At cross purposes: What the experiences of doctoral students reveal about doctoral education. A report prepared for the Pew Charitable Trusts, Philadelphia. www.phd-survey.org.

9. National Science Board.

10. Ferreira, M. M. 2003. Gender issues related to graduate student attrition in two science departments. *International Journal of Science Education* 25 (8): 969–989.

11. Ulku-Steiner, et al, Doctoral student experiences.

12. Ferreira, Gender issues.

13. Berkeley Graduate and Professional Schools Mental Health Task Force. 2004. Berkeley Graduate Student Mental Health Survey. www.ocf.berkeley.edu/~gmhealth/reports/gradmentalhealth_report2004.pdf.

14. Fox, M. F. 2000. Organizational environments and doctoral degrees awarded to women in science and engineering departments. *Women's Studies Quarterly* 28 (1–2): 47–61.

15. Nyquist, J. D., et al. 1999. On the road to becoming a professor: The graduate student experience. *Change* 31 (3): 18–27.

16. National Science Board.

17. Stephan, P., and J. Ma. 2005. The increased frequency and duration of the postdoctorate career stage. *American Economic Review* 95 (2): 71–75.

18. Stephan, P., and J. Ma. 2005. The increased frequency and duration of the postdoctorate career stage. Paper presented at the American Economic Association 2005 Annual Meeting. www.aeaweb.org/annual_mtg_papers/2005/0108_1430_1204.pdf.

19. Singer, M. 2004. The evolution of postdocs. *Science* 306 (5,694): 232.

20. Gwynne, P. 2004. Success factors for postdocs. *Science* 305 (5,691): 1,803–1,807.

21. Rutter, J. L., et al. 2002. Survey of mentoring experiences of NIH postdoctoral fellows. felcom.nih.gov/Mentoring/Survey.html.

22. Davis, G. Doctors without orders. *American Scientist* 93 (3, supplement). http://postdoc.sigmaxi.org/results.

CHAPTER SEVEN

A LAB OF HER OWN
WOMEN SCIENTISTS IN ACADEMIA

1. National Science Board. 2006. Science and Engineering Indicators 2006. 2 vols. Arlington, VA: National Science Foundation (vol. 1, NSB 0601; vol. 2, NSB 06-01A).

2. Marschke, R., S. Laursen, J. M. Nielsen, and P. Rankin. Demographic inertia revisited: An immodest proposal to achieve equitable gender representation among faculty in higher education. *Journal of Higher Education* 78 (1) (2007): 1–26.

3. Golde, C. M., and T. M. Dore. 2001. At cross purposes: What the experiences of doctoral students reveal about doctoral education. A report prepared for the Pew Charitable Trusts, Philadelphia. www.phd-survey.org.

4. Golde and Dore, At cross purposes.

5. Committee on Maximizing the Potential of Women in Academic Science and Engineering, Committee on Science, Engineering, and Public Policy. 2007. Be-

yond bias and barriers: Fulfilling the potential of women in academic science and engineering. Washington, D.C.: National Academies Press. www.nap.edu/catalog/11741.html.

6. Golde and Dore. At cross purposes.

7. National Research Council. 2001. From scarcity to visibility: Gender differences in the careers of doctoral scientists and engineers. Washington, D.C.: National Academy Press. www.nap.edu/catalog/5363.html.

8. Cataldi, E. F., E. M. Bradburn, and M. Fahimi. 2005. 2004 national study of postsecondary faculty (NSOPF:04): Background characteristics, work activities, and compensation of instructional faculty and staff: Fall 2003 (NCES 2006-176). U.S. Department of Education, National Center for Education Statistics. Washington, D.C.: GPO. http://nces.ed.gov/pubsearch.

9. The National Academy of Sciences has collected links to many universities' reports, including MIT's, at www7.nationalacademies.org/cwse/gender_faculty_links.html.

10. Umbach, P. D. Gender equity in the academic labor market: An analysis of academic disciplines. *Research in Higher Education* 48 (2) (2007): 169–192.

11. National Institutes of Health Office of Extramural Research. 2006. Success rates by institute. http://grants.nih.gov/grants/award/success/Success_ByIC.cfm.

12. National Science Foundation. 2005. About funding. www.nsf.gov/funding/aboutfunding.jsp.

13. Hosek, S. D., et al. 2005. Gender differences in major federal external grant programs. Santa Monica, Calif.: RAND Corporation. www.rand.org/pubs/technical_reports/2005/RAND_TR307.pdf.

14. Sprague, J., and K. Massoni. Student evaluations and gendered expectations: What we can't count can hurt us. *Sex Roles* 53 (11–12) (2005): 779–794.

15. Sonnert, G., and G. Holton. 1995. *Who Succeeds in Science? The Gender Dimension.* New Brunswick, N. J.: Rutgers University Press.

16. National Research Council, From scarcity to visibility.

17. Creamer, E. G., ed. 2001. *Working Equal: Academic Couples as Collaborators.* New York: RoutledgeFalmer.

18. Riger, S., et al. Measuring perceptions of the work environment for female faculty. *Review of Higher Education* 21 (1997): 63–78.

19. Committee on Maximizing the Potential of Women in Academic Science and

Engineering, Committee on Science, Engineering, and Public Policy. Beyond bias and barriers.

20. Ibid.

21. Niemeier, D. A., and C. Gonzalez. Breaking into the guildmasters' club: What we know about women science and engineering department chairs at AAU universities. *NWSA Journal* 16 (1) (2004): 157–171.

22. Brown, T. M. Mentorship and the female college president. *Sex Roles* 52 (9–10) (2005): 659–667.

23. Cataldi, Bradburn, and Fahimi, 2004 national study of postsecondary faculty.

24. Umbach, P. D. How effective are they? Exploring the impact of contingent faculty on undergraduate education. *Review of Higher Education* 30 (2) (2007): 91–123.

25. National Science Board.

CHAPTER EIGHT

BEYOND THE IVORY TOWER
WOMEN SCIENTISTS IN INDUSTRY AND GOVERNMENT

1. National Science Board. 2006. Science and Engineering Indicators 2006. 2 vols. Arlington, VA: National Science Foundation (vol. 1, NSB 0601; vol. 2, NSB 06-01A).

2. National Science Board.

3. Ibid.

4. Dey, J. G., and C. Hill. 2007. Behind the pay gap. Washington, D.C.: American Association of University Women Educational Foundation.

5. Ibid.

6. United States Government Accounting Office. 2005. Equal employment opportunity: Information on personnel actions, employee concerns, and oversight at six DOE laboratories. www.gao.gov/new.items/d05190.pdf.

7. Trial Lawyers for Public Justice. 2003. California Regents approve settlement in gender discrimination class action against Lawrence Livermore National Laboratory. www.tlpj.org/pr/llnl_settlement_112003.htm.

8. WIST Re-Evaluation Subcommittee, WIST Steering Committee. 2003. 10-year anniversary of women in science and technology at Argonne: An evaluation of its past, present and future. www.wist.anl.gov/docs/WISTRESCfinal report2.pdf.

9. Engineering Workforce Commission of the American Association of Engineering Societies, Inc. 2005. Engineering and technology degrees. New York: Engineering Workforce Commission.

10. England, P., et al. 2004. Does bad pay cause occupations to feminize, does feminization reduce pay, and how can we tell with longitudinal data? Presented at the 2004 annual meeting of the American Sociological Association. www.stanford.edu/dept/soc/people/faculty/england/BadPay.pdf.

11. Focus on the 100 Best – 2006 Hall of Fame. *Working Mother*. www.workingmother.com/web?service=direct/1/ViewArticlePage/dlinkFullArticle&sp= S142&sp=94.

12. It's elemental: Enhancing career success for women in the chemical industry. 2006. College Park, MD: University of Maryland. www.education.umd. edu/EDCP/enhance_site/It%27s%20Elemental.pdf.

13. Eaton, S. C. 2003. If you can use them: Flexibility policies, organizational commitment, and perceived performance. *Industrial Relations* 42 (2): 145–167.

14. It's elemental.

15. Deal, J. J., and M. A. Stevenson. 1998. Perceptions of female and male managers in the 1990s: Plus ça change . . . *Sex Roles* 38 (3–4): 287–300.

16. Smith-Doerr, L. 2004. *Women's Work: Gender Equality vs. Hierarchy in the Life Sciences*. Boulder, CO: Lynne Rienner Publishers.

17. McIlwee, J. S., and J. G. Robinson. 1992. *Women in Engineering: Gender, Power, and Workplace Culture*. Albany: State University of New York Press.

18. Smith-Doerr, *Women's Work*.

19. Heilman, M. E., and M. C. Haynes. 2005. No credit where credit is due: Attributional rationalization of women's success in male–female teams. *Journal of Applied Psychology* 90 (5): 905–916.

20. Heilman, M. E., and J. J. Chen. 2003. Entrepreneurship as a solution: The allure of self-employment for women and minorities. *Human Resource Management Review* 13 (2): 347–364.

CHAPTER NINE

THE FRONTIERS OF MEDICINE
WOMEN DOCTORS

1. Association of American Medical Colleges. Analysis in brief. 6 (7): October 2006. www.aamc.org/data/aib/aibissues/aibvol6_no7.pdf

2. American Medical Association. 2006. Physician characteristics and distribution in the U.S..

3. Frank, E., et al. 1998. Prevalence and correlates of harassment among U.S. women physicians. *Archives of Internal Medicine* 158: 352–358.

4. Nora, L. M., et al. 2002. Gender discrimination and sexual harassment in medical education: Perspectives gained by a 14-school study. *Academic Medicine* 71: 1,226–1,234.

5. Graduate Medical Education 2005–2006. 2006. *Journal of the American Medical Association* 296 (9): 1,154–1,163.

6. Xu, G., et al. 1995. A national study of the factors influencing men and women physicians' choices of primary care specialties. *Academic Medicine* 70 (5): 398–404.

7. Ibid.

8. Accreditation Council for Graduate Medical Education. 2007. Frequently asked questions about the ACGME common duty hour standards. www.acgme.org/acWebsite/dutyHours/dh_faqs.pdf.

9. Frank E., J. E. McMurray, M. Linzer, and L. Elon, for the Society of General Internal Medicine Career Satisfaction Study Group. 1999. Career satisfaction of U.S. women physicians: Results from the Women Physicians' Health Study. *Archives of Internal Medicine* 159: 1,417–1,426.

10. Association of American Medical Colleges. 2006.

11. National Science Board. 2006. Science and Engineering Indicators 2006. 2 vols. Arlington, VA: National Science Foundation (vol. 1, NSB 06-01; vol. 2, NSB 06-01A).

12. Nonnemaker, L. 2000. Women physicians in academia: New insights from cohort studies. *New England Journal of Medicine* 342: 426–427.

13. Jagsi, R., et al. 2006. The "gender gap" in authorship of academic medical literature—A 35-year perspective. *New England Journal of Medicine* 355 (3): 281–287.

14. Carr, P. L., et al. 1998. Relation of family responsibilities and gender to the productivity and career satisfaction of medical faculty. *Annals of Internal Medicine* 129 (7): 532–8.

15. Association of American Medical Colleges. Analysis in brief 7 (1): March 2007. www.aamc.org/data/aib/aibissues/aibvol7_no1.pdf.

16. Cull, W. L., et al. 2002. Pediatricians working part-time: Past, present and future. *Pediatrics* 109 (6): 1,015–1,020.

17. Barnett, R. C., et al. 2005. Career satisfaction and retention of a sample of women physicians who work reduced hours. *Journal of Women's Health* 14 (2): 146–153.

18. Cull, et al., Pediatricians working part-time.

19. See, for example, Xu, G., et al., A national study, and Carr, P. L., et al., Relation of family responsibilities.

20. Frank, E., L. Harvey, and L. Elon. 2000. Family responsibilities and domestic activities of U.S. women physicians. *Archives of Family Medicine* 9: 134–140. http://archfami.ama-assn.org/cgi/reprint/9/2/134.pdf.

21. Ibid.

22. Batchelor, A. J. 1990. Senior women physicians: the question of retirement. *New York State Journal of Medicine* 90 (6): 292–294.

23. Levinson, W., and N. Lurie. 2004. When most doctors are women: What lies ahead? *Annals of Internal Medicine* 141: 471–474.

CHAPTER TEN

HANGING UP HER LAB COAT
WOMEN LEAVING SCIENCE

1. Sax, L. J. 2000. Undergraduate science majors: Gender differences in who goes to graduate school. *Review of Higher Education* 24 (2): 153–172.

2. Golde, C. M. 1998. Beginning graduate school: explaining doctoral attrition. *New Directions for Higher Education* 101, 55–64.

3. Seymour, E., and N. Hewitt. 1997. *Talking About Leaving: Why Undergraduates Leave the Sciences.* Boulder, CO: Westview Press.

4. Ibid.

5. Ibid.

CHAPTER ELEVEN
GET 'EM YOUNG
ENCOURAGING GIRLS IN SCIENCE

1. More information about the program is available at www.techbridgegirls.org.
2. National Science Foundation. 2003. New formulas for America's workforce: Girls in science and engineering. www.nsf.gov/pubs/2003/nsf03207/nsf03207.pdf. Except where otherwise noted, examples of specific programs come from this publication.
3. Tenenbaum, H. C., and C. Leaper. 2003. Parent–child conversations about science: The socialization of gender inequities? *Developmental Psychology* 39: 34–47.
4. Crowley, K., et al. 2001. Parents explain more often to boys than to girls during shared scientific thinking. *Psychological Science* 12: 258–261.

CHAPTER TWELVE
WELCOMING WOMEN
IMPROVING SCIENCE FOR ALL

1. Yale News Release. 1997. Happy birthday to the oldest graduate school. www.yale.edu/opa/newsr/97-04-21-01.all.html.
2. Cohoon, J. M. 2000. Toward improving female retention in the computer science major. *Communications of the ACM* 44 (5): 108–114.
3. Ulku-Steiner, B., et al. 2000. Doctoral student experiences in gender-balanced and male-dominated graduate programs. *Journal of Educational Psychology* 92 (2): 296–307.
4. Fox, M. F. 2000. Organizational environments and doctoral degrees awarded to women in science and engineering departments. *Women's Studies Quarterly* 28 (1–2): 47–61.
5. The National Academy of Sciences has collected links to many universities' reports, including MIT's, at www7.nationalacademies.org/cwse/gender_faculty_links.html.
6. The University of Arizona ADVANCE. Dashboard for deans and department chairs. http://advance.arizona.edu/workgroup_info.cfm?a_ID=2&w_ID2=1.

7. Goldin, C., and C. Rouse. 2000. Orchestrating impartiality: The impact of "blind" auditions on female musicians. *The American Economic Review* 90 (4): 715–741.

8. Drago, R., and J. Williams. 2000. A half time tenure track proposal. *Change* 6 (6): 46–51.

9. Wax, A. L. 2004. Family-friendly workplace reform: Prospects for change. *The Annals of the American Academy of Political and Social Science* 596: 36–61.

10. University of Washington Center for Institutional Change. 2007. Results from and impact of the University of Washington ADVANCE Center for Institutional Change. www.engr.washington.edu/advance/resources/UW_ADVANCE_results_overview.pdf.

11. Academic Careers in Science and Engineering (ACES), Case Western Reserve University. 2007. Annual report for the National Science Foundation ADVANCE Project. www.case.edu/admin/aces/documents/Annual_Report_YR4.pdf.

12. Babcock, L., and S. Laschever. 2003. *Women Don't Ask: Negotiation and the Gender Divide*. Princeton, N. J.: Princeton University Press.

ACKNOWLEDGMENTS

First, I want to thank my editors, Brooke Warner for suggesting this project and helping get it off the ground, and Anne Connolly for her work at the end to bring everything together into a coherent whole.

Too many people to list helped me answer questions, discussed ideas with me, and offered support in many different ways. Kragen Sitaker, Desiree Phair, Jill Blackston, Ping Yee, and David Gibson provided insightful comments on early drafts of the manuscript.

Many thanks go out to the women I interviewed for this book. Talking about their experiences was not always easy, but I appreciate their candor and willingness to let me into their lives. Many thanks also go to the women who volunteered to be interviewed but with whom I was unable to sit down due to time constraints, as well as everyone who passed on information about my need for interview subjects to their friends, colleagues, family members, and others. Without them I would never have achieved such a diverse group of interviewees. Many of them also pointed me toward books, organizations, and other resources that were incredibly useful. Thanks go as well to Linda

Kekelis at Techbridge, Joyce Yen and Eve Riskin at the University of Washington Center for Institutional Change, and Annie Hanson at Discovery Creek Children's Museum for giving me access to their programs.

My siblings—Matt, Shannon, and Kelley—and my mom and dad have been a constant support, particularly my mother, who has never stopped believing that I could achieve great things.

And finally, thanks go to Andy Isaacson for all the ways he supported and inspired me during the writing of this book.

ABOUT THE AUTHOR

© JACOB APPELBAUM

Linley Erin Hall is a freelance writer and editor specializing in science and engineering. She is also one of the women who dropped out of science. Hall has a BS degree in chemistry from Harvey Mudd College (Claremont, CA) and a graduate certificate in science communication from the University of California, Santa Cruz. She worked as a science writer for the Ira A. Fulton School of Engineering at Arizona State University before becoming a freelance writer. Hall has written or edited four educational non-fiction books and writes articles on a wide variety of science and engineering topics. She lives in the San Francisco Bay Area.

SELECTED TITLES FROM SEAL PRESS

For more than thirty years, Seal Press has published ground-breaking books. By women. For women. Visit our website at www.sealpress.com.

SHE'S SUCH A GEEK: WOMEN WRITE ABOUT SCIENCE, TECHNOLOGY, AND OTHER NERDY STUFF edited by Annalee Newitz and Charlie Anders. $14.95, 1-58005-190-1. From comic books and gaming to science fiction and blogging, nerdy women have their say in this witty collection that takes on the "boys only" clubs and celebrates a woman's geek spirit.

THE ANTI 9-TO-5 GUIDE: PRACTICAL CAREER ADVICE FOR WOMEN WHO THINK OUTSIDE THE CUBE by Michelle Goodman. $14.95, 1-58005-186-3. Escape the wage-slave trap of your cubicle with Goodman's hip career advice on creating your dream job and navigating the work world without compromising your aspirations.

RECLAIMING OUR DAUGHTERS by Karen Stabiner. $14.95, 1-58005-213-9. Offers a message of hope and optimism to the parents of adolescent and preadolescent girls.

WOMEN IN THE LINE OF FIRE: WHAT YOU SHOULD KNOW ABOUT WOMEN IN THE MILITARY by Erin Solaro. $15.95, 1-58005-174-X. A wake-up call on the damage and repercussions of government neglect, rightist fervor, and feminist ambivalence about women in the military.

SINGLE STATE OF THE UNION: SINGLE WOMEN SPEAK OUT ON LIFE, LOVE, AND THE PURSUIT OF HAPPINESS edited by Diane Mapes. $14.95, 1-58005-202-9. Written by an impressive roster of single (and some formerly single) women, this collection portrays single women as individuals whose lives extend well beyond Match.com and Manolo Blahniks.

GETTING UNSTUCK WITHOUT COMING UNGLUED: A WOMAN'S GUIDE TO UNBLOCKING CREATIVITY by Susan O'Doherty, PhD. $14.95, 1-58005-206-1. This encouraging and practical book is about understanding blocks in the creative process and getting to the bottom of what causes them.